SLAVERY AND AFRICAN LIFE

AFRICAN STUDIES SERIES 67

GENERAL EDITOR
J. M. Lonsdale, *Lecturer in History and Fellow of Trinity College, Cambridge*

ADVISORY EDITORS
J. D. Y. Peel, *Professor of Anthropology and Sociology, with special reference to Africa, School of Oriental and African Studies, University of London*
John Sender, *Faculty of Economics and Fellow of Wolfson College, Cambridge*

Published in collaboration with
THE AFRICAN STUDIES CENTRE, CAMBRIDGE

For a list of other books in this series see page 235

SLAVERY AND AFRICAN LIFE

Occidental, Oriental, and African Slave Trades

PATRICK MANNING

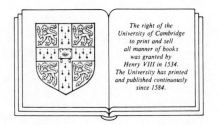

The right of the
University of Cambridge
to print and sell
all manner of books
was granted by
Henry VIII in 1534.
The University has printed
and published continuously
since 1584.

CAMBRIDGE UNIVERSITY PRESS

CAMBRIDGE
NEW YORK   PORT CHESTER   MELBOURNE   SYDNEY

Published by the Press Syndicate of the University of Cambridge
The Pitt Building, Trumpington Street, Cambridge CB2 1RP
40 West 20th Street, New York, NY 10011, USA
10 Stamford Road, Oakleigh, Melbourne 3166, Australia

© Cambridge University Press 1990

First published 1990

Printed in Great Britain by Redwood Press Limited,
Melksham, Wiltshire

British Library cataloguing in publication data

Manning, Patrick
Slavery and African life: occidental, oriental and African slave
trades. – (African studies series; 67).
1. Africa. Social conditions. Effects of slave trade,
1450–1899
I. Title II. Series
960'.22

Library of Congress cataloguing in publication data

Manning, Patrick, 1941–
Slavery and African life: occidental, oriental and African slave
trades/Patrick Manning.
    p.   cm. – (African studies series: 67)
Bibliography.
ISBN 0 521 34396 8 – ISBN 0 521 34867–6 (paperback)
1. Slave-trade – Africa. Sub-Saharan – History. 2. Slavery – Africa.
Sub-Saharan – History. I. Title. II. Series.
HT1321.M36 1990
380.1'44'0967 – dc20   89–34125 CIP

ISBN 0 521 34396 8 hard covers
ISBN 0 521 34867 6 paperback

CE

To Marjorie Murphy

Contents

Plates

Figures

Maps

Acknowledgements

Initial support for the research on this study came from a 1981 grant from the Social Science Research Council, for which I am happy to express my gratitude. Further funding came from the Northeastern University Research and Scholarship Development Fund. William S. Griffiths taught me Pascal and worked through the logic of the simulation program with me, as well as writing much of the program itself. The Johns Hopkins University History Department hosted me for a half year's research in 1981. The John Simon Guggenheim Foundation supported me for a year's research at the Population Studies Center at the University of Pennsylvania, where this study was completed. The simulation program has been operated on systems at Stanford University, The Johns Hopkins University, Bryn Mawr College, Northeastern University, and the University of Pennsylvania – too many systems for efficient work, but each one of them hospitably and effectively run. Of the many individuals who have provided me with useful advice, I must give first place to the late Joel Gregory, who encouraged me to fill out what I hoped would be a brief set of hypotheses into a full-scale article, and thus started the dominoes falling. To Joseph Miller, Stanley Engerman, Frederick Cooper, Martin Klein, Sara Berry, Christine Gailey, Paul Lovejoy, and Ronald Bailey, I offer my thanks for the comments and corrections they made to near-final drafts of the manuscript.

Prologue

Tragedy and sacrifice in the history of slavery

Tragedy is an imitation of an action that is serious, complete, and possessing magnitude . . . and effecting through pity and fear the catharsis of such emotions . . .

There are in tragedy . . . six constituent elements, viz. Plot, Character, Language, Thought, Spectacle and Melody.

Aristotle, *Poetics*[1]

To perform a sacrifice is, primarily, to try to outwit death . . .

When war becomes the servant of sacrifice, when a people decides to appropriate the lives of others in order to incessantly feed its gods, the religious system is lost in madness.

Luc de Heusch, *Sacrifice in Africa*[2]

The spectacle of slavery – with its chains, slave ships, and broken families – touched on every century of the modern era, including our own. This study of African slavery in the modern world focuses primarily on economic history. Yet the influence of slavery has extended beyond the economy to transform human emotions and trouble the human spirit. For this reason I have chosen to integrate spiritual and dramatic terms into this tale of costs and benefits: slavery was a sacrifice of Africans for the transformation of the wider world, and slavery was a tragedy for the people of Africa.

This is a brief book, given the immensity of the subject. In it, I have chosen the condensed and dramatic form of a tragedy, instead of the extended and narrative form of an epic. The tragic form, as given above in Aristotle's classic definition, is appropriate for several reasons. The seriousness of African slavery can hardly be in doubt. The story is complete in the sense that I shall discuss all the main dimensions of African slavery, though at the expense of much detail. As for magnitude, the form of the presentation is intended to reinforce the conclusion of the analysis: African slavery is of magnitude not only for its moral and philosophical meaning, but for its significance in modern economic history. Further, I shall make no attempt to segregate logic from passion. Instead, I shall seek directly to confront the

1

moral conflicts, the pain and suffering, in order to draw out of the reader pity – or empathy, to use the more modern term – for the victims of slavery on all sides, and fear that we may ourselves fall into a similar dilemma. The experiencing of these emotions, however, will arise from the context of a cold, hard analysis of demographic and economic facts.

The tragic experience of slavery in the modern world left Africans depleted in population, divided irremediably among themselves, retarded economically, and despised as an inferior race in a world which had built a vision of racial hierarchy based on the inspiration of their enslavement.

To portray the history of slavery as a tragedy is to emphasize that it is no morality play, medieval or modern. The cast of characters is not divided into innocent Africans pursued by evil Europeans, nor do I divide Africans themselves into the moral and the immoral. There were many innocents, particularly the children, and there were those who, overcome by consistent temptation, became truly evil exploiters of slaves. The protagonists here, however, are those who lived normal African lives, and who, in so doing involved themselves in slavery and in the slave trade. By removing African individuals and societies from any presumption of innocence, we bring them onto the stage as fully drawn historical actors: protagonists with the full range of emotions, goals, interests, flaws, insights, and blindness expected of tragic heroes.

Aristotle counsels us that these are the appropriate sort of heroes for a tragedy: he argues that the tragedy will fail to inspire pity and fear if it centers on a good hero falling into misfortune or on an evil hero rising. Instead, "We are left with the man whose place is between these extremes ... Such is the man who on the one hand is not pre-eminent in virtue and justice, and yet on the other hand does not fall into misfortune through vice or depravity, but falls because of some mistake."[3]

The mistake of our African protagonists was their willingness to participate in slavery and in the slave trade, even if they did so only to dispose of enemies in revenge, or in hopes of securing a fortune which might enable their family or their kingdom to grow and profit. The tragic results of these attempts to advance themselves at the expense of others emerge out of the logic of the plot itself, though over a period of more than a century rather than in a single episode. Developments in the story included the decline in the African population, the disruption of countless families, and the individual falls of the mighty.

The tragic climax came in the mid-nineteenth century, with the decline in external demand for slaves. Africans faced an array of choices, each one of which led necessarily to a tragic end. Those who sought to sustain African slavery achieved short-term prosperity, but then underwent conquest by Europeans. Those who sought to renounce slavery had either to accept conquest by their neighbors or ally with conquering Europeans and negate their own heritage.

The plot of a complex tragedy, again according to Aristotle, involves reversals of fate and episodes of recognition among characters. For Africans, the reversals were frequent enough at the individual level: warlords and merchants met sudden death at the hands of enemies; the reversals from wealth to indebtedness were no less significant. Cases of individual recognition by people separated by the misfortunes of enslavement were no doubt common enough: King Jaja of Opobo in Nigeria recognized an oath sworn by a man falling to the water from a boat, and was then reunited with the family from which he had been kidnapped and enslaved at the age of fourteen. But the most significant recognition for our story was the gradual realization by Africans of themselves as a people. At the beginning of the slave exports, Africans had no more common identity than did Europeans; they did not even share the European veneer of a common religious faith. Yet the course of the slave trade itself, with the accompanying development in European minds of a racialistic conflation of all black peoples into a single commodified work force, was perhaps the single greatest factor in the development of a Pan-African, racial consciousness. To the degree that Africans and Afro-Americans partook of that identity, they recognized each other during the nineteenth century at the height of their unfolding tragedy, but too late to halt the course of events.

The tragic hero of this tale, as is usual in classical tragedy, is male. This is because the surviving records of slavery give prominence to men, both as enslavers and as slaves. Moreover, it was the men who most clearly joined in the great gambit of the slave trade, only to experience later reversals which brought them tragedy and suffering. While I have not been able to bring women to center stage, I have sought to avoid relegating them to the passive role of victim. Women did participate at each stage of the drama, as slaves, slave owners, and as persons warning of the consequences of the tragic decision. We shall see, further, that women's lives were transformed fundamentally and repeatedly by the slave trade. The experience of slavery reinforced patriarchy – the domination of men over women – just as it reinforced the domination of men over men. Whether women or men suffered more, in the end, is difficult to tell.

I could go on and attempt to fit this story into even the most rigorous definition of tragedy. The thought and language of African protagonists not only stirs up emotions but adds magnitude to the presentation. The melody of the tragedy includes the work songs and dirges of the slaves, but also the martial music of African armies marching to battle. Certain of the heroes were great and noble individuals. For many cases one can argue that African participants in slavery failed but became more admirable in catastrophe. Without much doubt one can argue that the unhappy end – African poverty and division, compounded by most of a century of alien rule – was inevitable and issued from the decisions of the heroes in the face of a moral conflict, in which disaster was to result from any choice.

Perhaps this vision of African slavery as a tragedy will appear old-fashioned to some readers. Many have argued in recent years that tragedy can no longer be written, and that such horrors as the Jewish holocaust and the genocides of Armenia and Cambodia were more *pathetic* than tragic. I think that the response of the philosopher Walter Kaufmann to this objection is appropriate.[4] He argues not only that pathetic events qualify for modern tragedy but that they were important in ancient tragedy. He offers, instead, three more deeply seated reasons why modern-day observers feel that tragedies cannot be written: our contemporary infatuation with success and unwillingness to consider failure; a growing disbelief in great men; and, mainly, our contemporary unwillingness to observe drama centered on the immense and overwhelming human suffering that characterized Greek tragedy. If these are the reasons why audiences may wish to avoid tragedy, they are not, Kaufmann notes, reasons why tragedy should not be written. It is only the audience which experiences the tragedy which can partake of the catharsis that may result from it.

If the enslavement of Africans was a tragedy for Africa, it was also, from the standpoint of the wider world, a sacrifice. Africa's loss was the gain of the Occident – and of the Orient.

Sacrifice takes place in many ways and on many levels. African families performed sacrifices in memory of ancestors, to renew the earth's fertility, and to pay tribute to their rulers. Merchants and planters in Africa and elsewhere sacrificed the enjoyment of their current wealth for investments intended to bring later profit. Christians celebrated the ritual of the Eucharist, to participate in God's sacrifice of his son for the salvation of man. The meanings of these and other sacrifices came to overlap inextricably through the experience of slavery.[5]

An act of sacrifice entails distinct roles: the sacrificer who performs the act, the authority to whom the sacrifice is made, and – in the case of human sacrifice – the victim. The sacrificer offers up something of value in order to survive a threat, or to improve the conditions of a community. The victim gives up his or her life, but may leave behind the memory of having made a contribution to the community. The authority in whose honor the sacrifice is made receives it physically or symbolically, and benefits from the prestige of recognition.

If all could agree that slavery involved sacrifice, each tended to see his own sacrifice as central, and each tended to define the sacrificing community rather narrowly. African parents sacrificed their children involuntarily to the attacks of slave raiders, and reluctantly but sometimes voluntarily to the assault of famine and the demands of tax collectors. African monarchs and merchants handed their slaves over to European merchants, and accepted money and gifts in return. But they too could claim to be acting out the will of the gods. They could claim to be using their compensation to provide nourishment and hope for their communities, just as, in time of famine, one might sacrifice an ox in honor of the gods, yet divide the meat among the community.

4

The slaves themselves – the millions sentenced to death or transportation – were clearly and uniquely the sacrificial victims. Yet in another sense, those slaves who survived were also sacrificers, for they had to contribute their energies to the wealth of a new community. At the same time, plantation owners saw the sacrifice as their own, considering the sums they had to pay and the food they had to advance for slaves before they could achieve any profit. The fact that they defined the slaves as outside their community made it easy to ignore slave contributions either as victims or as sacrificers. Through such reasoning the planters, much like African merchants and monarchs, could see themselves as sacrificers rather than as exploiters.

The authorities on whose altars slaves were sacrificed were both temporal and spiritual. Slaves taken by the Aro, an elite religious clan of eastern Nigeria, were sacrificed to the great oracle of Arochukwu – "eaten" by it – as the first step of their journey to the coast. Secular African authorities – monarchs and warlords – benefitted as much as did African gods. In the New World, slaves were sacrificed to the worldly ambitions of merchants and planters. The victims, once baptized, contributed as well to the glory of the Christian God.

In this complex web of need and greed, the nature, the meaning, and the effectiveness of the sacrifice are seen to shift with the standpoint of the participants. Sacrifice, at its best, strengthens and ultimately rewards a community, brings honor to the victim, ennobles the act of sacrifice, and propitiates the authority for whom it is performed. But sacrifice need not achieve its aims. There is the waste of an investment with no return, and the waste of a human sacrifice which brings neither honor to the victim nor recognition to the sacrificer.

Slavery brought material benefit – growth, if not equitable distribution – to the New World. More than 10 million slave immigrants reached the New World, where they performed much of the earliest, dirtiest, and most exhausting work of constructing an economic system which has since prospered enormously.[6] Slavery brought material benefits to Africa as well: not only in the form of goods purchased in exchange for slaves, but also through centers of manufacture and culture such as the city of Kano in the Nigerian savanna, whose nineteenth-century brilliance was due to the labor of slaves. In each of these cases the sacrifice yielded a tangible gain, but with a disproportionate level of waste: the devastation of the areas raided for slaves, the many lives lost in transit to the New World, and the many more lives brought to an early end in bondage.

The spiritual benefits and costs of slavery are more difficult to trace, but are no less important. They were distributed inequitably and with ironic consequences. For a time, the sacrifice of Africans did contribute to the glory of the Christian God, to worship of the idol of the market-place, and to prostration before the secular icons of western civilization. Yet as time went on, the continued enslavement of Africans brought each of these into

5

question. Leaders of the Christian faith, prophets of the new industrial order, and philosophers of civilization's development each turned against slavery as the eighteenth century came to an end. Thus the sacrifice of slavery ultimately brought about its own repudiation and a change in the ideals of the western world. Ironically, however, in the course of their enlightenment western leaders forgot the contributions of slaves to Christian faith, to economic progress, and to civilization's advance. The very term "western civilization" serves to arrogate full credit for the present economic supremacy of the Atlantic nations to its European ancestors. Once the African sacrifice was forgotten, the rise of racism followed logically upon the end of slavery. Yet a further irony is that African gods and African ideals, having succumbed to the confusion of slavery, yielded for a time to conquest.

The dramatic images of tragedy and the religious images of sacrifice will recur through the book. The form and the analysis of the book, however, are focused firmly on social science. My analysis gives emphasis to four social scientific aspects of slavery in Africa: demography, economics, social institutions, and ideology. Further, since it is a historian who is drawing these materials together, the reader will not be surprised to find a strong emphasis on the factor of time: a given event can affect events which follow it in time, but not those which precede it.

This book is not only about the past. It also asks how the world of today should respond to the heritage of past inequities. To the extent that there is emerging a world community in this late twentieth century, it seems to rely on the notion that there should be equality of opportunity for all people, regardless of origin. Yet the reality of inequality confronts us daily: racial, sexual, and national discrimination, compounded by the vast economic gulf separating the wealthy nations from the poor. Many of these inequalities are inherited from past times, though some inequalities continue to grow. Slavery and the slave trade have all but completely passed from the face of the earth, yet their effects remain with us in racial, sexual, and economic inequality.

What sort of compensation should be granted to those who have suffered the exploitation of slavery, colonialism, or gender inequality? What sort of guarantees should be implemented to reduce levels of inequality? What ideas should we emphasize to encourage the equality of opportunity we seek? The great dialogues between north and south, between male and female, which will continue for the rest of our lives, require answers to these questions in order to reach conclusions which expand equality of opportunity. These answers must be sought in part in our study of the nature and causes of past inequality.

An understanding of Africa and its problems today requires that we recognize the extent of the damage inflicted by slavery, that we recognize the essential role of New World demand for slaves in inflicting that damage, and that we also recognize how much of the damage to Africa was self-inflicted. On the other hand, we must recognize as well the astonishing flexibility, mutability, and resilience of African societies in the face of such inhuman pressures. Surely those who withstood the distortions of life under slavery had lessons to teach a wider world.

1

The political economy of slavery in Africa

The story of slavery in the modern world is not a pretty story, nor an uplifting one. It is an unhappy chapter in our history which, one might think, is best forgotten, but scholars and readers continue to be fascinated with slavery, for slavery was not just an ancient institution which carried forth the inequalities of our earliest days, it was also an oppression important – and perhaps unavoidable – in the construction of our contemporary world. We live daily with the heritage of slavery, since black people in Africa, the Americas, and elsewhere are still victims of poverty and racial discrimination whose origins can be traced to the slave status of so many blacks in the past. But it is not only black people who carry forward the heritage of slavery. David Brion Davis, perhaps the most distinguished historian of modern slavery, has posed the issue in terms of the relationship between slavery and human progress.[1] That is, the accomplishments of which all of us in the late twentieth century are most proud – our economic advance, our progress toward freedom and equality – and which are in one sense a repudiation of slavery, came into existence in part because of the contribution of slavery and slaves to our economy, our society and our ideas.

Scholars have revealed a great deal of important information on slavery in Africa, and have published a number of good general studies.[2] But for most people outside of Africa, and perhaps even within Africa, the perception of the history of slavery focuses on the sugar and cotton plantations of the Americas, and leaves the African dimension of slavery as little more than a hazy outline. This book, therefore, is another attempt to summarize the impact of slavery on African life: an attempt to clarify African slavery and to set it in a world context.

The interpretive outlook that I will emphasize in the chapters below includes three interconnected points. First, there occurred a succession of transformations in African economic and social life from the seventeenth through the nineteenth centuries, and these transformations were centered on institutions of slavery. Thus the slave trade, often pictured as one long misfortune for Africa, was instead a series of unfortunate transformations.

8

My second main point is to show the degree to which these transformations were brought about through external impact. This external impact came mainly through European demand for slaves but also because of Middle Eastern and Asian demand. My third point is to show how these transformations were also the result of conflicts within African society – for instance, the conflict between the desire for individual aggrandizement and the desire for social welfare.

The plan of this study thus corresponds to an interpretation of African history in the modern period, and an interpretation of African history in the context of modern world history. Here I am using the term "modern" in the same way historians of Europe normally do, to refer to the period since 1500. This is a study of Africa in the period of maritime contact among the continents: the period of rising mercantile and industrial capitalism, and the period of national monarchies and nation states.

In order to make the presentation concise, I have concentrated the analysis on a few key points. First, the analysis emphasizes the demography of slavery, including the fertility, mortality, and migration of the slaves themselves and of the areas and populations from which they were drawn. Second, I emphasize the economics of slavery, and particularly the prices of slaves. The changing prices of slaves give an important indication of transformations in slavery more generally. Third, I emphasize the changing institutions of slavery in Africa. Here, the recent literature is particularly rich, and I am restricted to presenting only the most essential points out of a complex set of stories. In addition, I will give some attention to a fourth area, the ideology of slavery in Africa. The varying African beliefs which justified, limited, or condemned, slavery and the slave trade, while only sketchily documented, were none the less important.

The consideration of these several types of factors at once is an exercise in political economy. That term is less popular today than it has been in recent times, but it corresponds well to an analysis which, while based on the material conditions of life, also includes social structures, politics, and human consciousness as explicit elements in the analysis. It focuses on conflict and long-run change in the material and social conditions of human society.

The presentation also depends on being specific about geographic variation in African slavery and the slave trade. This requires being clear about the geography of the slave *origins* as well as of slave *destinations*. In the *origins* of slaves, I will work at three geographic levels: the *regional* level, with the slave-exporting portion of Africa broken into thirteen regions, as shown on map 1.1; *local* areas within those regions (such as the Fante, Asante, Brong, and Voltaic areas within the Gold Coast region); and three *sub-continental* zones, each consisting of an aggregation of several *regions*. These are the Western Coast, the Eastern Coast, and the Savanna and Horn.

As for the *destinations* of slaves, I have divided them into the *Occidental*

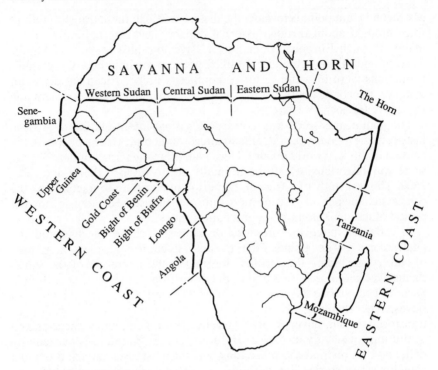

Map 1.1. Slave origins

trade, the *Oriental* trade, and the *African* trade. This terminology is in some ways old-fashioned, but it helps to make clear some important distinctions and some important unities in the history of the slave trade, for it is a terminology which is cultural in its connotation as much as geographic. Thus it permits one to emphasize a certain unity in the traditions of slavery in the western world (or the world under western rule), by including Europe, the Americas, South Africa, and the Mascarene Islands under the single category of the Occidental trade. Or, to compare it with the more common terminology, the Atlantic slave trade was most but not all of the Occidental trade; the Indian Ocean trade included both Occidental and Oriental aspects, with the latter being numerically predominant. What I have called the Oriental trade is sometimes called the Islamic slave trade: but religion was hardly the point of the slave trade, and such a terminology would suggest that one compares the Islamic slave trade to the Christian slave trade. Further, to use the terms Islamic trade or Islamic world in this way is implicitly and erroneously to treat Africa as if it were outside of Islam, or as a negligible portion of the Islamic world.

Finally, this threefold terminology forces us to consider the African slave trade – that is, the slave trade from one African region to another – on the

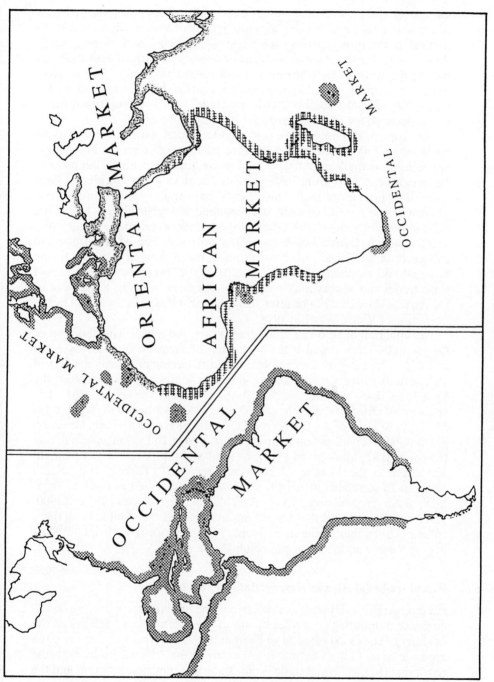

Map 1.2. Slave destinations

same level as the Occidental and Oriental trades. The reader must be wary of possible confusion, for this terminology is not universally accepted. In particular, the term "African slave trade" has been used to mean many things, including the trade in Africans or persons of African descent in any part of the world. Here, however, I will restrict the term "African slave trade" or "African trade" to trade in slaves within Africa, and I will use the terms "Occidental trade" or "Oriental trade" when referring to trade in slaves destined for markets outside sub-Saharan Africa.

The scope of this book extends to the Occidental, Oriental, and African trades since 1500. The Occidental slave trade began with the Portuguese appearance on the West African coast in the fifteenth century, but its most important years were from 1650 to 1850. The peak in the Occidental slave trade came just before 1800. The Oriental slave trade began before the rise of Islam in the seventh century, but remained at a relatively low level. The most important years in the Oriental slave trade were from 1750 to 1900, and the peak in Oriental trade came in about 1850. The African trade had existed on a small scale since early times, but it grew in response to the Oriental and especially the Occidental trades. (This interaction of export slave trades and slavery in Africa will be discussed in detail.) The peak of the African slave trade came after 1850, though it was virtually ended by the beginning of World War I in 1914.

The abolition of slavery required a century and a half. The abolition of Occidental slavery began with the freeing of slaves in England by court order in 1772, but was not complete until the freeing of Brazilian slaves in 1888. The British abolished slavery in their colonies beginning in 1834, the French in 1848, and the United States abolished slavery in 1865. The abolition of Oriental slavery began with the 1843 abolition of the legal status of slavery in India under British rule. Oriental slavery as a whole, however, did not become illegal until areas came under European colonial rule (Egypt in 1882, Morocco in 1912), or until Middle Eastern nations sought admission to the League of Nations after 1920 (Turkey, Iran, Saudi Arabia). In sub-Saharan Africa, some slaves were freed as early as 1835. Most of Africa came under European colonial rule between 1880 and 1900, but it was only by 1914 that further enslavement was prohibited in all these colonies. Even then, millions of people previously enslaved lived out their lives in slavery under European colonial rule.

Recent studies of African slavery: data and controversies

An interpretive essay such as this can only be undertaken by relying on the immense outpouring of studies on slavery in recent years.[3] Studies of the quantity of slaves exported have been published in great number since the appearance of Philip Curtin's 1969 census of the Atlantic trade, with the result that the Occidental trade is now known in remarkable detail, and the outlines of the Oriental trade are becoming increasingly clear.[4] Studies of slave prices, while of inherent difficulty because of the complexities of accounting (of the assortments of goods exchanged for slaves, of transport costs, and of exchange rates), have nevertheless advanced to the point where the main contours of African slave prices can be summarized.[5] Institutions and social conditions of slavery in Africa and the Americas have undergone detailed investigation by historians and anthropologists. For Africa a disproportionate number of the studies of slave life have focused on the late nineteenth century, the best documented period, but recent studies have broadened the temporal scope.[6] Studies of the ideology of slavery in Africa are not large in number, but the long dispute over abolition has created a large and insightful literature on slavery and ideology in the Atlantic world.[7]

In addition to the outpouring of regional African studies, another important development in the literature on slavery has been the linking of studies on Africa with studies on the New World.[8] The greatest importance of Curtin's census lies not in the precise numbers he came up with (though his estimates have been remarkably robust in the face of subsequent reviews), but in the fact that his book provided a forum which rapidly drew together scholarship on every aspect of slavery in the Atlantic basin, breaking down previous lines of national historiography and regional concentration. Curtin described his book as an "intermediate level of synthesis"; in fact it had a catalytic effect and remains a reference point. Studies of demography, work life, social conditions, profitability, ideology, and abolition in the New World are proving to be of great importance in providing guidance and comparisons for studies of Africa.[9] A similar process seems to be taking place, although at a more leisurely pace, for links between Africa and the Orient.[10]

But it would be misleading to present this profusion of studies on slavery as a great co-operative, positivist project of gathering and linking information. Conflicts and controversies underlie much of this work, and pursuit of the controversies helps to explain why much of the work has been done. Mention of two controversies will be sufficient to make this point. First is the controversy on the Williams thesis. Eric Williams, the distinguished Trinidadian historian, proposed a dual thesis in 1944: that slavery in the British West Indies had provided profits which were important in the growth of British industrial capitalism, and that the industrial capitalists, in turn, led in the abolition of slavery in order to ensure the primacy of wage labor.[11] The argument, in a sense, was that some sort of determinism could account for the impact of slavery and for its destruction. Repeated scrutiny of this thesis has led to numerous studies of the profitability of the Atlantic slave trade and West Indian slavery, and to detailed studies of abolitionist politics. Roger Anstey has argued that neither the slave trade nor slavery brought great profits to Britain. Seymour Drescher has argued that the slave trade and slavery remained profitable (though not sufficiently so to have caused industrialization), but he argued, like Anstey, that the campaign to abolish slavery was led by persons other than leaders in the rising capitalist enterprise.[12]

While the results have left Williams' assertions in doubt, the full potential of the Williams thesis has yet to be explored. In particular, the wider scope of recent work permits the thesis to be reformulated. That is, one may consider the role of slavery in the construction of the capitalist economic order throughout the Atlantic world – Africa, Europe, and the Americas – and also consider the approach of the capitalist class to slavery throughout the Atlantic. The reformulated Williams thesis would then argue that slavery throughout the Atlantic system contributed to the rise of capitalism in Europe and the Americas, and that capitalism in turn brought about the destruction of slavery throughout the Atlantic. One advantage of this reformulation is that it avoids excluding Africa from modern world history.

Second is the controversy on the Rodney thesis. Walter Rodney, a Guyanese scholar who did pioneering work in African history, argued in 1966 for the case of the Upper Guinea Coast that slavery had virtually no existence in the region until the Portuguese export of slaves caused African slavery to expand. Rodney later restated his thesis more generally for all of Africa.[13] John D. Fage, one of the founders of Africanist history in Britain, expressed admiration for Rodney's work but then developed a thesis which was in many ways contradictory to Rodney's. Fage argued that the export of slaves from West Africa may have slowed and perhaps halted population growth, but was insufficient either to have reduced population or to have brought significant social change to Africa. Fage also argued that the slave trade had brought a growth in centralized African states, and had to that degree led to social progress.[14] Most of the recent studies of the social and demographic impact of slavery in Africa can be linked to support of one or the other of these theses.

To reduce these complex issues to a crude choice: the question is whether the export slave trade had a great influence on African life and Atlantic life (as Rodney argued), or whether it had a small influence (as Fage implied).

Old disputes that live on

These are the materials and the debates which make up the recent literature on African slavery. But the debates are not new. The contradictions between the Rodney and Fage theses – between maximizing and minimizing the negative influence of slavery on Africa – can be traced back through two centuries of writings on African slavery. Nor is there any reason to expect contemporary scholarship to be so sophisticated as to be free of the outlooks and biases inherited from earlier times: our age, while methodologically more sophisticated, is psychologically no less partisan than earlier times.

A review of past controversies should help make explicit the conflicts inherent in more recent discussion of African slavery. In part to re-emphasize the emotionally and politically charged nature of this issue, I will review some of the high points in changing attitudes among writers on African slavery over the past two centuries, and demonstrate how changing social conditions in Africa – and also in Europe and the Americas – have caused writers to take sharply different positions on slavery and its impact. These earlier ideas remain with us: each has contributed to the sediment of reasoning and evidence on which contemporary writers draw. In part, looking at earlier statements will reveal more baldly the motives and biases now covered but not neutralized by more sophisticated methodology.

David Brion Davis has lucidly and convincingly shown that, until after 1750, there was no organized opposition to the institution of slavery, and therefore no real debate on the subject. He saw one crucial turning-point as the publication in 1754 of a pamphlet entitled *Some Considerations on the Keeping of Negroes* by John Woolman, a Quaker tailor from New Jersey, after his visit to Quaker slaveholders in Virginia and North Carolina. By 1758 the Philadelphia Yearly Meeting of Quakers agreed with Woolman that no Christian could own a slave without threatening his own salvation, since the master could not resist the temptation to exploit the slave. By 1761 the London Yearly Meeting excluded from its membership any persons dealing in slaves.[15]

Another example of this turning-point is the case of the French official Joseph Pruneau de Pommegorge, who wrote in 1752 a description of Senegal and Dahomey which described the cruelties of the slave trade and its politics, but without comment. By 1789, however, the same facts had a different meaning for the author. Pruneau submitted to King Louis XVI an equally detailed *mémoire*, since published, but now with a plea for the king's support for the abolition of the slave trade.[16]

The active defense of slavery rose at the same time as its critique. Under similar political conditions on the other side of the Channel, Archibald Dalzel, an English factor in West Africa, published in 1793 a *History of Dahomy* which described the same cruelties as Pruneau, yet attributed them to the inherent nature of African society rather than to the slave trade. He argued that the purchase of slaves had the merit of saving captives from otherwise inevitable execution.[17]

Dalzel won at least part of his point. Even the most successful example of anti-slavery iconography – the plan of the ship *Brookes* showing several hundreds of black slaves chained into place (see p. 153) – addressed only the issue of the Middle Passage and left aside the question of slavery in Africa.[18] Only gradually did anti-slavery activists in the Occident claim that slavery was destructive to life in Africa. In the 1830s Thomas Fowell Buxton, in his grand parliamentary proposal for the British abolition of slavery, estimated that one slave died in Africa for every one who reached the coast.[19]

Still, the assertion that slavery was greatly destructive to African life did not gain a wide audience until the second voyage of David Livingstone. Livingstone made his reputation as an explorer with his journey to what is

15

now Zambia in the 1850s. He returned for a second voyage up the Zambezi which failed in almost all its stated purposes of opening up trade and winning converts, yet brought him further fame because of his heart-rending descriptions of the incredible waste and carnage in the East African slave trade, which was rapidly expanding at that time. The work of other missionaries in East Africa, including the French Cardinal Lavigerie of the White Fathers, served to reinforce this view of African slavery.[20]

Beginning in the 1880s, and for reasons not primarily associated with slavery, European powers began their partition of Africa. Given the dominance of the Livingstonian image, the European campaign against slavery now became a part of the campaign for imperial conquest. Descriptions of slave raids, of human sacrifice, and of the senseless exploitation of slaves by African monarchs typically accompanied the celebrations of European conquests in Africa.[21] Humanitarians in the western world celebrated these African conquests as the introduction of civilization and the suppression of barbarity.

The establishment of colonial regimes at the turn of the twentieth century brought a remarkable turnabout in European descriptions of African slavery. European conquerors, who had previously seen African rulers as enemies, now found them to be allies. Whatever the realities of the situation, there is little doubt of the political motivations involved. The European objective was conquest, not social revolution, and the need for law and order in the colonies required that slaves be obedient. European rulers repressed slave raiding and the slave trade with considerable if not relentless energy.[22] The abolition of slavery itself was allowed to be phased in over a generation.

It was under these conditions that the collection of ethnographic reports began. Colonial governments delegated some of their abler and more energetic officials to collect information on the peoples who were now under their rule. These official ethnographers, who were well-informed amateurs generally lacking professional training, collected the data which forms the basis of the "ethnographic present," the information now coded into the great data sets of modern anthropology. Their reports on slavery, while at times including much useful detail, followed the standard format of a balance sheet. They listed the disadvantages of slave status, the protections accorded to slaves, and a summary indicating that the status of slave was not greatly inferior to that of a free person.[23] This description fits the political objectives of the administration. It also fits the social realities of the early twentieth century better than it fits the history of slavery in Africa.

With the end of the 1920s, a new breed of professionally trained anthropologists began to do field work in Africa. Because their aim was the development of social science theory, they tended to begin their work on a relatively small scale within simple societies, so that slavery played a small role in their work. With a few individual exceptions, it took until the 1960s before anthropology had taken African slavery to be a serious topic for analysis.[24]

When the first studies by professional historians of Africa began to appear in the 1950s, they presented an eclectic reflection of earlier writings. For the precolonial period, they tended to present the slave trade as a major motive force in African history, and they emphasized the great extent of African slavery in the nineteenth century. Yet, for the twentieth century, they treated slavery as an institution which withered away rapidly and with few social effects.[25]

As the Africanist tradition strengthened in the 1960s, the new historians sought increasingly to defend African society against the colonialist attempt to discredit it. In doing so, they adopted the functionalist approach of anthropologists, which justified the operation of African society and the strength of its institutions. According to this view, European slave merchants were simply not powerful enough to have determined the course of African history. As a result, early Africanist historians downplayed the importance of the slave trade and slavery as significant and causal factors in African history. Anthropological studies of African slavery, pursuing this functionalist approach, emphasized local peculiarities in slavery rather than the development of a continental system of slavery.[26]

Successive waves of postcolonial social and economic conflict brought forth new perspectives on African slavery. The period of nationalist movements up to 1960 caused Africans to emphasize their unity and the lack of stratification within African society. But after 1960, the emergence of class and ethnic conflict during the difficult period of consolidating new national states provoked African descendants of masters and slaves into identifying themselves as such, and into seeking out the historical roots of their contemporary conflicts. The contemporaneous renaissance of Marxian analysis out of the social conflicts of the 1960s in western countries encouraged scholars to apply class analysis and a world-economic approach to the newly available data on African slavery.[27] The latter emphasis on the world economy was reinforced by the oil crisis of the 1970s and the debt crisis of the 1980s, both of which caused scholars of various political viewpoints to seek out the historical roots of the increasingly integrated, if deeply conflict-ridden, world economy.

This hurried narrative of intellectual effort is intended to make clear that no study of African slavery is innocent of a political viewpoint, but also that most facts on African slavery can be fitted into contradictory paradigms. There is, nonetheless, a certain logic to the development of the literature. That is to suggest, for instance, that the debate on the Atlantic slave trade and slavery of the 1970s would have taken place even without the appearance of Curtin's census. The fact, however, is that the book did appear, and its particular timing, form, and quality moved the debate along.[28]

The two centuries of contributions mentioned and alluded to above remain a precious resource, despite the many contradictions among them. I hope to show, in the interpretation which follows, that most of the contradictions among these writers can be resolved – and many of the rest

17

can be explained if not resolved – by setting them properly in the context of conditions changing over space and time.

The remainder of this chapter consists, therefore, first of a summary of the main evidence on which my interpretation relies and, second, of a summary of the main conclusions I will attempt to support with the argument.

Evidence and methods in this analysis

The first type of evidence is demographic: the volume, sex, and age composition of slaves exported from Africa. The best evidence is on the total volume of slave exports, and it is summarized in figure 1.1. There is shown, for the Western Coast, for the Eastern Coast, for the Savanna and Horn, and for their total, an expansion, a peak, and a contraction in the volume of exports. While the timing of the movement for each of the sub-continental areas is somewhat different, the result for tropical Africa as a whole is a steady expansion of slave exports until the mid-eighteenth century, a plateau in the total volume of exports until the middle of the nineteenth century (with peak exports in the 1820s and 1830s), and then a

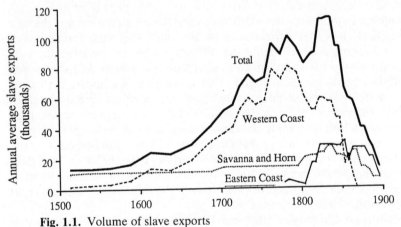

Fig. 1.1. Volume of slave exports

rapid decline to the virtual extinction of slave exports by the turn of the twentieth century.

The second category of data is economic, and within this category the best data are on slave prices, especially for the Occidental trade. Prices of slaves rose and fell in a pattern anticipating the changing volumes of slave exports. The prices shown in figure 1.2 are an average of real (or constant value) prices of slaves sold on the Western Coast of Africa. These prices declined in the mid-seventeenth century after an earlier peak, then rose dramatically at the turn of the eighteenth century, and remained roughly at that level for several decades. Slave prices declined sharply at the turn of the nineteenth century, fluctuated through the 1840s, and then declined again. The lower prices of the late nineteenth century, however, were much higher than slave prices of the seventeenth century.[29]

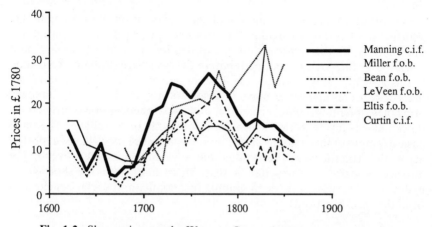

Fig. 1.2. Slave prices on the Western Coast of Africa

Meanwhile, in those areas of the New World where slavery remained legal, prices rose steadily during the nineteenth century in response to improved slave productivity. Thus, as a result of the increasing cost of moving slaves across the Atlantic, there emerged after 1800 a growing divergence of African and New World slave prices.[30]

The third category of evidence is institutional, and the most important institutional data for our purposes are those documenting the rise and fall of domestic African slavery. While the institution of African slavery can be traced back almost as far as historical records are to be found, there is clear evidence for many areas of the continent that, during the nineteenth century (and in some areas during the late eighteenth century), the scope and intensity of African slavery expanded greatly.[31] Slavery became, then, not just a social status accorded to some, but a way of life, a mode of production, and a social system. It was set in place at the beginning of the century, then destroyed in the course of the European conquests at the end of the century.

A fourth category of evidence is that on African ideas and ideologies regarding slavery. While much study remains to be done in this area, and while evidence is scarce from African societies where only a few people were literate, available evidence indicates that Africans had a contending and changing set of ideologies to rationalize their involvement with slavery. Most of these ideologies attempted to picture slavery as an extension of African family systems, but they defined families in varied and contradictory fashions.[32]

The methodology by which I will organize and analyze these categories of evidence is, as I noted above, that of political economy. That is, I will rely on standard principles of demography and standard principles of price theory, but I will integrate political, social, and ideological variables into the analysis.

In addition to this general methodological orientation, I must emphasize a further methodological axiom: the "window" principle. It is required, for this analysis, by the relative shortage of demographic and economic data collected on the African continent before the twentieth century. According to this principle, if we monitor the flows of persons and goods to and from the African continent, we may, in association with the use of standard principles of demographic, economic, and social theory, make projections on conditions inside Africa which are not directly observable.[33] The most basic example of this axiom's application is that, since most slaves exported across the Atlantic were young adult males, we may presume – even in the absence of African census data – that Africa had a relative shortage of males, and we may draw demographic, economic, and social conclusions from that presumption.

Theses on slavery and African life

What was the link between Atlantic capitalism and slavery? What was the link between slave exports and African society? Rodney and Williams sought to assert the existence of significant links in each of these areas, and an important place for Africans in the unfolding of the modern world. In a sense, one could say that the outline of my interpretation is an attempt to appropriate the heritage of the Rodney thesis and the Williams thesis: slave exports generated an expansion of African slavery, slavery in Africa and the Americas was an important contributor to capitalist construction, and capitalism brought about the end of slavery. On the other hand, I argue quite differently than either Rodney or Williams, and in a somewhat different context. Some of these conclusions are restatements of well-known scholarly consensus, while others are results of new research. All are discussed in detail in the chapters to follow.

The timing of the rise and fall of slavery

Slavery existed in most parts of the world in ancient and medieval times: Africa and the Middle East were no exception. The African and Oriental slave trades drew, at a modest level, on the Savanna and Horn in medieval times and into the modern period. The Occidental trade began along the Western Coast in the fifteenth century and grew steadily until the nineteenth century, though a key point in its expansion was passed in the mid-seventeenth century when the needs of sugar production came to dominate the demand for slaves. This expanded Occidental trade caused, in turn, the expansion of the African trade and of African slavery.

In the late eighteenth century, purchases of slaves along the Eastern Coast of Africa expanded, fueled initially by demand from the Occidental market. In the nineteenth century, Oriental demand grew significantly. Slave deliveries across the Sahara, Red Sea, and Indian Ocean expanded, and remained at their high level until 1870. Once again, now in northern and eastern regions, the rise of slave exports brought an expansion of the African trade and of African slavery.

The decline of slavery began in the west and proceeded to the east. Region after region was forcibly removed from the slave trade and then from slavery. Occidental demand began its decline with the Haitian revolution of the 1790s, and slipped further downward with the abolition of the slave trade by the Danes, British, Americans, French, and Dutch. From 1820 the Occidental trade was mainly restricted to Cuba, Brazil, and (in the Indian Ocean) French Reunion, but the volume of slave exports to these areas rebounded for another thirty years. After 1850 the Occidental trade was virtually over. The African trade expanded through most of the nineteenth century in compensation for declining Atlantic trade, reaching its peak in the 1870s. Oriental demand for African slaves, meanwhile, was progressively cut off by European constraints in the period from 1870 to 1900. African demand for slaves, finally, was halted with the European conquests in Africa, mostly in the years 1890–1905.

Economic mechanisms of the slave trade

Occidental demand for slaves resulted primarily from the determination of Europeans to profit from their conquests in the New World, and the need for labor in their sparsely populated colonies. Europeans focused this demand on Africans because of their relative immunity to disease, the low transport cost resulting from their relative proximity to the New World, and their low purchase price.

Africans supplied slaves at these low prices not because of an overall surplus of labor nor because of an inherent disregard for their own kind. Prices were low, for one reason, because they were prices at which merchants sold their slaves, rather than prices at which Africans would freely contract to migrate across the ocean. More fundamentally, prices were low because the low level of agricultural productivity set by hoe agriculture limited the value of labor even when it was scarce.

The process of enslavement resulted in a two-tiered price structure, distinguishing the very low price of a newly taken captive (a price based not on the value of the person but on the cost of capturing him or her), and the higher price of a slave ready to be put to work (a price based on the value of that slave's potential output). The fluctuations in both sets of prices determined the profits of African slave merchants.

Prices of slaves in the Occidental trade (as measured in real terms on the African coast) rose dramatically at the turn of the eighteenth century,

21

remained near their peak level until the late eighteenth century, declined significantly in the early nineteenth century, fluctuated for a time, and then declined to a level which was still well above that of the seventeenth century. A veritable world market in slave labor existed roughly between 1750 and 1850, encompassing the Occidental, African, and Oriental trades. The existence of this world market is demonstrated not by the existence of a single great slave market, but by the interconnection of many local markets and the shipments of slaves in different directions across many frontiers joining the African, Occidental, and Oriental markets.

African slavery expanded in the nineteenth century because of the sharply lower prices of slaves after export markets dried up, because of the expansion of African and overseas markets for agricultural and artisanal goods that could be produced by slaves, and in response to the perfection of African institutions for collecting slaves and for controlling them.

In the Occidental trade, the two most significant African imports in exchange for slaves were textiles and money. The slave trade thus expanded the money supply, but at the expense of scarce labor. It also brought imports of goods which undercut African industry. Money and textiles were elite goods, in the sense that the largest quantities were concentrated in the hands of the rich. On the other hand, few Africans could live without money or textiles. As a result, the prominence of these items in the slave trade reflects the degree to which all of African society, not just a privileged elite, was compromised in the slave trade. Further, the categories of money and textiles sometimes overlapped, as in Senegal and Angola, where certain imported textiles served as money. Other imported money took the form of cowrie shells, iron bars, brass manillas, and European coins.

The demographic and social impact of slavery on Africa

The forms and conditions of slavery in Africa varied widely, in accord with the multiplicity of its ethnic groups and the variety of its local conditions, but most forms of African slavery were influenced and conditioned by the slave trade. Along the Western Coast, the positive response to Occidental demand for slaves caused slaves to become more available. African demand for slaves then grew, and it focused mainly on female slaves, both because of their sexuality (their value in reproduction and their use as sex objects) and because their economic productivity could be utilized without entailing the degree of physical rebelliousness of male slaves. The combination of the Occidental preference for male slaves and the African preference for female slaves led to a pattern in which two-thirds of slave exports to Occidental markets were male, and only one-third were female.

Slave exports brought about substantial distortions in African sex ratios: along the Western Coast most male slaves were exported and the remaining population became dominantly female; in the Savanna and Horn most slaves exported to the Orient were female, so that the remaining population became dominantly male. The result of these imbalances was that the institutions of slavery, of marriage, and the sexual division of labor were placed under great pressure to change. Slave exports drew most heavily on the young adult population until the nineteenth century, when children were exported in particularly large numbers.

Total tropical African population was held in check during the eighteenth and nineteenth centuries by the slave trade. The continental loss of slave exports averaging nearly 100,000 persons each year for a century was compounded by the mortality of captives on the way to export, the mortality of captives retained within Africa, the concentration of captives in the fertile young adult ages, and the limits on compensatory increases in African fertility. The long decline in the population of the Western Coast, from 1750 to 1850, offset population growth elsewhere on the continent. In addition, the population on the Eastern Coast declined for fifty years in the middle of the nineteenth century; the population fell for shorter times in parts of the Savanna and Horn.

The effect of the slave trade on African politics was to build up the power and wealth of kings and warlords in the short run, but to create conditions of instability and collapse in many African polities over the longer run.

The slave population in Africa was roughly equal in size to the New World slave population from the seventeenth to the early nineteenth centuries (though slaves were a larger *proportion* of total population in the Americas than in Africa). After about 1850, there were more slaves in Africa than in the New World. The nineteenth-century growth of the African slave trade not only expanded the scale of African slavery, but caused a new set of institutional transformations. African sex ratios now tended to equalize, putting new pressure on the institutions of slavery, marriage, and the sexual division of labor. A slave mode of production flowered for a half-century, until it was ended under European colonization.

The abolition of slavery

The abolition of slavery in the Atlantic world correlates in a broad fashion with the development of industrial capitalism, though the causal relationships between the two remain in dispute. The abolition of slavery in Africa was an aspect of the world-wide movement for abolition, so the issues familiar to students of abolition in other areas reappear in Africa.

The abolition of the *slave trade* in Africa, while linked to the dominantly white humanitarian movement and to black opposition to slavery, became in practice an aspect of European imperial conquest of Africa.

The abolition of *slavery* in Africa – quite a different matter from the abolition of the slave trade – was slowed by the establishment of ties between European colonial rulers and African slave owners. But the abolition of African slavery was brought about, as elsewhere, by the

23

pressure of slaves, by moral pressure from Christian leaders and the educated elite, both black and white, and by pressure for development of a wage work force.

The heritage of slavery

Our understanding of the Atlantic heritage of slavery must advance to recognize the full contribution of African slaves and the full cost of African slavery. Slave production in the Americas provided a significant proportion of total output in the construction of the New World economy, even after 1850. Slavery was also central to the functioning of African economies in the eighteenth and nineteenth centuries. In Europe as well, slaves contributed directly and indirectly to economic expansion. If the contributions of slavery were great, the costs were even greater. The cost of slave production must include not only the cost to New World slave owners but the cost to African economies and the cost to the slaves themselves – notably through sheer demographic waste. When these factors are included, the overall rates of growth and profitability in the Atlantic economy are seen to be lower than if the calculation were done simply in terms of returns to proprietors' capital.

Similarly, we must recognize the economic and demographic contribution of Africans to North Africa, the Middle East, and the Indian Ocean. African slaves performed a significant portion of the menial and domestic work in those areas, especially from the late eighteenth to early twentieth centuries, and a larger portion of the regional population has African ancestry than is commonly recognized.

The heritage of slavery manifests itself even today in Africa: in the distribution of population, in marriage patterns, in continuing class distinctions, and in total population size, which remains relatively low despite its recent rapid growth. Further, while slavery ended in the early twentieth century, subsequent African labor systems retained important continuities with slave labor, including reliance on migration, on compulsion, on low pay, and on uneven sex ratios.

This heritage of slavery reaches us, of course, through the filter of subsequent events. The great events of the twentieth century – wars, colonial rule, and capitalist economic impact – have had immense transformative power in Africa. Yet these recent influences transformed an African world which had itself been dramatically restructured by the changing impact of slavery and the slave trade. The details of slavery's legacy may not always be obvious or easily summarized, but it would be a mistake to assume that the history of slavery has been rendered irrelevant by more recent events.

In the ideological arena, racism is the most pervasive and persistent Atlantic heritage of slavery. Racism resulted from slavery, and from the unique economic conditions which concentrated the impact of modern slavery on black people. While the interactions of slavery and racial prejudice are complex and subtle, there can be no doubt about this basic direction of causation. To phrase the point inversely, there is no way a simple European prejudice against Africans could have constructed a system so vast and so iniquitous. Beyond this basic direction of causation, however, slavery and racism reinforced each other through an intricate dialectic. An important instance of this dialectic is that the decline of slavery in the Atlantic world paralleled and in part provoked the most extreme outbursts of racial prejudice against black people, at the turn of the twentieth century. Racism, of course, has continued to exist well after the abolition of slavery, a fact which demonstrates that slavery is not the only factor propagating racist ideas. Nevertheless, the ideology of racism remains the clearest reminder that we still live with the heritage of slavery.

The unity and diversity of Africa

In the pages above I have already begun to offer conclusions about "Africa" and "Africans." The prudent reader should ask whether it is valid to attempt generalizations about so vast an area as the planet's second-largest continent and its millions of inhabitants.[34] Should one speak of one Africa or of many Africas? In fact I will do both.

Slavery helped, ironically, to create one Africa out of many. The irony is that the conditions of slavery, by the very arrogance and insensitivity of the oversimplified categorization of "the blacks," ultimately faced all black people with the same structures and the same dilemmas. These facts – the experience of slavery and the ideology of racism – brought responses among black people which led to the development of a Pan-African identity to match their common dilemma. Africans came to recognize each other as brothers and sisters, and to construct a common identity out of the repression and denigration they shared. The creation of one Africa, initiated by the impact of slavery, was taken to completion by the impact of colonialism (which brought another sort of oppression in the late nineteenth and twentieth centuries), and by the new forms of racism which developed in the twentieth century. The two sides to this process – the external action and the African reaction – together amount to what V. Y. Mudimbe has labelled the "invention of Africa."[35] In any case Africa, whether invented or inherited, is a reality of the modern world, and I have endeavored to develop a set of Pan-African generalizations for the pages of this book. They are a fundamental part of my interpretation, because they demonstrate the systematic moulding of African life by world-economic forces, they elucidate the continental trends that emerge as the resultant of disparate local trends, and they indicate where Africa has fitted into the emergence of the modern world economy.

Yet there remain many Africas. Africa – given the range of its languages, cultures, geographic and economic conditions – is the most diverse of the continents. Not even such powerful and systematic pressures as the New

World demand for slaves or the colonizers' demand for tax revenue and cheap labor were sufficient to make Africa homogeneous. The diversity continues.

Equally important to emphasizing the existence of African diversity is to demonstrate that such diversity has little to do with the isolation of African villages. The myth of African isolation, created centuries ago, will perhaps outlive us all. But it remains a myth. In fact the diversity of Africa continues to reproduce itself because different Africans, acting on the basis of their own specific environment, culture, and individual choice, have parried the external thrusts of slavery and colonialism in a panoply of directions. Thus there were and there remain many Africas, not because each village was isolated from all the rest, but because, in interacting with each other and with the outside world, distinct populations relied effectively on the specificity of local conditions and outlooks. As a result, the very diversity of Africa is one of the defining characteristics of continental and Pan-African identity.

As a result, in discussing slavery and African life, we shall have to keep our minds engaged at several levels: at the Pan-African level (where we focus on continental transformations and the role of Africa in the world economy), and at levels of regional and local distinctions (where we focus on the many variables held constant in the continental analysis). In addition, we must keep track of changes over time for each of the above. The reality of the past – that which we seek to reconstruct – carried on at all these levels. For the scholar or the student in social sciences, the point is perhaps that studying African affairs helps at once to develop broad conceptual rigor and sensitivity to the specifics of individual situations.

2

Why Africans? The rise of the slave trade to 1700

Why were Africans enslaved in such large numbers, and over such a wide area, that there grew up in western thought an almost automatic connection between black people and slave status? Why did the European conquerors of the New World need to import so much labor? Why did it have to be African labor? And why, finally, did the laborers have to be in slave status?

In fact, the connection that has been made between Africans and slavery is often overdrawn. Slavery has been an institution common to many – perhaps most – societies in recorded history. What distinguishes Africa and Africans with regard to slavery, however, is *modernity*. The enslavement of Africans increased in the modern period, a time when enslavement of most other peoples was dying out. This was true in the Occidental and Oriental areas which imported African slaves; it was also true in Africa, where slavery expanded from a somewhat marginal institution to one of central importance during the modern period.

Orlando Patterson, in his cross-cultural, transhistorical study of slavery, demonstrates the near-universality of the slave condition, touching on ancient Mesopotamia, classical Greece, medieval Korea, the Vikings of Europe, and Native North Americans, to name but a few of the societies he discusses.[1] Let us investigate this universality of slavery a bit further, in order to set African slavery in a broader context.

Slavery in the ancient, medieval, and modern worlds

In ancient times, slavery is best documented for the Mediterranean societies of Greece and Rome, though it is known in some detail for ancient Mesopotamia as well. Greek slavery was dominantly urban and artisanal. Slaves were mostly non-Greeks, captured in war or purchased, and they came to represent as much as one-third of the population in the leading Greek states. In Rome, such urban slave artisans, while of great importance in the economy, were outnumbered by a much larger rural population of slave agricultural laborers, so that as much as one-third of the entire population of Roman Italy was in slave status.[2] The slave population did not reproduce itself – both because of manumission and a low rate of reproduction – so that slavery could only be sustained by the continual capture of new slaves. If slave production was not especially efficient, the exploitation of slaves nonetheless produced a substantial surplus which, concentrated in the hands of a small elite, helped significantly to bring about the brilliant achievements of the ancient Mediterranean.

Slavery is also documented for ancient China and the civilizations of India, although the place of slaves in these economies seems to have been lesser than in Rome. In China, the presence of a large agricultural population under the administration of a strong central government (since the days of the Han dynasty beginning in the first millennium BC if not before) meant that there was no great shortage of servile labor, and little need for slaves. Slaves were but a small proportion of the population, probably under 5 percent, and they were owned mainly by the state.[3] Slavery in ancient India was likewise limited in its extent; conquest to obtain slaves and agricultural exploitation of slaves appeared there as well.[4]

With the medieval period (the period from roughly 400 to 1500 AD), slavery can be documented for a wider range of societies. Slavery in India and China continued for the medieval period, the institution expanded in medieval Korea, and debt-servitude came to be of significance in South East Asia.[5] For portions of India and China this slavery came under Islamic regulation. The Mongol conquests of the thirteenth century resulted in the enslavement of a great number of people, and in the extension of large-scale slavery to new areas, notably to Russia. Two of the Mongol successor states, the Il-Khanids of Persia and the Khanate of the Golden Horde in Central Asia, adopted Islam, and in those areas as well slavery came under Muslim regulation.[6]

In the Mediterranean slavery survived the fall of Rome, though its extent diminished and it was eventually replaced, in many areas of Europe, with serfdom. Slavery in the Mediterranean, however, came to be dominated by a new order: that of the rapidly expanding Islamic world. A controversy has long raged as to whether Islam served more to spread slavery or to restrict it. Did the institutions of Islam have the effect of expanding slavery by recognizing and codifying it, or did Islam limit the extent of slavery by legislating against the abuse of the slave?[7] The answer seems to vary with the time and the place. The latter argument is convincing for the case of the Arabian peninsula and, to a lesser degree, for the whole area of the Umayyad Caliphate: slavery had existed since the most ancient times in what became the Islamic heartland, so that the Qur'ān and religious law served to limit the abuses of slaves with such injunctions as the encouragement of slave owners to manumit their slaves at death. But with the passage of time and the extension of Islam into further areas, Islam seems to have done more to protect and expand slavery than the reverse. In an early example of this influence, the Muslim conquerors of Egypt levied an annual tribute on the Christian kingdom of Dongola in the middle Nile valley: this tribute, known as the *baqt*, was paid by the rulers of Dongola to the rulers of Egypt from about 650 AD until the fourteenth century, and required Dongola to furnish some 400 slaves each year. Throughout the medieval period, much larger numbers of slaves were drawn into the Islamic heartland from Africa, the Caucasus, the Black Sea, and other areas.[8]

In the medieval era, Islam spread to significant areas of sub-Saharan Africa. These areas must therefore be viewed as part of the Islamic world and not, as is too often the case, as irrelevant appendages to it. While it is known that Mali and Borno exported slaves across the Sahara, it may also be the case that slavery expanded within those societies by the same logic that sustained the institution elsewhere in the Islamic world.[9]

Slavery in most of Europe declined in the medieval era, as the Roman heritage of slavery was gradually transformed into medieval serfdom. But European slavery went beyond the heritage of Rome: the Vikings, especially during the period of their emigration, conquests, and long-distance trade, held slaves in fairly large numbers.[10]

During the crusades – the Mediterranean religious wars of the eleventh through fifteenth centuries – Christians enslaved Muslims and Muslims enslaved Christians. These Crusades continued longest in the west, where the long Christian *reconquista* of the Iberian peninsula, along with wars in North Africa and piracy in the Mediterranean, served to keep slavery alive and well. Indeed, the Spanish and Portuguese voyages of discovery may be seen, in part, as extensions of the Crusades.

Meanwhile, the association between sugar and slavery took form in the medieval Mediterranean, and spread slowly from east to west. The Belgian historian Charles Verlinden has provided magnificent documentation of the early days of sugar production in Syria and Palestine, of its adoption by European Crusaders, of the use of slaves to perform the heavy labor of planting, cutting, and refining, and of the concentration of sugar production on islands, beginning with Cyprus, and then moving to Malta, the Balearic Islands and later, with the early Atlantic voyages, to the Canaries, the Madeiras, and particularly to São Thomé.[11]

With the modern period, after 1500, slavery contracted in some areas of the world, in Europe, in China, and in parts of the Islamic world. One outstanding exception to this regression of slavery was Russia. Russian slavery was unusual in several respects: the slaves were Russian slaves of Russian masters, and they were often self-enslaved. That is, persons without land and unable to gain an existence sold themselves into slavery as a last resort. This system expanded greatly in the sixteenth and seventeenth centuries, and was replaced by the "second serfdom" of Russian peasants.[12] Another case of modern expansion of slavery was in the Dutch East Indies, where Dutch planters enslaved Indonesians for work on sugar and coffee plantations. Slavery, however, was gradually replaced with other forms of servile labor as the Dutch regime proceeded.[13] The demand for slaves in the Islamic heartland of the Middle East and North Africa remained at much the same level as the medieval era shaded into the modern, but the points of origin of the slaves moved southward: Black Sea slaves tended to be replaced by African slaves. In the New World, Spanish and Portuguese conquerors enslaved Indians as well as Africans in Central and South America during the sixteenth century, but by the seventeenth century almost all slaves in the Americas were of African origin.

The net result of all these transformations in the extent of slavery can be summarized by saying that, in 1500, Africans and persons of African descent were a clear minority of the world's slave population, but that by 1700 Africans and persons of African descent had become the majority of the world's slave population. African slavery is a phenomenon of the modern world.

To explain why African slavery grew to such an extent in the modern period, and why it lasted so long, we will turn first to a narrative of its expansion, and then draw from the narrative some specific consideration of the demand for and the supply of African slaves.

The Occidental demand for African slaves

As the Portuguese first worked their way along the African coast from around 1440, they captured and purchased slaves which they took to Portugal and to such Atlantic islands as the Azores, the Madeira Islands, the Cape Verde Islands, the Canaries, and São Thomé. The slaves in Portugal were surprisingly numerous, but they were only part of a larger slave labor force including Arab and Andalusian (or Spanish Muslim) captives. The islands, on the other hand, which had been generally unpopulated, became miniature models of what was to develop in the New World.[14]

It is only with the New World that one can explain the European demand for large numbers of slaves. As the Spanish and Portuguese *conquistadores* strode across the Americas, they expropriated wealth and shipped it home until there was little left to seize. Soon enough, they found that they would have to satisfy their thirst for wealth by going beyond expropriation: they would have to *produce* wealth. But since these *conquistadores* had no intention of performing the work themselves, their desire to produce entailed the creation of a labor force under their control. Such a labor force would have to be both productive and cheap, for otherwise the cost of production and transportation would prevent the resulting goods from being sold on the distant markets of Europe, and no profit would be realized. The first impulse of the Spanish was to enslave the Native Americans, but their high mortality and their continuing hope of escape made them unsatisfactory slaves.[15]

Epidemiology is one major factor which pointed toward a demand for African labor. The introduction of Old World diseases to the isolated New World populations decimated them. Smallpox, plague, typhus, yellow fever, and influenza carried away large numbers. While one may doubt the very high estimates of pre-Columbian population proposed by Dobyns and Borah (they estimate as many as 100 million inhabitants of the New World in 1492), their estimated low point of some 5 million Native Americans in the early seventeenth century can be accepted as plausible.[16] With such a rate of extinction, it is remarkable that the cultures and societies of the New World survived.

Of the Old World populations, the Africans had the misfortune and the advantage of living in the most disease-ridden area.[17] Malarial mortality rates for African children took a very heavy toll, but those who survived to maturity had near immunity from malaria, from other African diseases, and also from many of the diseases known in Europe. For European adults not previously exposed to African malaria, on the other hand, the death-rate in the first year of exposure ranged from 30 per cent to 50 per cent; death-rates from New World malaria were slightly lower. So it was that Africans, all other things being equal, had the lowest mortality rate of any population in the New World.

All other things were not equal, of course. The full picture of the Occidental demand for slaves must include not only this epidemiological factor, but other aspects of demography, institutional factors, and such economic factors as labor cost and the demand for slave produce, especially sugar. Since the slaves were given the heaviest work, a minimum of physical care, and poor social conditions, they died in large numbers and failed to bear enough children to reproduce themselves.

This leads us to consider the nature of the work as a cause for the demand for African labor and the demand for slaves in particular. Much of the work done by slaves was on sugar plantations and in mines, though they also provided a great deal of domestic service. We have already seen for the Mediterranean how the particular intensity of labor in sugar production always seemed to point to slavery. For mines as well, a coerced labor force presented great advantages for the owners. Africans mined gold in Brazil and various minerals in lowland Spanish territories.[18] (In one important exception, the silver mines of the *altiplano*, the Spanish relied on a work-force drawn from the local population – miners whose descendants are now the tin miners of Bolivia.)

Slaves did more than cut cane and mine gold: there was always a range of agricultural, domestic, and artisanal tasks to be performed. This range of tasks is one of the reasons for the remarkable stability in the age and sex composition of slaves purchased by Europeans from the fifteenth through the nineteenth century. For example sixteenth-century Spanish settlers in the Canary Islands bought slaves ranging widely in age but averaging just over 20 years of age, of whom just over 60 per cent were male; prices of male slaves averaged 5 per cent higher than those of females.[19] These figures were similar to those for African slave exports over two centuries later. While the range of slave tasks was wide, the slaves were often

31

prevented from becoming skilled artisans. But from manumitted slaves and free mulattos in sixteenth-century Peru and Mexico, for instance, there grew up classes of artisans whose ambitions and competitiveness brought down upon them wrath and restrictions from their Spanish competitors. This ethnic competition among whites, mulattos, and free blacks for artisanal work was to show up repeatedly in New World colonies.[20]

African disease resistance, the economic advantages of slavery in sugar and mine work, and the need to replenish lost slaves with new ones set the pattern for the demand for slaves. But new developments were required for the amplitude of this demand to increase. Among these was the entry of the northern European powers into competition for power on the oceans. Early in the seventeenth century the Dutch, followed by the English, French, as well as the Danes, Swedes, and Brandenburgers, scoured the oceans for treasure, trade, and colonies.[21] When the Dutch took much of Brazil in 1630, they showed little interest in European settlement and instead got right to work on extending Brazilian sugar plantations, implementing a number of significant and cost-saving technical improvements as they did so. They also began to seek out new sources of African slaves. The Dutch experience in Brazil, while it ended with their expulsion at the hands of the Portuguese in 1654, was the harbinger of the new order. British and French colonies in the West Indian islands began with the settlement of Europeans but within a generation sugar showed itself to be the most remunerative crop and a slave population progressively crowded out the white settlers.[22]

One may ask why the European demand for sugar increased so rapidly at this time. Part of it was the reduction of the cost in sugar brought by improved technology and perhaps cheaper shipping. More importantly, European consumption habits were changing, with the advance of urbanization. With changes in the countryside, bee-keeping had been undercut and production of honey reduced.[23]

With these factors now in place, sugar plantations expanded steadily, and with them increased their need for slave labor. The flow of slaves to the New World, which came to exceed the number going to the Orient in about 1650, continued to increase for a century at a rate of about 2 percent per year.

The supply of African slaves

This continuing upward spiral of slave purchases was possible, however, only because of the relatively low prices at which African slaves could be bought. Transportation costs for moving Africans to the New World were lower than for Europeans, but this was not a major factor. So the explanation for the concentration of modern slavery on Africans is not complete until it accounts for the supply of slaves from Africa.

Could it be, as some have argued, that Africa was simply burdened with a surplus population? Was Africa overpopulated in relation to its resources? Were thousands – ultimately millions – of Africans incapable of making valuable contributions to their societies? Or, to put it more gently, is it possible that the captives were removed from Africa without significantly reducing African levels of production?[24] The error in such approaches becomes apparent immediately when one considers Africa's relative abundance of land and labor, the two great factors of production in agricultural societies. For most parts of precolonial Africa, land, rather than labor, was abundant. African patterns of shifting cultivation, preserved well into the twentieth century, demonstrate the ready availability of land. Farmers typically opened up new fields every second year, and left their previous fields in fallow for ten years or more. Labor, in comparison to land, was relatively scarce, and its utilization involved difficult choices. The opening of new fields was limited not so much by the shortage of land as by the shortage of labor. And if labor was not initially in short supply, it certainly should have become so in the wake of the disorientation and depopulation that was to come in the eighteenth and nineteenth centuries.[25]

To argue in this way, however, is to propose a paradox: if labor was the limiting resource in Africa, why did Africans agree to sell so many million able-bodied persons to be carried away from their homes? A clue to the solution is suggested in a cynical old saw: "Every man has his price." Or, to update the language a little, European slave buyers were able to make African merchants an offer they could not refuse.

The resolution of this paradox relies on an insight offered by Jack Goody in one of his wide-ranging, cross-cultural studies. Goody divided the peoples of the world acording to their technology, into peoples of the plow and peoples of the hoe. Peoples of the plow – in Europe, North Africa, and the Middle East – were able, thanks to an efficient technology, to produce a relatively large amount of agricultural output and to support relatively large urban populations. Peoples of the hoe, regardless of their individual levels of energy and initiative, were doomed by their technology to produce smaller amounts of agricultural output. The reasons for the technical inferiority of African agriculture, in turn, were technical rather than social – the difficulty of using draft animals because of tsetse fly and sleeping sickness, and lateritic tropical soils, easily leached, which generally respond poorly to plowing.[26]

Thus, to the degree that a person is valued in terms of the value of goods he or she can produce, the value of an African in African society – even where labor was the limiting resource – was less than that of a European in European society. Since agricultural labor was the primary producer of value in early modern society (in Africa, Europe, and elsewhere) the value of an agricultural worker's productivity set the value of labor in general in a given society.[27]

The logic of African supply of slaves depends, therefore, on the notion that slaves in the New World were more productive than free producers in Africa, with a margin large enough that New World slave owners could pay for the costs of transportation, mortality, and seasoning of their slaves. As long as African agricultural technology, constricted by the limits of the hoe, was trapped at a level of productivity below that of Europeans, European buyers were able to pay consistently more than the value of an African person's produce at home.[28]

So far I have argued that the value of a person (in this case the price of a slave) is determined most fundamentally by his or her productivity: the additional value that person can produce. But every price is a compromise, accepted provisionally by buyer and seller, and prices of slaves were influenced by many more factors than productivity. These additional factors in price determination can generally be classified either as market factors or as institutional factors.

Normally a key element in the price of a commodity is the cost of its production. The problem here is that slaves were "produced" by their families, but were then carried off without the family ever gaining compensation. That is, the economics of slave capture, as Philip Curtin has noted, are the economics of theft.[29] To the captors, the "cost" of a captive was the cost of turning a free person into a captive (that is the cost of capturing, transporting, and sustaining the captive), rather than the much higher cost of "producing" the captive (that is, the cost of raising and educating a person, borne by his or her family). The initial captors sold their captives at low prices precisely because of their low costs of acquiring slaves. This was a market factor, in the sense that these captives were sold at prices well below the normal value of a laborer because they were stolen. But it was also an institutional factor, in the sense that the institutions of enslavement – the structures permitting the theft of humans from their families – made labor appear cheap.[30]

Prices of slaves in Africa were also held down by the limited demand for slave labor or for slave-produced produce: while monarchs relied on slaves to produce for the palace entourage, few other Africans had the wealth to sustain many slaves, nor could they find purchasers for goods the slaves might produce. Yet another type of market factor was the relative preference of European buyers for male slaves, and the preference of African buyers for female slaves.

One key institutional factor keeping African slave prices low was the political fragmentation of the continent. For even given the attractive prices slave purchasers might offer African merchants, there can be no doubt that many Africans, arguing on the basis of personal and societal welfare, opposed the enslavement and export of slaves. Such reactions are reflected in the policy statements and the actions of sixteenth-century kings in Jolof, Benin, and Kongo.[31] Yet they were insufficient. One way or another, European slave buyers could always find an African who would supply them with slaves. It only required a few greedy or opportunistic persons, who felt they should enrich themselves rather than resist the inexorable pressures of supply and demand, to keep the slave trade alive. Those suppliers, in turn, rapidly became wealthy enough to become a focus of power to whom others had to accommodate.

On the other hand, big men, slave merchants, warlords, all had, through their own greed, inspired feelings of cupidity and revenge in their allies and enemies. So the fortunes built up by slave exporters, while impressive, were often short-lived, as their allies or enemies expropriated them. In yet another reversal, however, the leaders of a successful movement of revenge against African slavers found themselves in control of captives, and then found it to their advantage to sell these captives as slaves for export.[32]

There are, however, records of efforts – some successful – to restrict the scope of enslavement. The rise of the kingdom of Asante in the Gold Coast region, for instance, brought a virtual end to the export of slaves from the area it governed. On the other hand, the state was active in buying and capturing slaves from surrounding areas, with the result that the total volume of Gold Coast slave exports grew in the decades following the rise of Asante. Similarly, the Oyo empire of the Bight of Benin was able to prevent the export of slaves from within its borders as long as it remained strong. However, with the nineteenth-century decline and collapse of Oyo, exports of Yoruba slaves skyrocketed. The nearby but smaller kingdom of Danhomè expanded dramatically at the beginning of the eighteenth century, and at least discussed the policy of attempting to halt slave exports – a policy that was certainly relevant for a region whose population was declining as a result of slave exports. But Danhomè itself was rendered tributary by Oyo and prevented from conquering its whole region, so that the situation was frozen for a century with implacable enemies within easy reach of one another, and the toll in warfare and slave exports continued to be inordinately high.[33]

These examples of the relentless growth of slave exports show that slave exports in many ways fit the model of primary exports from Third World countries in recent years: as prices rose, so did the quantity of slaves supplied. But slaves were unlike exports of rice or palm oil, in that the "producers" of slaves could not simply plant more of their resource to meet increases in demand. The expansion of the slave trade can more accurately be compared to the case of overfishing, where the resource is ultimately unable to renew itself, especially given the long time required to bring a human to adulthood. Those who harvested the slaves were motivated by the higher prices, but the real producers – the families of those to be enslaved – received nothing in reward.[34]

If African agricultural productivity had been as high as that in the Occident, prices for African labor would have been bid up until only a trickling stream of laborers flowed across the Atlantic, rather than the great rush of laborers who crossed the ocean in the holds of slave ships. But the low level of African productivity did not in itself make the slave trade inevitable. Indeed, it is at least an interesting thought experiment – a counterfactual – to consider what would have happened if Europeans had engaged Africans as wage or contract laborers, i.e. if African political fragmentation had not been a factor. African workers would still have been cheaper than Europeans and might have emigrated if offered a sufficiently high remuneration. The Europeans engaging this labor, in paying a higher remuneration, would have earned lower profit levels, which would have reduced the growth rate and the extent of the New World economic system to that degree. African merchants would not have received the earnings from the sale of slaves. On the other hand, after a time, African families would have received remittances from the migrants to the New World (much as European families of the nineteenth and twentieth centuries received remittances from sons and daughters in the Americas). Further, most of the mortality and disorder accompanying enslavement might have been avoided; more generally, Africa would have experienced in much less severe form the contradiction between the grasping for private gain and the achievement of public social welfare. The great private gains to be won through slavery, however, meant that this contract-labor alternative was passed by.

Yet perhaps (the reader may argue) it was not economic logic that brought Africans to sell slaves, but rather social tradition. After all, had not Africans sold slaves across the Sahara for centuries? Was not African participation in the Occidental trade but the continuation of an established pattern? Indeed, Paul Lovejoy has emphasized the Islamic links in the earliest Portuguese slave trade along the West Coast of Africa.[35] This set of facts might encourage us to treat the slave trade not as an economically or socially rational (if inhuman) activity, but as an addiction or as a contagion, a behavior based on non-rational motivation. In such a view slavery, once begun, continues to replicate itself until it runs out its course, regardless of economic or social consequences. We shall return to this view later. Here we may simply note that while it does help to explain the propagation of slavery, it cannot explain slavery's origins. The motivation of revenge and the logic of contagion served to catalyze the spread of enslavement, but did not cause it.

Instead, of course, we may seek to explain the reasons for the African export of slaves to the Orient. The explanation of the Oriental slave trade breaks down into two parts: in medieval times, the reasons for the movement of African slaves to the Orient before the Atlantic trade became significant; and in modern times, the reasons why the slave trade to the Orient increased after the expansion of the Atlantic slave trade. I shall sketch an explanation of the medieval Oriental trade here, and return in chapter 5 to discuss the modern trade.

The medieval Oriental demand for slaves was based in large part on the desire for domestic servants, though the demand also included demand for soldiers, laborers, and eunuchs. As long as there were alternative sources of supply, African slaves joined slaves of other origins in the Orient. The differential in productivity provides some explanatory power for the movement of slaves to the Orient; most of the slaves were women who were involved in domestic services in the Orient, but many of them had come from agricultural work in Africa. Market forces appear to be more important in this case: the development of market forces in general and a market for slaves in particular caused slaves to move toward the Islamic heartland even when productivity differences were not great.[36]

We have considered the causes of the slave trade, particularly that linking Africa and the Occident. This combination of forces for the European demand for slave labor and African willingness to supply slaves at a relatively low price set in place, by the end of the seventeenth century, a powerful mechanism for large-scale slave migration. Before looking at the African effects of this migration in the next chapter, let us pause to consider one remarkable and well-hidden effect of the slave trade in the Americas. The New World demographic results of this migration, after three centuries, are striking, particularly when it is remembered that Africans had an epidemiological advantage over Europeans. By 1820, some 10 million Africans had migrated to the New World as compared to some 2 million Europeans. But in 1820, the New World white population of some 12 million was roughly twice as great as the black population.[37] The relative rates of survival and reproduction of whites and blacks in the Americas were sharply different.

3

Slavery and the African population: a demographic model

Between 1650 and 1700, the Occidental trade rose to dominate African exports, and began to influence the aggregate size and composition of the African population. The previous chapter discussed the way in which the Occidental trade grew to such significance; this chapter and the following chapter analyze the impact of both the Occidental and Oriental trades on the African population in the eighteenth and nineteenth centuries. That is, these chapters will trace the ways in which the expanding Occidental and Oriental trades each caused the expansion of the African trade.

I have chosen to analyze the impact of the slave trade on Africa here through the device of a model, a simplified and schematic representation of past reality. Though some readers might find it surprising for a historian to use a model so explicitly, the use of models is not unusual in the least. No historian, in presenting a picture of the past, can avoid sketching a distorted image, for it is not possible (nor in this case desirable) to reproduce the full drama of the past. Perhaps it is better, rather than speak of distortion, to say that every historian constructs a *portrait* of the past. For as surely as a painter is restricted to two dimensions in representing the three dimensions of life, a historian is prevented from representing the dimension of time in the exact form it took in the real world of history. Many choices remain, however, in defining each portrait. Just as paintings may be classified into schools or styles of representation and abstraction, so also may the work of historians be characterized according to their approach to representing the past, or to abstracting from it. I have chosen, in relying on a formal model, to emphasize a logically consistent interpretation of African slavery which downplays nuance and detail in return for comprehensiveness. This will provide a different historical portrait than one emphasizing individual successes and failures, or one emphasizing the complex interactions of many different factors in the history of slavery.[1] This is an attempt to tell a broad but simple story of demographic and economic change in the slave trade. This particular model has some properties which give it an individual character, as will be discussed below, but it is not fundamentally different from social science models in general, nor is it fundamentally different from the usual sort of historical reasoning.

38

The demographic model summarizes the effects of the slave trade on the African population. I present it at three levels of complication. First, I introduce the model in its simplest, static form: a cross-sectional slice of the slave trade at its late-eighteenth-century height. The variables in this static model are the prices of male and female slaves and the levels of fertility, mortality, and migration in the slave trade. The results of the model provide estimates of changes in the size and structure of African populations and of slave populations in the Occidental and Oriental worlds. Second, I discuss the model in comparative statics form, allowing for changes over time. The changes over time are reflected in changing levels of these same price and demographic variables; the results yield predictions of changes in population size and structure over the period from 1650 to 1900. Third, I present the model in interactive form, allowing the variables to influence each other as the process of enslavement unfolds. Here, in particular, I discuss the possibility that fertility and mortality interacted with each other, and with such factors as famine and epidemic. The results suggest the degree to which these more complex considerations change the results of the simpler forms of the model.

In this chapter I focus on the *direction* of the effects of the slave trade on the African population. Estimates of the actual *magnitude* of the demographic effects are presented in the following chapter.

The direction of demographic effects: the static model

Why did the Occidental trade leave a large and visible population of African origin in the New World, while the Oriental trade has left few visible traces in the Middle East population? Which of these two export slave trades had the greatest effect on Africa? How large was the slave population of Africa? A simple, static form of the demographic model provides responses to these questions.

The cast of characters in this initial version of the model, as well as in subsequent modifications, includes groups to be known by such descriptive titles as Sources, Captors, Captives, New Exports, and Domestics. That is, the African populations are divided into age and sex groupings, and they are also divided into further analytical categories. The largest two groups are the *Sources* (who lose more people than they gain through enslavement), and the *Captors* (who gain more slaves than they lose). Crudely, these were the Raided and the Raiders, the losers and the winners in the grim game of enslavement. As we shall see, it is not always possible to divide African populations into Source and Captor groups, as the two roles often overlapped or were exchanged with time. Even such a powerful Captor state as Danhomè lost a share of its population to those with whom it warred. Nevertheless, the distinction between Sources and Captors seizes the essence of the relationship for a short-run, cross-sectional analysis. The next group consists of the *Captives*, those taken from the Sources by the

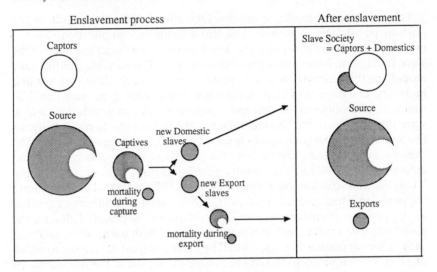

Fig. 3.1. The model in schematic form

Captors. The Captives, if they survive, are eventually added into either the *Domestic* slave population (in Africa) or the *Export* slave population (in the Occident or the Orient). The final two categories to be introduced are aggregates of the African population. A *Slave Society* includes the total of the Captors and the Domestics populations – the masters and their slaves in Africa. The *Regional* population includes all those remaining in Africa – Sources, Captors, and Domestics.

For ease and clarity of presentation, it is assumed in this initial static model that a large group of slaves is taken in a single year. The effects of this enslavement are then considered both in the immediate aftermath and fifteen years later.[2] We will observe the impact of enslavement on each *cohort* (an age group in a population as it is followed through time), both immediately after enslavement and after fifteen years.

The analysis relies, as is already evident, on a variety of demographic rates, including rates of birth, death, enslavement, and migration. Here it is important to emphasize the distinction between *crude* rates and *age-specific* rates. The crude birth-rate is defined as the ratio of births to total population size: thus a crude birth-rate of forty per thousand means forty births per year per thousand in the total population. An age-specific birth-rate is defined as the ratio of births to total female population within a given age rate: thus an age-specific birth rate of 300 per thousand for women between the ages of twenty-five and twenty-nine means 300 births per year for each thousand women in that age group. In addition to rates of birth and death, rates of enslavement and migration may also be calculated in crude and age-specific terms: thus a crude annual rate of enslavement of ten per thousand (one percent) might, if sufficiently concentrated, also be consistent with a rate of forty per thousand (4 percent) for persons aged between twenty and twenty-four.

The advantages of using both types of rates to describe a population are easily seen: as the age and sex structure of a population changes, crude rates may change while age-specific rates remain the same, or vice versa. For example, if death-rates declined among children but increased among old people, the crude death-rate might remain unchanged. On the other hand, if age-specific death-rates remained unchanged but the number of births increased, the crude death-rate might actually increase, especially for cases where the death-rates for young children are high compared to the population as a whole.

To recall our terminology, the division of slave exports into the Occidental and Oriental trades refers to the *destinations* of the slaves. This differs slightly from the regions of African *origins* of the slaves, which are those of the Western Coast, the Savanna and Horn, and the Eastern Coast. The regions of slave origin and of slave destination were closely linked, however, in the pattern of enslavement: slave exports from the Western Coast were dominantly male, and slave exports from the Savanna and Horn were dominantly female. To complete the pairings, slave imports to the Occident were dominantly male and dominantly from the Western Coast, while slave imports to the Orient were dominantly female and dominantly from the Savanna and Horn.

Two areas – the Eastern Coast and Senegambia – delivered slaves to both the Occidental and Oriental markets, thus complicating the pattern.[3] The complex movements of slaves from the Eastern Coast are discussed in a later section, after the simpler form of the model is presented for the Western Coast and the Savanna and Horn.

The model also assumes a large African slave trade, since all those captured but not exported were sold into slavery in Africa. The African trade thus grew along with the Occidental and Oriental trades. It reached a volume at least half that of the Occidental trade, and greater than that of the Oriental trade.

For readers reluctant to work through the demographic details of the model – the accounting of births, deaths, and migrations under slavery – a compact summary of the results concludes this section.

The Western Coast

Captives, we assume, are taken from the Source population in a given year. The Captives include persons of both sexes and all ages, but a disproportionate number of Captives are young men and women, from fifteen to thirty years of age, as these are the most valuable. The Captives undergo a heavy initial mortality, corresponding to losses in warfare and deaths from disease and exposure while being moved within Africa.

The Captors retain half of the female Captives as Domestic slaves, and sell the rest to European slave merchants who export them; the Captors sell almost all of the male Captives to be exported across the Atlantic. The exported Captives, male and female, suffer another severe mortality in the course of the difficult voyage across the Atlantic – the Middle Passage – which averaged two months at sea. The survivors join the Occidental slave population.

The reason for the difference in the destinations of female and male Captives is the difference in prices by sex. For male Captives, the prices paid by European slave merchants were higher than those paid by African purchasers of slaves. For female Captives, the prices paid by African purchasers were nearly as high as those paid by European purchasers.[4] To state this contrast in other terms: Europeans paid higher prices for male than for female slaves, while African purchasers paid higher prices for female than for male slaves.

Approximate age pyramids for the Sources and the Captors are shown in figure 3.2, followed by age pyramids for the Sources, for Slave Society (Captors + Domestics), and for Occidental slaves in the immediate aftermath of enslavement and export (fig. 3.3), and for these same groups fifteen years later (fig. 3.4).

In the aftermath of enslavement, the Source population declines by the amount of those captured and those who die in the course of enslavement. The age-specific birth-rates of the Sources are assumed to remain the same after enslavement, on the argument that unchanged family structure tends to keep them the same. The crude birth-rate, however, declines since fertile women are now a smaller portion of the total population. Fifteen years later, therefore, a relative dearth of children under fifteen will remain. Meanwhile, the aging of the cohort of those who were children at the time of enslavement brings more women to childbearing age, and the crude birth-rate increases. On the other hand, another wave of enslavement at this later time would again reduce the relative size of the fifteen to thirty age group, and reduce the crude birth-rate.

The Captors sell almost all the men and half the women Captives to the European slave merchants. In keeping half the women as Domestics, the Captors create around themselves a larger Slave Society population. Most of the women of marriageable age among the Domestics are brought into polygynous relationships (marriage or concubinage), and many of them may end up in harems of the political and military elite. The few male slaves in the Slave Society may find wives because of the excess of women.[5] The crude birth-rate rises because of the larger percentage of fertile women in the total Slave Society population. The children – or, more often, the grandchildren – of Domestic slaves by their free masters tend to become free, gradually escaping slave status. Returning in fifteen years, one will find a relatively large number of children under fifteen, and an equality of sexual balance in their cohort as opposed to the predominance of women in the

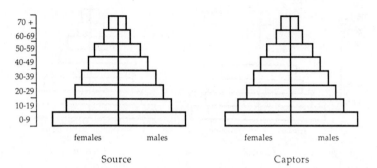

Fig. 3.2. Western Coast: before enslavement

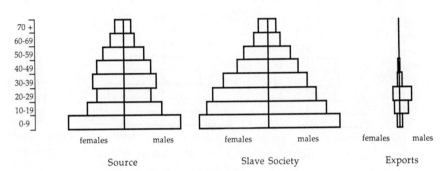

Fig. 3.3. Western Coast: immediately after enslavement

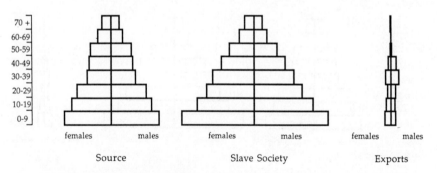

Fig. 3.4. Western Coast: fifteen years later

cohort of their mothers. The arrival of women captured in another wave of enslavement would again provide a surplus of women of childbearing age and restore the crude birth-rate to a higher level; without new Domestics, the crude birth-rate will fall below its initial level.

The Exports from the Western Coast, who comprise an initial Occidental slave population, are in the ratio of two males for every female, and

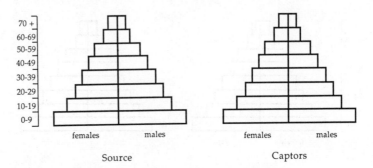

Fig. 3.5. Savanna and Horn: before enslavement

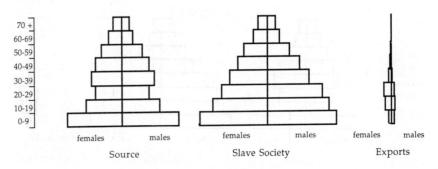

Fig. 3.6. Savanna and Horn: immediately after enslavement

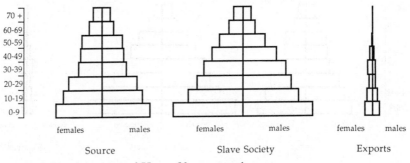

Fig. 3.7. Savanna and Horn: fifteen years later

dominantly in the age group from fifteen to thirty. The crude birth-rate tends to be generally low in the Occidental slave population because of the shortage of women.[6] Most slave marriages and sexual relations in the Occident are with other slaves, and most children of slave women remain slaves, so that their descendants remain mostly African and slave rather than interracial and free. The Occidental slave population remains predominantly male, except for the equal number of boys and girls born to slave mothers. Returning in fifteen years one will find that the crude birth-rate has fallen sharply, and that the slave population is divided into children who have an equal sexual balance, and adults who are dominantly male. The addition of new Export slaves would reinforce the excess of male adults, but it would also increase the number of births. In either case, African patterns of polygynous marriage are virtually impossible to maintain among Occidental slaves because of the shortage of women.

The Savanna and Horn

As with the case of the Western Coast, we assume for the Savanna and Horn that Captives are taken from the Source population in a given year, that the Captives are disproportionately young men and women from fifteen to thirty years of age, and further that they suffer an initial wave of mortality upon capture.

Captives sold to slave merchants from the Middle East and North Africa are dominantly female, in a ratio of two females for each male. The reason for this sexual disparity, as for the Western Coast, is differences in prices and demand. In this case, however, the demand for female slaves exceeds that for male slaves both in the African Savanna and in the Orient. Further, the relative preference for female slaves in the Orient is even greater than in Africa.[7] That is, the prices for female slaves are higher than for male slaves both in the Savanna and in the Orient, but the premium paid for female slaves in the Orient is even higher than in Africa. As a result it is assumed that two-thirds of the female Captives become Exports sent to the Orient, while one-third of the female Captives remain as Domestics. For the males (for whom the initial mortality may be greater than females because of their lesser values), we assume that one-third are exported while two-thirds are retained.

The results of enslavement for the Sources are the same in the Savanna as on the Western Coast: total population declines, age-specific fertility remains the same, and the crude birth-rate falls. A smaller number of children is produced for the next generation, but the sexual balance remains undisturbed. This would be the case unless, as one might argue, fewer male than female slaves are taken, in which case the Source population would end up dominantly male.[8]

The Captors of the Savanna sell two-thirds of the female Captives and one-third of the males to North African and Middle Eastern merchants. Thus the Captors, in making Domestic slaves of the retained Captives (with nearly twice as many males as females), create a larger Slave Society population. The Domestic slave women become wives and concubines of their masters, and notably of leading figures in the society. Slave males marry only infrequently, since their masters take the women. The Domestic slave men are settled in slave villages, where they live a life that may be

45

characterized as that of a nearly all-male barracks.[9] (As we will see in chapter 4, however, the historical magnitude of this Savanna and Horn surplus of male slaves was not usually large.) The crude birth-rate in the Savanna Slave Society increases because of the additional women obtained, but it declines because of the excess of men obtained: the net change in the crude birth-rate is thus small. The children of Domestic slaves in the Savanna generally remain in slave status.

Returning in fifteen years, one will find that the Slave Society population has grown, in addition to its intrinsic growth, as a result of the progeny of slave women, and that the sexual balance of the new generation will tend to reduce the relative shortage of females. By this time, the number of women of childbearing age has declined, and the crude birth-rate declines as well. The addition of Domestics from a new wave of enslavement would again increase the population, and would again lower the crude birth-rate.

The slaves exported to the Orient are in the ratio of one male for every two females. The crude birth-rate of the Oriental slave population rises, in comparison to its ancestral population, because of the higher percentage of fertile women. But, in the Orient as in the African Savanna, slave men do not marry, while slave women do.[10] The result in the Orient is the tendency toward disappearance of slaves as a social group: biologically, through assimilation of African slaves into the dominant population, and socially, through the manumission of children of free fathers. The children shown among the Oriental slaves in figure 3.7, therefore, were biologically only half African and socially free. While in the Occident the offspring of slave-free unions become an identifiable social caste, the "mulattos," who are kept distinct from the whites, in the Orient the offspring of slave-free unions are not particularly distinguished from other free persons. With the passage of time the proportion of the Oriental population with some slave ancestry grows quite large, but the number of persons in legal captivity remains restricted.[11]

Returning in fifteen years, one will find that the crude birth-rate for the population of Oriental slaves and their children has declined, and that the sex ratio in the children of slave women is equal. The arrival of new slaves would again increase the proportion of women and the crude birth-rate.

Summary

The simple principles set forth here explain many of the characteristics and interrelations of slavery in Africa, the Occident, and the Orient. Here is a summary of the demographic predictions of the model, as discussed above, for the late eighteenth-century Western Coast and for the Savanna and Horn, and comparing each population before and after a wave of enslavement.

The Sources (Western Coast and Savanna): Population declines, age structure becomes younger, a sexual balance is maintained (unless the

Savanna Source populations become dominantly male), and no additional incentive for polygyny exists.

The Captors and Slave Society (Western Coast): Population increases, age structure becomes slightly older, a shortage of males develops, polygyny is reinforced heavily, little male slavery exists, male slaves may marry, and children or grandchildren of those enslaved often become free.

The Captors and Slave Society (Savanna): Population increases, age structure becomes older, a surplus of males develops, polygyny is reinforced but only among the privileged strata, male slavery is reinforced, male slaves do not marry, and children of slaves generally remain slaves.

The Occidental slaves (from the Western Coast): Except as modified by arrival of new Exports, population declines, age structure becomes older, a large surplus of males develops, and a disincentive for polygyny exists. Slaves have children with other slaves, and the slave-descended population remains distinct.

The Oriental slaves (from the Savanna and Horn): Except as modified by the arrival of new Exports, population increases, age structure becomes older, a surplus of females exists among the slaves and in the population as a whole, so that an incentive for polygyny exists. But slave women have children with free men, and slave men do not marry, so that the slave-descended population tends to become free: it loses its distinctiveness and is assimilated.

The number of persons enslaved and retained in Africa, according to this model, is over half of the total number of slaves exported in the Occidental and the Oriental trades. The relative sizes of slave populations in Africa, the Occident, and the Orient, however, depend on rates of birth, death, and especially on manumission of slaves. The logic of this demographic portrait of enslavement is slightly different for the Oriental than for the Occidental trade, mainly because of a greater demand for female slaves in the Orient.

Mere statement of the model brings forth many of its implications. To summarize these implications in strong terms: the slave trade caused a reduction in the population of Africa. It brought a major shortage of men on the Western Coast and a noticeable shortage of women in the Savanna and Horn. The slave trade substantially shifted patterns of marriage and family structure in Africa and among Africans abroad. The sexual division of labor and other aspects of African work life underwent significant modification as a result of slavery. Further, the slave trade led to the export of much larger proportions of the African population than one might imagine from the size of today's black populations outside Africa: the shortage of African women in the Occident meant that imports of millions of slaves brought only minimal population growth; the intermarriage of

African women in the Orient meant that their offspring were not distinctively African.

The simple, cross-sectional version of the model above provides predictions not only of conditions in the late eighteenth century but also of changes in conditions before and after that time. (This is, in fact, a "prediction" of the past, a development of hypotheses about past history, which may ultimately be tested on available data.) For instance, if the rise of slave exports brought uneven sex ratios and a changing division of labor, then the later decline of slave exports (in the nineteenth century) must have brought a return to balanced sex ratios, and with it a second period of revisions in the division of labor. With this sort of observation, we have entered the realm of comparative statics.

Changing levels of enslavement: the comparative statics model

My objective in this section is to sketch out the predictions of the model for the period 1600–1900 for three sub-continental zones (the Western Coast, the Savanna and Horn, and the Eastern Coast).

To make the model's predictions more properly historical, we must introduce the factor of time explicitly. That is, we must progress from statics to comparative statics, from a single timeless portrait to a series of portraits, sketched to incorporate the changes in conditions over time. I will introduce changes in prices, in levels of demand and in population size, and follow their implications. The story linking one portrait to the next forms the web of the model's predictions.

The Western Coast

Slave exports from the Western Coast of Africa began in the fifteenth century at a tiny level, but grew at an average 2 percent per year from that time until the mid-eighteenth century, by which time they reached a level exceeding 70,000 slaves per year. In this same period, slavery in the societies of the Western Coast grew from an institution of minimal importance in the sixteenth century to a greatly expanded and greatly transformed institution in the eighteenth century. The demographic model, along with data on the prices and age-sex composition of slave exports, give clear evidence of this change. That is, in the long run, Occidental demand for slaves created African demand for slaves.

In the early, Portuguese-dominated days of the Atlantic slave trade, the number of slave exports was too small to affect the African population except on a local level, such as on the Upper Guinea Coast and in Angola.[12] Ultimately, however, the process of collecting slaves for sale to the Europeans brought two key economic changes in Africa. It stimulated new demand for slaves among Africans, and at the same time it increased the cost of obtaining slaves. These changes are reflected in the rapid rise in slave prices in the eighteenth century (see fig. 1.2). As African slave merchants passed their cargoes on to the Europeans, they developed a taste for female slaves which eventually turned into a broad social demand for slave women. As a result, the proportion of female slaves exported declined with time. Males were generally under 60 percent of slave exports in the seventeenth century, and over 60 percent of slave exports in the eighteenth century.[13] The effect of these competing demands in driving up slave prices was compounded by other effects. An absolute shortage of potential slaves came about as Source populations began to decline. The remaining Source populations increased the costs of enslavement by learning better ways to escape and to defend themselves. Slaves were captured in areas steadily more distant from the coast, a factor which affected the age and sex composition and the price of slaves exported. Further, state officials learned new techniques for taxing the movement and the maintenance of slaves, and thus increased the costs to merchants of supplying slaves.[14]

The early export of slaves was mainly restricted to a few areas: Senegambia, Upper Guinea, the kingdom of Benin, and Angola. The Aja-speaking area of the Bight of Benin became a leading exporter of slaves in the mid-seventeenth century. By the eighteenth century, as slave prices rose, slave exports were drawn more evenly from the whole coast.[15]

From the mid-eighteenth to the mid-nineteenth centuries, an average of over 60,000 slaves was exported each year from the Western Coast. This represented a crude export rate of some two to three per thousand population per year. The African growth rate (the crude rate of natural increase) was some five per thousand per year, which might seem to compensate for the loss. But the loss was concentrated among young adults to the degree that the Western Coast lost, through mortality and export, some twelve per thousand among its young men and seven per thousand among its young women.[16] Since the young women in particular were the group from whom succeeding generations had to come, it becomes clear how the pressure of forced migration caused the population to be reduced not only in the most affected areas, but for the Western Coast as a whole.

With the coming of the nineteenth century, however, area after area dropped out of the business of exporting slaves: the Gold Coast by 1810, the Bight of Biafra by 1840, and virtually all the coast but Loango and Angola by 1850. The end of slave exports led to major changes in each of these regions. The total population ceased declining and began to rise.[17] The inequality in the sex ratio came to an end, and the larger number of men available meant that marital patterns and the division of labor changed. In addition, the collapse of export demand for slaves meant that the price of slaves fell.

The result, which will be discussed more fully in chapter 8, was the development of a large class of male and female slaves on the Western Coast, where slaves had previously been dominantly female. A new economic order, based on ownership of land and slaves in Africa, rapidly came to assume significance in the production of palm oil and kernels and peanuts for export, and of domestic products as well.[18] In response to the higher domestic demand for slaves, prices of slaves ceased falling by 1850 and remained stable for several decades. This expanding system of African slavery was brought to an end only when European conquerors removed the protection of the institution at the end of the nineteenth century. For Angola and Loango, however, the transatlantic slave trade continued longer than in other areas. As a result, the rise of a new slave system in those regions was restricted to the latter part of the nineteenth century.[19]

The Savanna and Horn

The slave trade across the Sahara and the Red Sea is very ancient: its existence is well documented from the early days of Islam, and slave exports from Africa clearly took place before that time. The volume of this trade in these early days was not as large as it was to become later. For the seventeenth century, I have followed Ralph Austen's estimate of 10,000 slaves per year. The flow of slaves was certainly smaller in earlier centuries, but it just as surely fluctuated in its volume and in its regional orientation. Relatively large numbers of black slave soldiers are reported for Morocco in the seventeenth and eighteenth centuries, for instance.[20]

The work of the historian Charles Verlinden encompassed the whole of Mediterranean slavery in the early modern period. He showed that slaves were drawn to Christian and Muslim territories not only from Africa, but from the Balkans, Russia, and the Caucasus, and also included Christian and Muslim captives of piracy and holy war. The great expansion of the Ottoman empire at the beginning of the sixteenth century cut off the supply of Black Sea slaves to Europeans; whether it did so for the Muslim Middle East is harder to tell. It may be that the Oriental demand for African slaves increased from this time forth.[21]

The Oriental trade brought changes to the African Savanna and Horn, though to a lesser degree than along the Western Coast. That is, while external demand was demonstrably the main factor in the development of slavery along the Western Coast, it is not possible to make a similarly strong statement for the Savanna and Horn. Exports of 10,000 slaves per year, according to the assumptions of the static model, would have brought about a domestic African slave population of perhaps half a million, or 5 percent of the total population of the Savanna and Horn.[22] The actual extent of slavery in the Savanna and Horn, however, was greater than this. In Mali, Songhai, Sennar, and Abyssinia, reports of significant slave raiding and substantial slave holdings abound for the medieval and early modern years.[23] That is, the autonomous African demand for slaves in these areas exceeded (and perhaps preceded) the derived demand, that which can be attributed to the influence of Oriental demand.

This autonomous African demand for slaves, in turn, might be explained by any of three sorts of reasoning. First, it may be that the Savanna and Horn demand for slaves had long existed for purely domestic reasons. The most basic limit on this sort of reasoning is that there must be a market for slaves or slave produce sufficiently well developed to cause people to go to the trouble of capturing and holding slaves. Second, it may be that the long commercial contact with the Orient had built up an African demand for slaves in earlier times, so that the large Savanna slave populations of the seventeenth century are a reflection of a much earlier Oriental influence. Third, it may be observed that the African Savanna was not only in contact with the Islamic world, it was *part of* the Islamic world. To the degree that Islam supported the institution of slavery directly through legal protection and regulation, and indirectly through its characteristic sustaining of a broadly linked commercial system, African Islam can be hypothesized to have elicited the expansion of slavery in the Savanna and Horn even beyond the influence of the Oriental market.[24]

At the turn of the nineteenth century, however, the Oriental demand for African slaves increased, and the number of slaves exported from the Savanna and Horn nearly doubled. Three areas were particularly deeply involved in this expanded trade: the Middle and Upper Niger, the Eastern Sudan, and the southern portion of the Horn. Warfare was the main means of obtaining slaves in the first two; slaves were obtained more peaceably in the third. Egyptian and Arabian sources make clear the strong preference of men in those countries for Oromo and Nilotic women.[25]

In this period the crude rate of slave export was roughly one per thousand per year, an export rate well below the crude rate of population increase of about five per thousand per year. For the young adult population, however, this corresponded to age-specific rates of loss of 1.7 per thousand for males and 3.5 per thousand for females.[26] Thus, even though the Oriental trade was smaller in absolute and relative terms than the Occidental trade, it was still large enough to threaten and in some cases reverse the growth of population in the Savanna and Horn. This was so particularly because most of the slaves exported were female, and with their loss went the reproductive potential of their societies.

The expansion of this export trade left the Savanna and Horn with a growing surplus of men, who were enslaved in large numbers but who were cheap because demand for them was not high. These men slaves were thus available to be used in an expanding system of plantation labor. This plantation sector expanded most notably in the nineteenth-century Sokoto Caliphate, but also in the eastern Savanna under Sennar and then under Egyptian rule. Islamic slavery, in the African Savanna, thus came to have a different and more male-dominated character than the Islamic slavery of the Middle East.[27]

The pressures of formal and informal European control of North Africa and the Middle East reduced the demand for slaves from the Savanna and Horn late in the nineteenth century. As this happened, the sex ratio returned to equality, the population grew, and slave prices declined. The quantity of slaves demanded in local markets rose as prices fell, and the increased availability of women meant that it was easier to provide slave wives to male slaves: this became a useful measure for social control. In the Savanna and Horn as on the Western Coast, the late nineteenth century brought yet another expansion in the scale of slavery and the growth of classes of slaves and slave owners. The timing and the nature of the transformation differed between the two great zones, but in both cases the contraction of the export slave trade led to the expansion of Domestic slavery. A further development, which we shall have to investigate separately, was the substantial surplus in female rather than male slaves, especially in the Western Savanna, at the end of the nineteenth century.[28]

The slave trade of the Eastern Coast

The Eastern Coast is a relatively small zone which began its large-scale slave exports rather late. During the nineteenth century, however, it combined the experiences of the Western Coast, the Savanna and Horn into a dizzying and disastrous sequence of events. The dramatic expansion of the East African ivory trade at the same time gave the Indian Ocean slave trade a special twist. The Eastern Coast contributed to both Occidental and Oriental trades, though the Oriental trade dominated.

Slaves had been exported from Swahili-dominated ports to South Arabia, the Persian Gulf, and India for centuries, though only in small numbers. These exports were not sufficient to stimulate the expansion of slavery, and as late as the mid-eighteenth century domestic slavery had only a very minimal development in East Africa except in the Portuguese-linked *prazos* of the Zambezi valley and, to a lesser degree, among the Shona of Zimbabwe and the Swahili of the coast.[29]

The first major increase in slave exports came in the late eighteenth century when French merchants began to seek slaves in Mozambique for the expanding sugar colonies of the Mascarene islands (Reunion and Mauritius). Brazilian merchants soon joined this market, expanding their purchases significantly at the turn of the nineteenth century. Then, with the assertion of Omani supremacy over the Swahili-speaking region of the coast, an active slave trade to the Persian Gulf and India sprung up. Very rapidly, new systems of slave supply were set up in the interior of East Africa. Many of the slaves exported from Mozambique came from populous regions near to the coast. But the coast of Tanzania was thinly populated, and the slaves who went to Zanzibar and beyond came in large part from interior regions. A series of severe droughts and epidemics added to the nineteenth-century turmoil of the Eastern Coast.[30]

The Eastern Coast exported slaves to both Oriental and Occidental markets. Overall the proportions of men and women among Eastern Coast exports were relatively even. It is tempting to suggest that the Oriental trade dominated in the north, in Tanzania, and that the Occidental trade dominated in Mozambique. According to this reasoning, as women were exported from the Swahili-controlled coast, the male slaves who were left behind became available for use on plantations, most notably on the clove plantations of Zanzibar and Pemba, and on the food plantations of the Kenya coast. By the same reasoning, a disproportionate export of male slaves from Mozambique to Madagascar, the Mascarenes, and the New World left a large number of female slaves under the control of wealthy Gaza and Yao men. But the incredible mobility of the East African slave traders and their captives was such that it is unlikely any neat patterns held, and the region became a patchwork, leaving some areas with shortages of men and other areas with shortages of women.[31]

The export trade from the Eastern Coast reached nearly 30,000 per year in the first half of the nineteenth century, or two to three per thousand per year in the total population. For young adults, the age-specific rates of loss through export and mortality reached seven per thousand for both males and females.[32] These rates of loss, while they held for no more than fifty years, were sufficient to bring a substantial reduction of the region's population during the middle years of the nineteenth century.

Though East Africa was less well known to Europeans than most other areas of the continent, European explorers, missionaries, and merchants entered the East African interior during the height of the slave trade, and provided substantial documentation on its effects. The export trade had grown only shortly before their arrival, and their descriptions show that it was impossible for East African societies to have accommodated to the effects of the slave trade without undergoing serious damage.[33]

Suppression of this trade began in the 1870s, and colonial conquest followed soon after. So for East Africa (in contrast to areas to the north and west) there were few opportunities for the evolution of a large-scale system of slave economies. Frederick Cooper has provided ample documentation of the most extensive system of slavery in the region, that of Zanzibar and nearby areas of the Swahili Sultanate of Zanzibar, which rose and fell in a pattern quite analogous with the African plantations of the Western Coast and of the Savanna and Horn.[34] That is, it was like the plantations of the Savanna and Horn in that slavery grew along with the export of large numbers of slaves, mostly female; it was like the plantations of the Western Coast in that the expansion of slavery was facilitated by the downward trend of nineteenth-century slave prices.

The telescoping of events on the Eastern Coast remains the region's most outstanding characteristic. Within a single century, the Eastern Coast underwent a range of experiences which in other areas of Africa had been played out across several centuries. Even the latter phases were hurried: where the Western Coast had several decades between the end of slave exports and the colonial conquest, during which domestic slavery was transformed and expanded, the Eastern Coast virtually escaped this stage.

Recovery from the ravages of slave exports took place as part of the early colonial era, rather than as a separate episode.

Changing levels of fertility and mortality: the interactive model

Up to this point I have assumed that the levels of African fertility and mortality remained unchanged throughout the slave trade. That is, the changing demography of African slavery was caused by changes in prices and levels of demand for slaves. In addition, I have assumed any factors not mentioned in the model to have remained unchanged or to have been of negligible importance. Under these assumptions, I have argued that slave exports brought serious limitations to the African population. By implication, I have argued that the African population would have been significantly larger if it had not been for slave exports. Only by increasing their fertility or by reducing their mortality could Africans have escaped the sharply negative effects of the slave trade.

In this section we reconsider both the assumptions and the conclusions reached above. Were there other factors which tended to offset the loss in African population through the slave trade? Is it possible that birth-rates might have risen sufficiently to overcome the loss of slaves? Did new crops and farming techniques improve nutrition and reduce mortality enough to enable the population to grow despite the slave trade? Were the limits imposed on population size by drought and disease so serious that the slave trade caused little further change in population? Was the mortality among Captives reduced through the efforts of slave traders? These are examples of possible interactions among variables which might minimize the analysis given in previous sections.

By the same token, interaction among the variables associated with the slave trade might have magnified the effects I have suggested above. The status of slavery might have reduced fertility and increased mortality among slaves both inside and outside Africa. The expansion of polygyny might also have reduced fertility among African women. The slave trade might have interacted with drought to increase mortality, and it might have expanded warfare and its mortality.

All of these interactive effects are logical possibilities, and we shall investigate each of them in this section. The conclusion I will advance, however, is that each of these effects is small in magnitude. The demographic impact of the slave trade, as suggested in the static and comparative statics model, thus provides a good approximation to the real historical changes.

Let us begin by considering possible changes in African fertility. It has been suggested that Africans increased their fertility in response to the impact of the slave trade.[35] This task, as I shall demonstrate, was more difficult than might first appear. To begin with, African populations were what demographers call "natural fertility populations." That is, there were no conscious efforts to restrict births of married women, although the institution of prolonged breast-feeding (which postpones conception) had that effect. Virtually all adult women were married or in concubinage. Under these conditions, fertility could have increased only in response to some major social or physiological change.[36]

The persons lost to enslavement were, dominantly, young adults. Thus the source populations were put in the position either of asking parents of teenagers to start another family when they were well past their prime childbearing years, or of asking for additional children precisely from the young adult group most seriously reduced in numbers. In this sense, enslavement had the demographic impact of a war rather than of a famine or epidemic.

In the longer run, given African family patterns, the problem was compounded, as is demonstrated by a comparison with European families. In the European family structure, marriage was relatively late in life and not all women married. European families could thus respond to demographic crisis by increasing fertility in two ways: women could marry younger and in larger proportion. In African family patterns – if we may safely project nineteenth- and twentieth-century patterns back into earlier days – women married soon after puberty, and virtually all women married. African women could increase fertility rates only by spacing their children more closely or by continuing to have children until a later age. But given African lactation practices – children are generally nursed past the age of two, which tends to inhibit the conception of further children – spacing births more closely was likely only with the death of the earlier child, and surviving children were still widely spaced.

There is a well-known demographic phenomenon in which, after a famine or an epidemic, birth-rates are observed to increase. Such increases in births, however, seem to result not so much from conscious decisions to replace lost children as from the end of post-partum amenorrhea. That is, menstruation of the mother resumes once her child dies and breast-feeding ends, and she is again at risk of becoming pregnant. This sort of replacement of lost children cannot, therefore, apply to the older children lost to enslavement. For women to continue childbearing until a later age seems to have been the main option for increasing fertility, and this would have run up against the common practice of women abstaining from sexual relations once they had become grandmothers.[37] Overall, it is not clear that, by an act of the will, African women struck by the influence of the slave trade could have overcome the previous limits on their fertility.

The slave trade increased the proportion of polygynous marriage on the Western Coast, because it reduced the ratio of adult men to women. Since polygynous marriage may have meant less sexual contact for women than monogamy, one must ask whether fertility declined as a result. In fact, modern studies of polygyny suggest that fertility is virtually unchanged in households of as many as four or five co-wives.[38] A reduction in the frequency of sex may not significantly reduce the number of births. The exception to this conclusion, however, comes with the great harems of hundreds of wives assembled by monarchs, warlords, and merchants in the era of the slave trade. While the fathers had scores of children, the mothers had fewer children than average. Even this factor was of little importance in the aggregate, however, unless the harems represented a significant proportion of the total female population.

If fertility was inflexible, is it possible that African mortality declined in the era of the slave trade to permit a higher rate of natural increase and avoid population decline? Possible arguments for declining mortality include better nutrition as a result of new food crops, and perhaps improvements in security or reduced severity of disease.

The expansion of maize production in Africa, following its introduction from America in the time of the Portuguese, is sometimes argued to have led to population growth.[39] Such a conclusion is premature. Maize was adopted only in some regions of Africa, but these corresponded to areas of heavy slave trade, notably the Bight of Benin, where it partially displaced yams. Maize, however, was neither more productive nor more nutritious than the crops it replaced. Yams contain a wide range of nutrients, and they produce more calories per hectare than maize, even with two maize crops per year. The advantage of maize is that it is much more easily stored and transported than yams. Its advantage was therefore in nourishing a population of slaves in movement rather than in increasing the size of a peacetime population.

The case for the benefits of manioc is perhaps stronger, if only for Angola and Loango. Joseph Miller has collected numerous references to the spread of manioc cultivation along with the expansion of the slave trade in eighteenth-century Central Africa. Its advantage was that it could grow in most soils, and could be left in the ground for many months before harvesting. Still, manioc was more likely to have prevented a rise in mortality than to have reduced it. Elsewhere, manioc did not become a significant component of total calorific intake until the nineteenth-century decline of the slave trade. In general, nutritional change is unlikely to have reduced African mortality in the slave trade era.[40]

In the Savanna, women faced the same limits on increasing fertility as did the women of the coast. Changes in food crops for the Savanna were even more minimal than for the coast, and the increase in warfare entailed by the expansion in enslavement can only have rendered many areas more insecure. For the Savanna too, in sum it is unlikely that mortality declined in the era of heavy slave exports.

A secure existence was provided in some parts of the Western Coast by the growth of strong states – Asante and Oyo would seem to be examples for the eighteenth century – and it is understandable that mortality rates might have fallen within those borders. But this higher level of protection was more than counterbalanced by the insecurity in other areas. Many stories of flight to safer if less fertile lands can be traced to the eighteenth and nineteenth centuries: the migrations of the Akan peoples surrounding Asante and of the Aja peoples surrounding Danhomè, as well as the seemingly endless wars and migrations of Angola, all reflected insecurity and low productivity.[41] The same conditions of migration and instability were more favorable to the spread of epidemic disease than to the reduction of epidemics.

The eighteenth- and nineteenth-century peak of the slave trade was also a time of relatively frequent famine and epidemic related to drought, particularly in Senegambia and Angola, which are less well watered than the intervening areas of the Western Coast. The human disaster of the slave trade interacted in various ways with the natural disaster of drought. To a certain degree the two offset each other: Africans who would otherwise have starved were sold into slavery, and the remaining population was able to recover more rapidly. Joseph Miller has argued in detail that the capriciousness and inhospitability of the landscape – that is, famine and drought – did more to limit the growth of Angolan population than did the slave trade. The high level of Angolan slave exports between 1785 and 1795 corresponded to a particularly severe drought. But the two also reinforced each other. The slave trade interfered with cultivation; the migration it caused spread disease; the loss of young adults reduced average productivity.[42]

The pressures of drought, famine, and epidemic were at least occasionally severe for the Savanna and Horn. A great drought in the Central Sudan during the mid-eighteenth century caused widespread displacement, loss of herds, and no doubt many deaths. Charles Becker has recorded a series of droughts in the Senegambia.[43] These droughts, and the recoveries after them, caused significant fluctuations in the size and location of Savanna populations, and were perhaps as influential as the slave trade in determining population size. But they were not independent of the slave trade. With drought and famine, the destitute sold themselves and their children into slavery; with recovery, the wealthy and powerful sought slaves to provide them with labor and service. On the other hand, the wars and displacements brought by enslavement reinforced or perhaps even caused famines, and the movements of slaves in weakened condition could only serve to spread disease more widely. As fugitives from wars and raids abandoned cultivated lands in wooded areas, tsetse flies returned along with the recrudescent bush, and brought sleeping sickness which rendered these areas dangerous for both humans and large animals.

The status of slavery may well have influenced both fertility and mortality for the worse. New World records clearly suggest that the mortality of first-generation African slaves was higher than that of slaves born in the Americas.[44] If the same was true in Africa, then population growth was further restricted by this factor. New World records on slave fertility are more ambiguous. In the Caribbean, slave fertility was lower than that for free persons, and it was particularly low on sugar plantations, where the work was hardest and longest. In North America, on the other hand, slave and free fertility were virtually identical.[45] In the Middle East, slave fertility is likely to have been lower than that for free persons. A significant number of slave women were held in a sort of domestic servitude where they did not marry. For Africa, we are left with the presumption that slave fertility may have been lower than that for free persons, but we have no evidence that the effect was large.

One further interactive effect to consider is that the mortality of Captives may have been reduced with time, thus enabling slave merchants to make a better profit. In the transatlantic Middle Passage, slave mortality was mainly a function of the length of the voyage, and average mortality did decline from the seventeenth to the eighteenth centuries, but it rose again during the nineteenth-century years of illegal slave trade.[46] There is too little evidence on rates of mortality in the Oriental trade to hazard a guess as to the direction of their change.

Captive mortality within Africa depended heavily on the distance and time of their march to the point of export. Captives on the coast of West Africa and of East Africa had to march up to 200 kilometers before being shipped overseas; Captives in Angola and Loango had to march distances averaging 500 kilometers. Captives crossing the Sahara had to march from 300 to 1,000 kilometers to reach the desert edge, and the trek across the Sahara could be as much as 1,500 kilometers. Did rates of Captive mortality change over time within Africa? There are some stories which suggest that this might have been so: the development of a taxation system in Angola in which slaves had to be handed over, or the case of enslavement by kidnapping in the Bight of Biafra, in which mortality was low. On the other hand, some late-nineteenth-century levels of Captive mortality were very high, especially as reported for slave raids in the Western and Central Sudan. No doubt levels of Captive mortality varied sharply from region to region within Africa, as they varied significantly among regions contributing to the Middle Passage.

In sum, there is little justification for accepting a functionalist view that, since Africa was able to supply a large and growing number of slaves for export, African society must have been able to sustain the losses without population decline or other serious disruption. On the contrary, we have strong evidence to suggest that significant areas of the African continent experienced population decline and social disruption during precisely the century when most other continents were beginning to undergo demographic and economic growth. The likelihood of an offsetting increase in fertility was low, as eighteenth-century African women seem to have had levels of fertility near their twentieth-century levels, although their general level of health must have been lower. Similarly, the likelihood of an offsetting decrease in mortality was equally low: it was only in the mid-nineteenth century that mortality levels all over the world began to decline, for reasons not yet well understood.[47]

A sketch of African slavery

To review very briefly the demographic model and our first evaluation of it, we may say that the model predicts substantial inequalities in African sex ratios, the threat of population decline whenever slave exports rose to a locally high level, and contrasting structures for the slave populations of the Western Coast, the Savanna and Horn, and the Eastern Coast. By the same reasoning, we have seen the contrasting composition of the African slave populations delivered to the Occident and the Orient. The model implies that slavery was new for the Western Coast and the Eastern Coast, where it was imposed and extended as a side-effect of supplying export demand, while the importance of pre-existing slavery was greater in the Savanna and Horn. For all areas of the continent, the greatest impact of slave exports on total population and on the sex ratio fell during the eighteenth and nineteenth centuries; this great impact was then reversed with the decline of slave exports in the middle and late years of the nineteenth century.

Additional factors surely modified the demographic impact of slave exports on Africa. There is no doubt that local changes in fertility and mortality, particularly those associated with droughts, famines, and epidemics, caused different variations in African population than have been predicted here. These other factors, however, were not powerful enough nor variable enough to overwhelm the seriously negative and distorting impact of slave exports on the African population.

4

The quantitative impact of the slave trade, 1700–1900

The technique of portraiture now changes. The model of African slavery set forth in the last chapter was a still life, or a series of still lifes when it was used in a comparative statics approach. Now we turn to moving pictures: the resulting images of African slavery, while presented with less complexity, will change clearly over time. The moving pictures, further, are sketched with the aid of a computer. As computer art, they are systematic rather than eclectic; sharp lines and deep perspective replace the shadings of the hand-drawn image, as we move from an emphasis on the *direction* of the effects of the slave trade to an emphasis on the *magnitude* of the effects. But since the artist is the same, the reader should expect to see, in this new medium, different aspects of the same message. In particular, this chapter will reveal the decline in population for region after region, and it will also point out the occasionally dramatic discrepancies in African sex ratios during the years of the export slave trade.

Method and presentation of the simulation

The projections given in the pages below were constructed with the aid of a computer simulation which carries out, in much greater detail, the analysis of the demographic impact of slave exports discussed in chapter 3. The simulation model is described in appendix 2: it is based on the principle that the relatively well-known data on the size and composition of the export slave population provide a window through which one may, by inference, project the size and composition of the population remaining in Africa.[1] The types of information used in this projection may be reduced to four:

1 The size and composition of the export slave population. These figures are reconstructed from shipping records, slave import records in the Occident and Orient, and slave export estimates from Africa.[2]
2 The size of the African population in each region. These populations are estimated by backward projection from colonial-period population figures.[3]

3 The fertility and mortality of the African population. These rates are estimated based on evidence from past and present populations of Africa and Europe.[4]

4 Estimates of the specific incidence of enslavement, and of captive mortality, export, and retention. These estimates are based on assessments drawn from the descriptive literature on African slavery.[5]

In sum, from what is known about slave exports and from what can reasonably be assumed about the size of the African population and the process of enslavement, it has been possible to estimate the size and composition of each African regional population. The model predicts these populations by working backwards from recent times to 1700, but the graphs below can be read in either direction. These estimates have been simplified in some important ways. For each portion of the Western Coast, I have assumed a single sex ratio and age composition of slave exports, and a uniform range of intrinsic population growth. But then, allowing for regional variations in population size and in the number of slave exports, I have used the simulation to calculate the rate of population growth and the sex ratio in each region for each ten-year period. I have made similarly uniform assumptions for the various regions of the Savanna and Horn (but now assuming that most slave exports were female). For the Eastern Coast I have assumed a mixture of the two approaches.

Because the size of the African population in precolonial times cannot be known with any exactitude, the analysis was performed based on two estimated populations – one high and one low – for each region. The results, as shown in the graphs below, give high and low estimates of changes in African population sizes and sex ratios. The solid lines show the volumes of slave exports, based on documentary research; the dotted lines are estimates from the computer simulation. For each region, the figures show the level of regional slave exports by decade (solid line), the high and low estimates of regional population as influenced by slave exports (heavy dotted lines), and the high and low estimates of the ratio of adult men to women (light dotted lines).

The reader will observe two interesting properties of the graphs: see figure 4.2, for instance. First, when the solid line representing slave exports lies below a dotted line representing population, the regional population continues to grow, albeit at a reduced rate. When the line representing slave exports lies above a line representing population, however, the drain is sufficient to cause regional population to decline. This property was achieved by adjusting the scales of the variables. The second property is that the high and low estimates of regional population get closer to each other (both relatively and absolutely) as one goes back in time. This property is inherent in the logic of back-projecting of populations exporting known numbers of slaves. Since a given number of slave exports might cause a small population to decline but allow a larger population to grow, the two estimates of population are necessarily closer together at the earlier time than at the later time. That is to say that the projection fortuitously contains a self-correcting mechanism which preserves its value in more distant times. As a result, these projections may be pushed back into the seventeenth century without a corresponding decline in confidence.

The adult sex ratios shown in the graphs are for the slave society populations (the totals of captors and their domestic slaves) in each region. In the source populations, meanwhile, the adult sex ratios remained roughly equal.[6]

The simulation also projects the relative size of the slave population for each African region. As I have argued in chapter 3, Occidental and Oriental demand for slaves brought about, as a by-product, an increase in the number of persons enslaved and retained in Africa. In the discussion for each African region, I have given a simulation-based estimate of the proportion of the regional population held in slavery at the peak of the export slave trade. In addition, for the four regions of the Savanna and Horn, I have given a second and larger figure on the proportion of slaves. These are cases where an autonomous, domestic demand increased the number of slaves beyond those who would be held as a by-product of the external demand for slaves. For the eighteenth and early nineteenth centuries, such autonomous domestic demand was in most other cases small. In the years after 1850 (to be discussed in chapters 5 and 7), domestic demand grew to become the primary cause of the enslavement of Africans.

Further, for each region I have listed an estimate of the average distance the captives had to travel on foot before leaving the African continent, or before crossing the Sahara. The estimates, ranging from 100 kilometers in the Bight of Biafra to 1,000 kilometers in the Eastern Sudan, provide a reminder that the mortality of captives varied from region to region. In addition, the average forced march of nineteenth-century captives was longer than that of captives in the seventeenth century. I did not modify the estimates of population shown in the graphs to account for this factor. Nevertheless, the reader may readily conclude that the long marches of captives in, for instance, Angola and the Eastern Sudan made the impact of slave exports correspondingly more severe in those regions.[7]

With this introduction, we may turn to region-by-region discussion of the results. For each of thirteen African slave-trading regions, I present a graph of slave exports, population size, and sex ratio. (See map 1.1 for the thirteen regions.) Since these thirteen regions are large – most are larger than modern African nations – I also discuss the variety of local experience within each region. Then I summarize the results for the three sub-continental zones: the Western Coast, the Savanna and Horn, and the Eastern Coast. Finally I total the results into an estimate of the global impact of slave exports on tropical Africa, but also distinguishing the separate impacts of the Occidental trade and the Oriental trade, and the magnitude of the African trade.

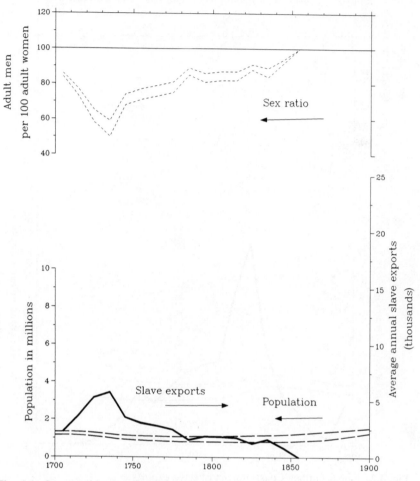

Fig. 4.1. Senegambia: impact of slave exports

The Western Coast

The export slave trade of the Western Coast, a trade dominated by the transport of male slaves and young adults of both sexes, was the largest of the three great exporting zones, and it had the most serious demographic impact.[8]

Discussion of the Western Coast begins with Senegambia. Figure 4.1 shows the total number of slaves exported across the Atlantic each decade, and the demographic impact of that total on a population taken to live within the frontiers of modern Senegal, Gambia, Mauritania, and the western portion of Mali. The results indicate that Senegambia underwent a modest population decline during the early eighteenth century, and that the

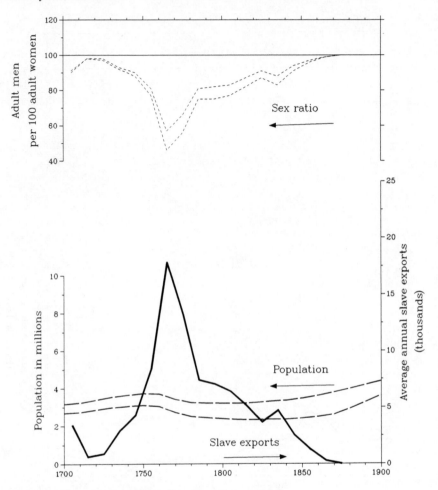

Fig. 4.2. Upper Guinea Coast: impact of slave exports

sex ratio fell to as low as 60 men per 100 women during the time of population decline.

The situation for Senegambia is complicated by the fact that this region (along with the Western Sudan or upper Niger valley) exported slaves both to the Atlantic and across the Sahara desert. The average march to the Atlantic coast was about 100 kilometers in the seventeenth century, but grew to over 300 and perhaps as much as 600 kilometers in the eighteenth century as Bambara captives from the Niger valley came to displace Wolof captives from the coastal region as the largest ethnic group among slave exports.

For the early period, slave export figures give support to the assertion of Boubacar Barry that, during the seventeenth century, the kingdom of

Waalo was declining in population as a result of losses to the Atlantic slave trade, and that there existed reasons for the king of Waalo to seek to withdraw the region from slave exports.[9] From the early eighteenth century, the wars of Mamari Kulibaly and his successors in the Segu state brought an increase in Bambara captives sent across the Atlantic and also across the Sahara. We shall return to consideration of this more complex period when we discuss the impact of the Oriental trade from both Senegambia and the Western Sudan.[10]

For the Upper Guinea Coast, including the areas of modern Liberia, Sierra Leone, Guinea, and Guiné-Bissau, slave exports were sufficient to reduce regional population from the 1750s through the 1790s, and to halt growth for two succeeding decades. The average slave march to the coast in this region was relatively short, less than 200 kilometers. The sex ratio fell very sharply in the 1760s and remained below eighty men per 100 women for the rest of the century. In the same period, the proportion of slaves in the regional population may have risen above 15 percent.[11]

A word of commentary is perhaps worthwhile on how to interpret the meaning of a slave population equalling 15 percent of a regional total. Let us remember that a region was – to simplify – divided into a source population which had little slavery, and a slave society population into which the slaves were concentrated. If slaves were 15 percent of the regional population, they were well over a third of the slave society population. Meanwhile the source populations felt every year the pressure of raids and other forms of enslavement which diminished their numbers. Finally, and by no means least, were the captives who perished in the course of enslavement and those who were exported from the region. They were under one percent of the regional population each year, but the annual repetition of enslavement brought large effects.

The Gold Coast was one of the great centers of European involvement on the Western Coast of Africa from the mid-fifteenth century. That involvement, however, centered almost entirely on the purchase of gold until the mid-seventeenth century. During this time, the Gold Coast imported slaves – from Benin kingdom and from Ardra – rather than exporting them. With the growth in the market for slaves, the export of slaves began on the eastern portion of the Gold Coast, and slowly expanded toward the west.[12] But the seventeenth-century export of slaves, which was sufficient to bring about a drastic reorganization of politics and warfare in the region, was dwarfed by the quantity of slave exports in the eighteenth century. Slave prices had risen so high that the region, while still producing gold in quantity, became an *importer* of gold (as well as an exporter) as Brazilian merchants bought slaves with gold from Minas Gerais.[13]

The rise of Asante after 1700 meant that the total number of slave exports from the region increased, but that now they tended to be taken from the periphery of the Akan population rather than from its core as before. The average slave march to the coast rose from perhaps 100 kilometers in the

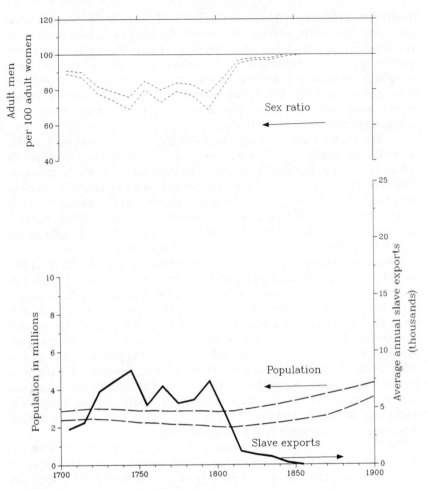

Fig. 4.3. Gold Coast: impact of slave exports

seventeenth century to as much as 300 kilometers in the eighteenth century. Figure 4.3 shows that slave exports were sufficient to cause a regional population decline of from 5 percent to 10 percent from 1720 to 1760, a decline in the sex ratio to eighty or even seventy-five, and that the late eighteenth-century peak in slave exports brought a further decline in regional population. In the nineteenth century, the vitual halt of slave exports from the Gold Coast permitted the population to grow again. Meanwhile, the high eighteenth-century levels of enslavement kept the slave population of the Gold Coast at well over 10 percent of the total population for much of the century.

For the Bight of Benin, the population declined almost without interruption from 1690 to 1850. This is the most serious long-term population

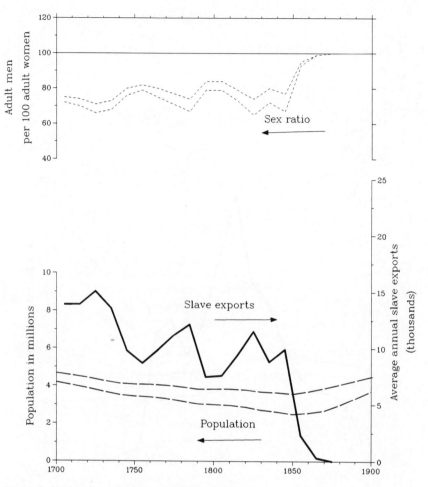

Fig. 4.4. Bight of Benin: impact of slave exports

decline projected for any of the African regions. In addition, according to recorded ethnic designations of slaves exported from the region, the overwhelming majority of these slaves were from the Aja (or Gbe-speaking) peoples of the coastal fringe in the period up to the late eighteenth century. Whereas Asante gained hegemony in the Gold Coast and thus brought to an end the depopulation there, Danhomè was prevented from gaining hegemony over the Bight of Benin by Oyo, which rendered Danhomè tributary in the 1730s and kept it within reach of hostile neighbors for nearly a century: the fratricidal wars which resulted produced an immense quantity of slaves.[14] Modern disputes continue as to whether the slaves exported from the Bight of Benin came from the coastal area, or whether most were sent from the interior by Oyo. In my view, the slave

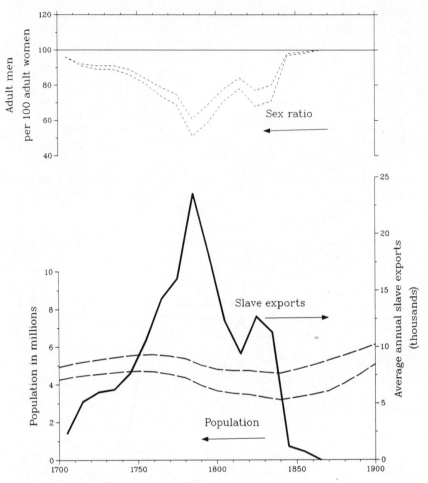

Fig. 4.5. Bight of Biafra: impact of slave exports

march to the coast never averaged more than 200 kilometers for this region.[15] Meanwhile, for the Bight of Benin as a whole, the disproportionate export of male slaves was such as to reduce the sex ratio to seventy adult males per 100 females; in the regions where the slave trade was concentrated, the proportion of males fell to sixty-five or even to fifty for every 100 females.[16] This intensive Occidental trade brought with it an expanded African trade: some 20 percent of the region's population may have been in slavery in the first half of the eighteenth century, and the proportion declined only slightly in later decades.

The rise of the Sokoto Caliphate at the turn of the nineteenth century and, more importantly, the subsequent collapse of Oyo, brought slaves of Nupe, Hausa, and particularly Yoruba origin into the Atlantic trade: a resultant decrease in the Yoruba population may thus be projected for the early nineteenth century. The African slave population may have risen beyond 15 percent of the regional population in this period.[17]

Slave exports from the Bight of Biafra did not rise to a high level until the mid-eighteenth century, but from that time this region became one of the main sources of slave supply. Despite the region's dense population, the number of exports was sufficient to reduce the population for the last four decades of the eighteenth century and in the early years of the nineteenth century. Captives marched a relatively short distance to the coast, averaging just over 100 kilometers. For the period of intensive exports, the slave population of the region may have risen to 20 percent of the regional total, and the sex ratio dipped occasionally below seventy men per 100 women.

Recovering the political history of the Bight of Biafra – and with it the local impact of slave exports – is difficult. The timing of the rise of the Aro clan and its oracle to prominence in slave exports remains unsettled. David Northrup has argued that Igbo slaves whose origins can be traced came from all over Igbo country in roughly equal numbers, which would imply that the late-eighteenth-century decline in population was shared by all regions. On the other hand, the relative importance of Ibibio slave exports in earlier days, along with the fact that Aro and other Igbo clans moved into areas previously occupied by Ibibio, might be taken as evidence that the eighteenth-century slave trade led to a substantial decline in the Ibibio population.[18]

Slave exports from Loango and Angola, which are often lumped together into the immense region of West Central Africa, are here broken into two regions, each of which remains very large.[19] From the Loango coast, figure 4.6 reflects the heavy impact of slave exports in the early eighteenth century, and the even heavier impact in the last half of the century. The second wave of exports, along with later peaks in the nineteenth century, corresponds to the entry of Bobangi traders into a large-scale slave trade on the Zaire river, as well as to periodic diversions northward of slaves collected south of the river in Kongo. The slave march to the coast rose from perhaps 300 kilometers in the early days to over 600 kilometers in the later period. The result was not only a serious reduction of the region's population, but a dramatic reduction in the sex ratio so that, for the region as a whole, there were at times more than two adult females for every adult male in the slave society populations. This extraordinary level of enslavement may, at its peaks, have brought as much as one-third of the total regional population into slavery.[20]

Angola exported more slaves, over a longer period of time, than any other region on the Western Coast. The region is defined for our purposes as containing modern Angola and the Kivu and Shaba regions of Zaire. While slave exports in the sixteenth and seventeenth centuries were probably suficient to reduce the population of the coastal Angolan areas from which they came, it was only in the late eighteenth century that the

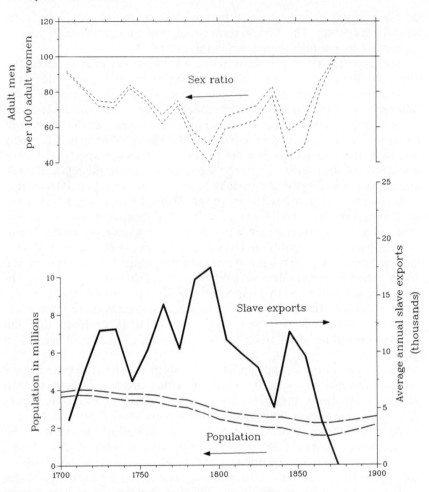

Fig. 4.6. Loango: impact of slave exports

slave trade had expanded enough in volume and geographical scope to reduce the total regional population. The slave march to the coast averaged perhaps as much as 300 kilometers in the seventeenth century, but lengthened to 600 or 700 kilometers in the nineteenth century, a four-month journey for a slave coffle. Angolan slave exports continued to expand in the nineteenth century, at a time when they were declining in most other areas of the Atlantic coast, and the result was a sharp decline of the region's population.[21]

The adult sex ratio in the remaining slave society population was reduced to sixty or below in the early nineteenth century, and to even lower levels in coastal areas which tended to achieve high concentrations of females. As a by-product of the steady increase in Angolan slave exports, the domestic

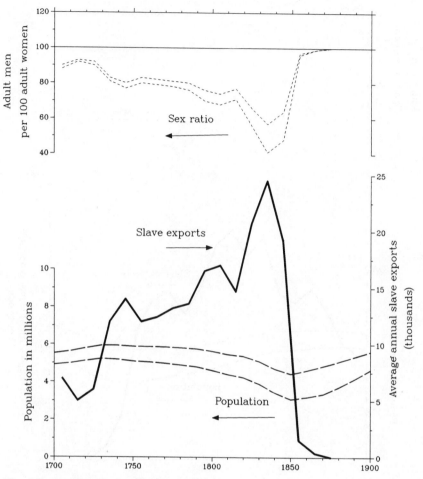

Fig. 4.7. Angola: impact of slave exports

slave population grew as well. By the mid-nineteenth century it had reached well over 20 percent of the regional population.

To summarize for the Western Coast of Africa as a whole, figure 4.8 shows that population growth was slowed by the export of slaves even before the eighteenth century, but that from about 1730 to 1850 the population of the Western Coast as a whole was reduced by the influence of slave exports, and that the overall sex ratio was reduced to under ninety men per 100 women for the Western Coast as a whole, and to less than eighty for the slave-holding populations. The local and regional variation within this aggregate was, as we have seen, very great. But to set Africa in the context of the Atlantic economy, it is this aggregate figure which is relevant. The African slave population created in the wake of this Occidental

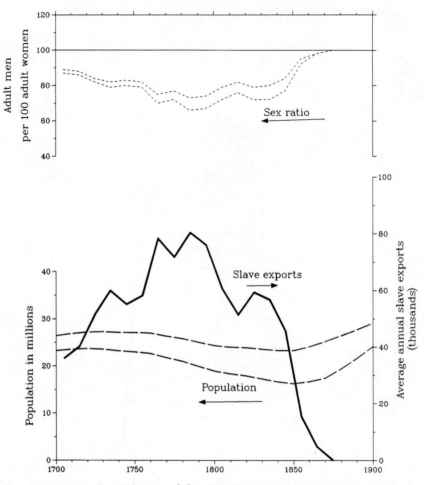

Fig. 4.8. Western Coast: impact of slave exports

trade rose, at the turn of the nineteenth century, to perhaps 15 percent of the total Western Coast population: that is, roughly 3 million persons in slave status. This was virtually equal to the number of slaves then living in the New World, and only somewhat less than the total of 4.2 million slave and free persons of African birth or descent living in the Americas.[22]

The Savanna and Horn

The estimated impact of slave exports on the population of this great region must be calculated with a greater margin of error than for the Western Coast: not only is the size of the African population uncertain, but the size and composition of the stream of slave exports is less well documented than

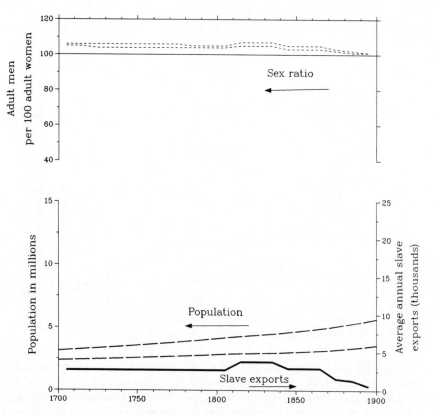

Fig. 4.9. Western Sudan: impact of slave exports

for the Atlantic trade. Since these two types of uncertainty have a similar impact on our calculations, however, they may be combined in practice by widening the difference between the high and low estimates of regional population.[23]

The number of slaves exported per year from the Savanna and Horn was far smaller than the annual number of slaves exported from the Western Coast, yet the proportionate impact of slave exports on the Savanna and Horn was occasionally severe. The first reason is an obvious one: the population of the Savanna and Horn was (in 1700, at least) smaller than that of the Western Coast. The second reason is more significant and more interesting: since most slaves exported from the Savanna and Horn were female, the loss of reproductive power for an average slave exported was higher than that of the Western Coast. Let us consider these results region by region.

We have already embarked upon discussion of Senegambia and the Western Sudan, the regions from which slaves went in similar numbers

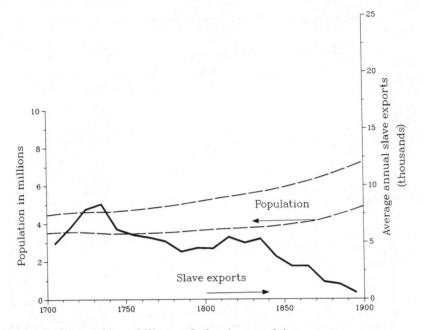

Fig. 4.10 Senegambia and Western Sudan: impact of slave exports

across both the Atlantic and the Sahara. In figure 4.1 I showed the impact of the Occidental trade on the population of Senegambia. Figure 4.9 shows the impact of the Oriental trade on the rest of the Western Sudan. That is, it compares the estimated total number of slaves exported across the western portion of the Sahara to the population within the limits of modern Burkina Faso and the eastern half of Mali. This estimate shows a halt to population growth in the early nineteenth century, and a significant slowing of growth before and after that time. Slaves exported across the Sahara were marched an average of 300 kilometers to the desert edge; the march across the Sahara was more than 1,500 kilometers long.

In fact, the two regions of Senegambia and the Western Sudan were not fully distinct. Many slaves from Senegambia went across the Sahara; many slaves from the Western Sudan crossed the Atlantic. Their total is shown in figure 4.10. The overall impact of slave exports on the two regions was thus, in effect, the sum of figures 4.1 and 4.9. That is, the total population of the two regions was halted in its growth in the early eighteenth century, and growth was very slow for the next century. The population of the combined regions showed a shortage of males in the eighteenth century, and a shortage of females in the nineteenth century. The level of exports in the combined regions suggests a resulting domestic slave population of near to 10 percent of the regional population. But beyond the impact of slave exports, the wars associated with the rise of Masina on the middle Niger

74

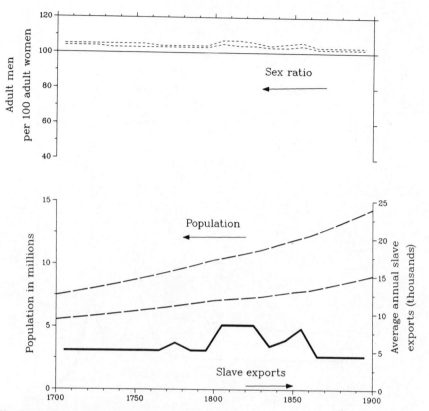

Fig. 4.11. Central Sudan: impact of slave exports

from 1810, and with the campaigns of al-hajj Umar Tal on the upper Niger from 1850, suggest that the total number of persons enslaved in the Western Sudan and Senegambia may have been 20 percent of the regional population.[24]

The Central Sudan, dominated by what is now northern Nigeria, was the most densely populated of the Savanna regions. It could thus export large numbers of slaves (as was certainly the case in the nineteenth century), without necessarily reducing the regional population. The number of slaves sent from the Central Savanna to the Atlantic trade, while by no means negligible, was far smaller than the number sent across the Sahara. Slaves exported to the Orient were marched an average of some 600 kilometers to the desert edge, and then made the long trek across the Sahara. Even larger was the number of persons enslaved in the region who remained in Africa; some within the Central Sudan, some sent to the Sahara, some sent to the Bight of Benin, and some sent east but especially west in the Savanna. Of these, the number whose enslavement may be thought of as a by-product of

75

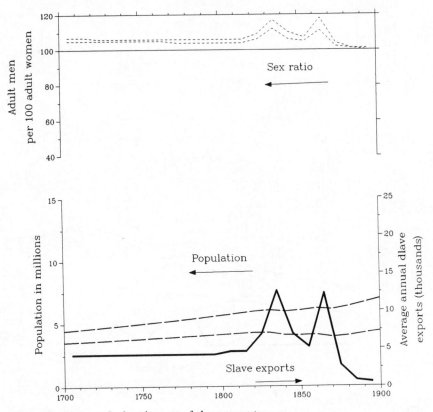

Fig. 4.12. Eastern Sudan: impact of slave exports

the Oriental trade reached a total of perhaps 5 percent of the Central Sudan's population in the mid-nineteenth century. An additional 5 to 15 percent of the region's population fell into slavery with the nineteenth-century expansion of the African demand for slaves.[25] Meanwhile, the adult sex ratio showed a modest surplus of males, with a ratio of perhaps 105 men to 100 women. In sum, therefore, slave exports slowed the growth of the Central Sudan, but they were never able to stop it.

Quite a different result must be reported for the Eastern Sudan. Here a combination of a smaller population and more intensive exports combined to bring about population restriction and perhaps decline for the period from 1800 to 1850. The market for slaves in the receiving regions – Egypt and Arabia – was much stronger than was the North African market for slaves from the Central Sudan. The well-documented stories of slave raiders from Khartoum, Dar Fur, and Baghirmi pushing far to the south to collect slaves in murderous raids make clear the sub-regional breakdown: slaves were certainly taken in the northern portions of the region, but the political

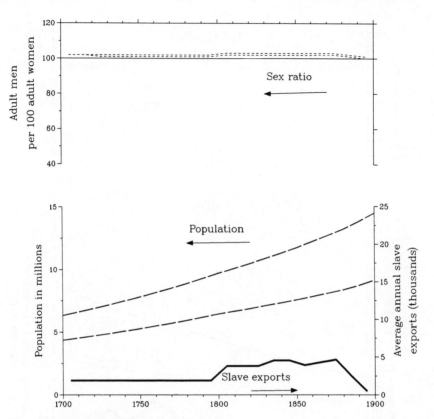

Fig. 4.13. Horn: impact of slave exports

power of the sultanates and the Muslim justification of enslaving non-Muslims combined to put great pressure on the populations of the southern portion of the region. The great distances involved served only to magnify the effects of these raids: exported captives had to march an average of 1,000 kilometers before reaching the desert edge or the Red Sea coast.[26] The slave population held in the Eastern Sudan became large in the early nineteenth century. Some 10 percent of the region's population was enslaved and retained as a by-product of the Oriental demand, and perhaps another 10 percent was held in slavery as a result of African demand. The adult sex ratio among slaveholders and their slaves rose to peaks of 115 men per 100 women.

For the Horn, the ratio of slave exports to regional population was lower than for the Eastern Sudan, but the proportion of females exported was exceptionally high. A large number of the captives came from the Sidama areas in the south-west of modern Ethiopia, as well as from the Oromo peoples – groups involved in a nineteenth-century expansion of warfare.

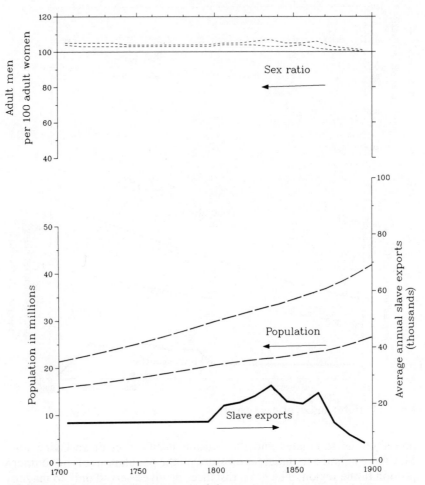

Fig. 4.14. Savanna and Horn: impact of slave exports

Their march to the coast averaged some 600 kilometers. Still, the population of the Horn was able to grow at a modest rate through the worst period of slave exports.[27] The slave population of the region may have reached 10 percent of the total in the mid-nineteenth century.

Summing up the results for the whole of the Savanna and Horn, the result is that the population of this zone was slowed in its growth betweeen 1800 and 1850, but that it was not reduced. During this period some 10 to 15 percent of the population of the Savanna and Horn was held in slavery, that is, a population of over 3 million slaves. The surplus of males became significant in the Eastern Sudan if not in other Savanna regions.

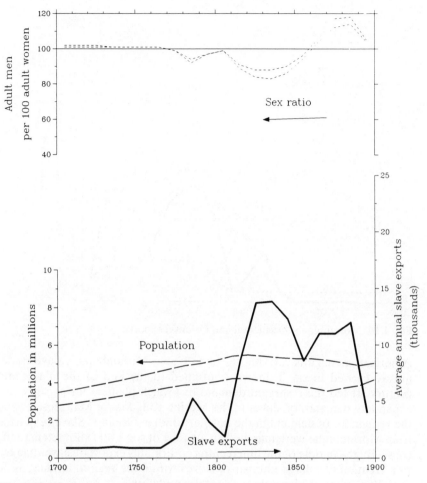

Fig. 4.15 Mozambique: impact of slave exports

The Eastern Coast

This is the smallest but most complex of the three African sub-continental zones, because of the rapidity of the expansion and contraction of the slave trade there, and because it fed both into Oriental and Occidental markets. For the nineteenth century, export figures are relatively sure for the Occidental trade and somewhat less so for the Oriental trade.

Mozambique exported small numbers of slaves from early days, but a new development began in the mid-eighteenth century with the arrival of significant numbers of Occidental slavers. They came, first, to obtain slaves for expanding French plantations in the Indian Ocean. Then came Brazilian merchants unable to obtain slaves in Angola, followed by Spanish and

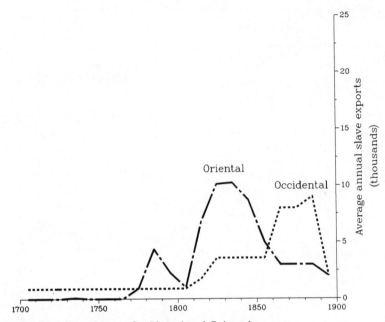

Fig. 4.16. Mozambique: Occidental and Oriental exports

American merchants carrying slaves to Cuba. Mozambique's slave trade, mostly carried in small dhows, continued to the end of the nineteenth century. It fed the resurgent demand of French planters for *engagés*, the expanding demand for slaves in the Merina Kingdom of Madagascar, and the remainder of demand in the northern Indian Ocean.[28] Slaves exported from Mozambique were marched an average of some 400 kilometers to the coast. By the middle of the nineteenth century, this export of slaves had led to a creation of a large number of slaves within the region, amounting to over 10 percent of Mozambique's total population.

The export trade from the Tanzania coast, directed by Swahili merchants and drawing on a hinterland including modern Tanzania, much of Malawi, and north-eastern Zaire, drew heavily on a large but sparsely populated area. The balance of slaves exported was female. In addition, the rapid rise of the trade in the nineteenth century meant that mortality from disease and from exposure in the long transit to the coast – averaging some 600 kilometers – was unusually high.[29] Figure 4.17 shows the decline in regional population from the 1830s through the 1860s. This export of slaves generated an African slave population of roughly 10 percent of the total regional population, though the slaves were distributed very unevenly over the area of Tanzania.

In addition, Madagascar itself experienced significant enslavement and exported thousands of slaves during the nineteenth century. These exports

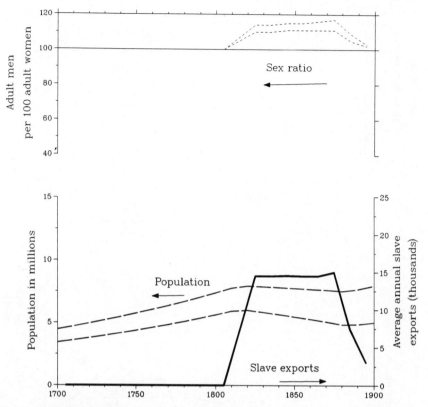

Fig. 4.17. Tanzania: impact of slave exports

came both as a response to European and Oriental demand, and as a result of the wars of expansion of the Merina state. In addition, captives brought to the island from Mozambique were divided in three directions: some were settled there as slaves, some were re-exported to Oriental markets in the Persian Gulf and India, and others went to the Occidental islands of Reunion and Mauritius. While comprehensive estimates of the volume of Madagascar's slave trade have not yet been proposed, it seems unlikely that slave exports reduced the island's population.[30]

In sum, the Eastern Coast underwent a fairly serious decline in population, but for a relatively brief time in the nineteenth century. During that time, domestic slaves rose to over 10 percent of the region's total population, that is, to nearly one and a half million.

The African continent

The Occidental trade, as measured by its average annual number of exports, was far larger than the Oriental trade, though the Oriental trade

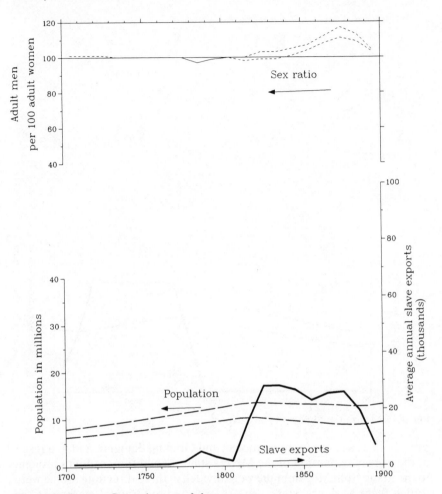

Fig. 4.18. Eastern Coast: impact of slave exports

began far earlier and lasted a short while longer. The Occidental trade had the effect of reducing the African population in the region from which it drew for over a century. The Oriental trade, by drawing predominantly on women, significantly slowed growth in the region from which it drew for much of the nineteenth century. One outcome was a reversal in the relative population size in two great zones. In 1700 the Western Coast had a population of roughly 25 million, while the Savanna and Horn had a population of under 20 million. By 1850, however, the Western Coast population had declined to roughly 20 million, while the Savanna and Horn population had grown beyond 25 million.

Some areas of tropical Africa were virtually unaffected by the export

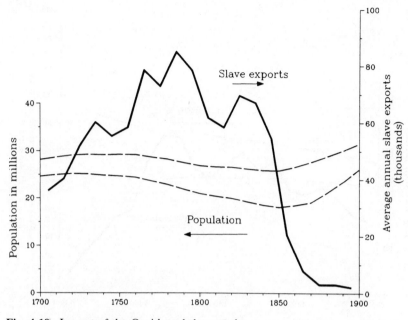

Fig. 4.19. Impact of the Occidental slave trade

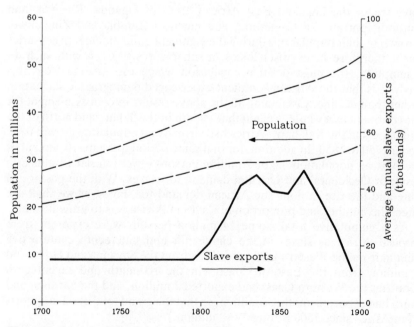

Fig. 4.20. Impact of the Oriental slave trade

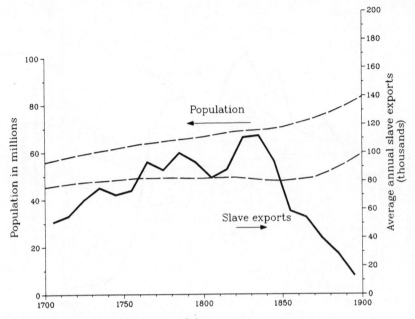

Fig. 4.21. Tropical Africa: impact of slave exports

slave trade: the highland East African areas of Uganda, Rwanda, and Burundi, portions of Cameroon, and much of Zambia and Zimbabwe. Growth in their populations during the eighteenth and nineteenth centuries might therefore have offset losses in other areas.[31] Even with such an assumption, the most positive conclusion which can emerge from this analysis is that the African continent experienced demographic stagnation rather than decline. Combining all the above results into an assessment for the continent as a whole, we find that – south of the Sahara and north of the Limpopo and the Kalahari – Africa had virtually no population growth from about 1750 to 1850. In addition, for that same period, perhaps 10 percent of the African population – 6 or 7 million persons – were in slave status as a result of Occidental and Oriental demand for slaves. With the passage of time and the rise in domestic African demand for slaves, as we shall see later, the number and proportion of slaves in Africa was to grow further.

As a cumulative total, some 14 million persons were exported from tropical Africa as slaves in the eighteenth and nineteenth centuries: 9 million from the Western Coast, 3 million from the Savanna and Horn, and 2 million from the Eastern Coast. (In the sixteenth and seventeenth centuries the Western Coast had exported 2 million, and the Savanna and Horn had exported another 2 million, so that the grand total of slave exports from Africa since 1500 is roughly 18 million.)

What would the population of Africa have been without the losses of the

84

slave trade? Throughout the simulation analysis, I have assumed an intrinsic growth rate for African populations of five per thousand or 0.5 percent. If the populations of 1700 had been able to grow at this, their assumed normal rate, the 1850 population of sub-Saharan African would have been roughly double that which actually lived in 1850: that is, it would have been nearly 100 million instead of roughly 50 million. Most of the difference was concentrated in the regions of the Western Coast, which suffered more heavily than the rest of the continent.

Even if we make more restrictive assumptions, it remains clear that the population of Africa would have been much larger if there had not been slave exports. Let us imagine that, in the absence of slave exports, average African growth rates were reduced to three per thousand. This amounts to making two further assumptions. First, that the African slave trade went on, even without the export of slaves, and that it brought about significant mortality. Second, that other ecological factors – droughts and famines – intervened to reduce population growth. Even in this case, the 1850 population would have been about 70 million rather than 50 million for sub-Saharan Africa.[32]

The century from 1750 to 1850 was precisely the era in which European and American populations began a high rate of growth; Asian and North African populations continued to grow at previous or slightly enhanced rates. One cannot be certain how a larger African population would have changed African history: for instance, whether Africans would have been able to face European colonial adventurers more effectively. What is certain is that the losses to the slave trade left Africa with a smaller proportion of world population in 1900 than it had in 1700. Those losses, further, came about not because of some impersonal force of nature, but because of direct African involvement in economic contact with the Atlantic, Mediterranean, and Asiatic economies.

From 1850 slave exports declined and population began to grow again, as is suggested in most of the graphs in this chapter.[33] In one sense, the return to growth provides a reminder that populations can recover, even when hard hit. What the graphs do not show, however, is the number of Africans held in slavery. The last half of the nineteenth century brought yet another slavery-related trial through which African populations had to go: the final stages of the African slave trade.

In chapter 5 and especially chapter 7, I present an interpretation of the period from 1850 to 1900. To anticipate some of the conclusions to be found there: with declining slave exports, sex ratios moved rapidly toward equality in most regions. Population ceased declining and began to grow, although the slave trade continued and in some cases expanded. The demographic effects of slavery remained severe after 1850, because of the mortality and migration brought about by slavery. Equally important in this later period, however, were the economic and social effects of slavery: the expansion of African slave-labor economies, and the accompanying oppression of the slaves.

5

The economics and morality of slave supply

Why did Africans supply slaves for sale, either on domestic or intercontinental markets? As I argued in chapter 2, the prices offered by European merchants were high enough that some Africans could not resist profiting from the sale of slaves. But this reasoning is insufficient to explain why the slave trade should have continued at a high level for over two centuries. How could Africans have continued to export slaves from region after region, even when the total population declined as a result of those exports?

Many Africans saw the consequences of slavery, and some fought bravely against its continuation and expansion. Certain whole societies managed to avoid tainting themselves with slavery. On the whole, however, enough Africans participated actively in the capture, commerce, and exploitation of slaves to prolong these forms of oppression into the twentieth century. Explaining African complicity in slavery is a complex matter, and I can only hope to offer a simplified beginning. The answers I will suggest in this chapter are gathered under four general headings: (1) Africans were unaware of the damage the slave trade was doing to the continent; (2) they were unable to escape the social pressures to participate in the slave trade; (3) they were unable to escape the economic pressures to participate in the slave trade; and (4) they did not think enough about the consequences of their actions. That is, I will discuss the limits on African knowledge, the constraints of social institutions, the pressures of economic logic, and the dilemmas of African moral judgment. I shall show how these intermediate factors led Africans to succumb to temptation, to pursue narrow self-interest, or to follow the path of least resistance – in short, to respond to the relentless pressures of demand from those wishing to purchase slaves. The net result of these factors, as I shall argue, was to facilitate, to rationalize, and also to disguise the flow of slaves.

The difficulty of knowing

To begin with, few people in the eighteenth and nineteenth centuries knew that the African population was declining, for the statistical data and

86

comparative framework were missing. In England Thomas Malthus, one of the founding figures of the science of demography, began his writings on population in the late eighteenth century, in the midst of a great controversy over whether the English population was growing or declining. We now know it to have been growing rapidly, at a rate of over one percent per year. But if the population growth rate for little England was unknown at the time, despite the many available records, how could anyone have been sure that the population was declining for the immense Western Coast of Africa?[1]

Further, African population decline, while serious, was far less serious than the depopulation of the Americas and of Oceania. In the Americas, the total population fell from scores of millions to under 10 million between 1500 and 1700, and only then did it begin to recover. Most of the New World's demographic devastation, however, was brought by diseases over which there was almost no possible control: smallpox, measles, typhus, pneumonia, and other such diseases, which were introduced from the Old World by European conquerors and merchants.[2] Africa too suffered from new diseases, especially smallpox, though less drastically so than the Americas. The decline in the African population came later (from 1730 to 1850 on the Western Coast, and later on the Eastern Coast), and it was smaller in absolute and relative terms than that of the Americas. The African decline was therefore less striking, though it was perhaps equally tragic, in that it was brought about through conscious human agency (that is, through the slave trade) more than through the biological reflexes of disease.

One further and important reason why it was not possible for Africans to know about the decline in their population was that they did not then accept the notion of a common African identity. It would be unfair for us to project back into the past the Pan-African and racial consciousness which is characteristic of the twentieth century. Africans, while they could recognize racial and cultural groupings as well as anyone else, did not have a consciousness of themselves as a unitary group in the eighteenth century. Quite the contrary, it was the experience of slavery and the attendant racial discrimination which brought Pan-Africanism and black race consciousness into being. And while Pan-Africanism today condemns, of necessity, not only the European demand for and use of slaves but also the African participation in slavery, there existed no possible realistic basis for such a vision of African unity in the early days of the slave trade.

Significant areas of Africa escaped, at least for periods of time, any devastation and depopulation from the slave trade: people of such areas as the interior of modern Cameroon and Gabon were perhaps ignorant of the damage being done elsewhere. At the village level of those areas which suffered more seriously, on the other hand, even without modern statistics, the loss of population through mortality and slave exports was quite evident. Such was the case among the Mahi people of the central Bénin

Republic, whose numbers were reduced in the nineteenth century. In response to such losses, villages under attack defended themselves, families ransomed captured relatives, and large African states attempted to prevent the export of their subjects as slaves.[3] Yet even where they were aware of their demographic decline, the only principles on which Africans opposed slavery were the narrow self-interest of a family, ethnic group, or state. With the exception of those peoples whose law did not provide for slave status, there was no principled African opposition to slavery: the ideology of anti-slavery did not even begin to develop until the mid-eighteenth century, and even in that time there was almost nowhere in the world one could go without finding evidence of fundamental social oppression, or cruel and unusual punishment.[4]

Social pressures to participate in slavery

As the continental volume of African slave exports grew toward a peak sometimes exceeding 100,000 slaves per year, more and more social institutions were developed and refined to facilitate the collection and transportation of the slaves. Here we will categorize those as institutions of capture, institutions of enslavement, mercantile institutions of transport and commerce, and state institutions of protection, regulation, and taxation. In addition, the African societies incorporating slaves required structures for that incorporation, institutions which paralleled the New World process of "seasoning."[5]

The recruitment of slaves – that is, the enslavement of persons in Africa – took place in many different ways. One important means of recruitment, to which we shall return in chapter 6, is that many people were born into slavery. Sometimes, but not always, being born into slavery provided the slave with some added rights and protections in comparison to those enslaved after birth, who were usually foreigners. In other cases, non-slave relations of dependency shifted subtly into slavery. Of the many loyal dependents of Angolan rulers, for instance, some suddenly found themselves shackled and exported when their lord's debts were called in by merchants. In most cases, however, the act of enslavement was explicit and forcible. Meanwhile, the slave populations of Africa, the Occident, and the Orient were almost never able to maintain themselves. The result was a continuing demand for new slaves.[6]

The mechanisms of capture were many. They included (in rough order of their significance) warfare, in which the slaves resulted as prisoners of war and booty; razzia or raids, aimed particularly at the capture of slaves, but also of other booty; kidnapping on an individual level; court proceedings in which persons were enslaved for violating the rules of society; witchcraft accusations in which persons were enslaved for carrying on illicit supernatural activities; exactions of tribute, in which tributaries were required to render up some of their own to a higher authority; and self-enslavement or sale of one's kin in the wake of famine or epidemic. These mechanisms were of varied importance in different times and climes. Further, the various mechanisms of capture entailed different dynamics of capture, enslaving different types of persons, and imposing different levels of mortality on the captives.

Warfare was the most prominent means for the capture of slaves. For the Bight of Benin, for instance, the seemingly endless wars of the late seventeenth and early eighteenth centuries coincided with the heaviest export of slaves from that region. For seventeenth-century Angola, John Thornton has retrieved descriptions of wars involving armies of several thousand on each side, with a baggage train enclosed within each army consisting mainly of women, so that each side represented, in Thornton's phrase, a "preselected population" ready for export. Slave merchants waited nearby to purchase the vanquished from the victors.[7]

On a different scale from wars were slave raids. Here the balance of forces was less equal and less effort went into political justification for the raid. The wanderings of the Ngoni in nineteenth-century East Africa may be classified as half conquest, half raid. The annual wars of Danhomè in the nineteenth century were mostly great slave raids. The razzias of Bambara kings and of smaller groups in the Western Sudan brought in a large number of slaves. For a detailed description of a slave raid, we may turn to Gustav Nachtigal's 1872 description of a Baghirmi raid on the village of Kôli.[8] There were cases where Europeans led the raids – in Senegambia, Upper Guinea, and Angola – but European-led raids counted for little in the aggregate.[9]

A still smaller scale of slave procurement was kidnapping. Here isolated individuals, usually young and particularly female, were captured and whisked off for sale by small bands. This is the way in which Olaudah Equiano was enslaved in Igbo country in the eighteenth century, and it was perhaps the main method of slave procurement in the Bight of Biafra. The price of venturing out alone could be high. Kidnapping took place to some degree all over the continent. It would seem that the level of captive mortality in kidnapping was less than in warfare and raiding.[10]

Quite a different mechanism of enslavement was judicial enslavement. The more prominent slavery became, the more common it became for the punishment of enslavement to be meted out to serious offenders, for murder, incest, or for threats to authority. The most famous such institution was the Aro oracle of the Bight of Biafra, where the oracle rendered decisions in great disputations brought before it, but consumed the defeated party. That is, those condemned were eaten by the oracle and were then spewed out as slaves and marched to the coast for export. In Portuguese Angola, which Jan Vansina has described as an African state, plaintiffs in any court case who wished to appeal to the next level were called upon to pay a fee in slaves in order to get a hearing.[11]

Tribute and taxation represented another method of slave recruitment.

The famous *baqt* paid by Dongola to the rulers of Egypt for several centuries included some 400 slaves per year. The tribute paid by Danhomè to Oyo from the 1730s to 1818 included eighty-two slaves per year. Tribute-payers sometimes enslaved strangers to pay as tribute, but at other times they were forced to choose among their own. Those condemned to judicial enslavement, when they were influential, sometimes arranged to send substitutes.[12]

Accusations of witchcraft could also end in the enslavement of the accused, and this mechanism of enslavement was relatively common in the areas of Loango and Angola. Indeed, once slave exports from the area ended, the general level of anxiety about witches seems to have risen, since they could not be disposed of so easily, and the tendency was to execute them instead. Condemnations for witchcraft were thus, in effect, decisions made by popular courts.[13]

Famines and epidemics led families to such desperation that they offered children, adults, or whole families into slavery as a last hope for survival. This self-sacrificing method of enslavement, normally kept to a minimum, rose to importance when hunger became severe. The waves of slave arrivals at Zanzibar were clearly amplified by the incidence of famine in the interior. Similarly in Angola, repeated famine and associated epidemics drove down the prices of slaves and increased their flows to the coast. The same is true for eighteenth-century Senegambia and for the Central Sudan. These famines, of course, were more than simple natural disasters: the previous conditions of the slave trade caused enough dislocation of agriculture to make famines more common.[14]

Warfare and razzia tended to capture a cross-section of the source population, though the death-rate of young male captives was relatively high because they were most heavily involved in fighting. Kidnapping tended to result in the capture of young and economically active (because mobile) persons, captured while away from centers of population. Court proceedings and witchcraft accusations were more likely to yield mature adults. Tribute exaction probably resulted in the enslavement of persons who were physically or socially marginal, except to the degree that the overlords were able to insist on the supply of slaves meeting specific criteria. Famine and epidemic resulted in the enslavement of a high proportion of children.

Finally, there are cases where enslavement can be seen as a form of voluntary emigration. European observers on the Horn in the nineteenth century found large groups of young Oromo women walking to the coast, guarded only by a few men. They announced themselves to be looking for husbands, and most would go to Arabia. Behind them they left some villages with overwhelmingly male populations. A somewhat similar case is to be found in the Ivory Coast and Burkina Faso, where the nineteenth-century pattern of Voltaic women going south as slaves to marry men of the lagoon region has been succeeded by a twentieth-century movement which, except for the abolition of slavery, is the same.[15]

The act of capture put the captive into the hands of a captor. The process of rendering a captive into a slave involved the imposition of both distance and socialization. Only rarely did the captor become the owner of the captive. A captive of war, razzia, or even kidnapping might still be ransomed, and captives of high social standing were often ransomed. More commonly, the captor sold the captive to a merchant, or rendered the captive over to a higher authority, as when soldiers passed their captives over to the agents of their king. The need to feed captives, in particular, was a factor encouraging captors to pass their captives on rapidly and for modest compensation. Assuming, however, that the captors sought to profit from their booty, their gain from the sale of captives should not have been less than the physical and monetary cost of their making the capture.

This cheap captive became a more expensive slave after several conditions were satisfied. As Claude Meillassoux has written for the case of the Western Sudan, the captive was desocialized, depersonalized, degendered, and decivilized upon capture. Once the captive was too distant from home to hope for escape, cut off from family, and dependent on the whim of the owner, he or she was forced to accept a subordinate role in the adoptive society. The captive, now reborn as a slave, took up a new trade: as laborer, concubine, or domestic. He or she was held within a family group, but had no rights: slaves became and remained the *other*.[16] These new slaves now acquired a higher value, based on the level of their productivity.

The function of merchants involved transporting captives from the areas of supply to areas of demand, and passing them off as slaves at their next point of sale. This merchant-function was performed most obviously by large-scale merchants, such as the Ovimbundu merchants of Angola, the Maraka merchants of the middle Niger valley, and including the great Swahili caravan leaders of nineteenth-century East Africa. But the function was also performed by small operators, who passed individual slaves from hand to hand in numerous transactions; and it was performed by state trading agencies and by states acting on their own account. The sale price at the completion of the merchant's function reflected the value of the slave to the purchaser, and this depended most fundamentally on the social and economic productivity of the slave. At the same time, this slave selling price had to cover the merchants' cost of transporting, feeding, and perhaps even clothing the slaves. Very likely, however, for the eighteenth century and some of the nineteenth century, the selling price of the slave exceeded the purchase price of the captive by a substantial amount, thus allowing for a margin of mercantile profit.[17]

The most striking evidence for this thesis of African commercial profit on slave exports lies in the increase of slave prices on the Atlantic coast. Prices in the late eighteenth century were five or six times higher than in the mid-seventeenth century. The cost of capture may have risen, but not at this rate. That is, slaves were marched a longer average distance to the coast in the eighteenth century than in the seventeenth, but not five or six times longer. One is left to conclude that African profits rose. I do not wish to argue, however, that merchants collected all of this windfall profit: state authorities, for instance, were able to intervene with tolls and taxes, in exchange for protection of the trade, which diverted a significant portion of the profits from merchants to monarchs. For the moment, it is difficult to assess the share of this profit which went to each, or the mechanisms and institutions through which this division was achieved.

Trade in slaves, more than that in non-human commodities, required the support and protection of political authorities. Where states defended the property rights of slave merchants and defended their caravans, it was difficult for slaves to escape or for their families to rescue them. Similarly, to hold a servile population within an African society required political authority to maintain order and subjugation. But state regulation of slavery, that is, state protection of private slave traders' and masters' rights over their slaves, is not the same as state monopoly of the slave trade nor state ownership of all slaves. Thus in Asante and Danhomè, the kings exercised rights and responsibilities over all slaves, but they did not own all the slaves within their realms.[18]

Many of the captives were retained within Africa. By the logic of the demographic model utilized in chapters 3 and 4, roughly one-third of all surviving captives were retained in Africa in the period up to 1850. After 1880 almost all captives remained in Africa. Throughout, merchants and transporters conveyed slaves both to the African market and to the external market. For expanding groups such as the Chokwe and the Yao of Central Africa, captives were set directly into the social order of their captors, without an act of sale; the Yao nevertheless also sold slaves in the external market.[19]

These structures of capture and distribution provided the social pressures encouraging new generations of Africans to participate in enslavement. Alongside the institutions of enslavement developed the institutions of slavery itself. African institutions for the social and economic exploitation of slavery also began as innovations, but were passed on to later generations as rules of society: slavery and the slave trade became "traditional."

The economic logic of slave supply

In an attempt to untangle the economic logic which propelled Africans into supplying millions of slaves for sale, I shall focus on the prices of slaves.[20] Through a comparison of the changing prices and quantities of slaves sold, we may learn about the choices and alternatives facing participants in the slave trade. Specifically, in this section we consider how slave exports compared with the value of other African exports, whether the slave trade encouraged monopoly or competition among merchants, whether the slave trade expanded African warfare, how strongly slave suppliers responded to price increases, and how the differing prices of men, women, and children reflected the varying demands for slaves of each category.

Slave prices followed some clear trends from the sixteenth through the nineteenth centuries. We shall have to proceed cautiously, however, so as not to exaggerate the dependability of the data. Slave prices were complex and variable at best, and they are poorly documented. Prices paid by Africans to Africans were only infrequently recorded.[21] Prices paid by Atlantic merchants to African sellers were more frequently recorded, but they remained complex. Even when payment was made (or at least recorded) in cash, the historian must convert these prices by the appropriate exchange rate to a common basis of comparison, such as British pounds at their 1780 value.[22]

Most often, Atlantic merchants purchased slaves in lots, rather than as individuals, and they often paid in wide assortments of goods rather than in cash. On the eighteenth-century Gold Coast, for instance, an assortment of goods was established as an equivalent of a trading "ounce," and an ounce was given an equivalent in a number of slaves. At Luanda, the largest and most unique African slave port, Portuguese merchants provided import goods and credit, Luanda-based Luso-African merchants owned the slaves during their transatlantic voyage, and Brazilian shippers provided the transport.[23] In both these cases, the cost of a lot of slaves on the African coast must be calculated as the purchase price (in Europe, usually) of the goods exchanged for the slaves (this is known as *prime cost*), plus the cost of shipping the goods to Africa. (The shipping cost, while roughly as great as the cost of the goods, is itself difficult to document.) The price per slave, then, is this total cost divided by the number of slaves in the lot. Prices are usually reported as prime cost per slave: most of the prices displayed in figure 1.2 were calculated in this way.[24] A better measure would be prime cost plus transport cost of import goods per slave: this measure would rise more slowly with time than prime cost per slave, since transport costs declined with time.[25]

Further, the values of slaves varied significantly by sex and especially by age. Young adults fetched the highest prices, while prices of infants and the old fell very low. The "average price" of a lot of slaves depended in part, therefore, on the age and sex composition of the group. Some estimates of slave prices have attempted to correct for these variations, usually by adjusting prices and reporting them as prices for "prime males," that is, young adult males in good health.[26]

Quite aside from these difficulties of measuring slave prices, there was a great variety of influences combining to set the price levels. As I argued in chapter 2, the level of productivity – the value of the output of an African man or woman – was the most basic determinant of slave prices. But when we note, for instance, that the average price of slaves rose by a factor of from five to six over the course of a century, we can be sure that this does not mean the productivity of African workers increased by a similar factor. That is, we shall have to account for a variety of market factors and institutional factors which caused fluctuations in the prices and quantities of slaves sold.

In short, I have begun this analysis with two cautions. First, African slave prices are known in general, but only imprecisely. (Further research, of course, has the potential of reconstructing slave prices in greater precision.) Second, our analysis of how slave prices were determined must go beyond simple considerations of cost and productivity, and must include a number of other market and institutional factors.

Let us turn to the main trends in prices. The reader may find it helpful to refer to figure 1.2 (which summarizes some available price data) to complement this discussion of long-term trends. Prices are presented in terms of the value of an English pound in 1780 (a date chosen because it is roughly halfway through the period of highest Occidental slave exports), and they refer to prices on the African coast, in regions actively involved in slave exports across the Atlantic.

During the sixteenth century, prices for average slaves gradually increased from an average £10 in 1550 to £14 in 1600. Prices remained unchanging until the 1630s and then fell, dipping below £5 in the 1670s. Prices then rose to £25 in the 1730s, and fluctuated about that level into the 1790s. With the Napoleonic wars, prices fell to £15 and remained stable or declined slightly thereafter. By the 1860s prices for the few remaining slaves exported across the Atlantic averaged just over £10.[27]

If we go through this same narrative of prices at a more leisurely pace, we can point out some additional details related to these price variations. Thus, during the sixteenth century, Portuguese and Spanish purchasers, buying mainly in Senegambia and the Upper Guinea Coast, paid prices gradually rising from £10 to £14. By the early seventeenth century the focus of slave exports had shifted to Angola, where prices also reached an average of £14. The entry of Dutch, English, and French competitors beginning in the 1640s brought new demand and a high volume of slaves. Paradoxically, prices fell. In geographical terms we may say that new areas were brought into the slave trade: the Bight of Benin and later the Gold Coast. In economic terms we may say that Africans had a positive supply response to the higher demand for slaves. African suppliers committed themselves more fully to slave exports by supplying larger numbers at any given price.

From the 1690s to the 1730s prices rose sharply. During this time several supply areas – the Bight of Benin, the Gold Coast, Senegambia, the Upper Guinea Coast, and perhaps the coastal region of Angola – underwent varying degrees of decline in population. The higher prices corresponded, in simplest terms, to a relative scarcity of slaves. For the following four decades total Occidental slave deliveries rose very slowly; during this period the Bight of Biafra became a large supplier, and its additional supplies held prices stable at roughly £25. The 1780s, the peak decade in the Atlantic trade, brought sizeable increases in slave exports from the Bight of Biafra and Loango.

With the French Revolution, the Napoleonic wars and the British abolition of the slave trade, New World demand and African slave prices declined to £15 from the 1790s to the 1810s. From the 1820s, rising New World demand stemmed mostly from Cuba and Brazil, and concentrated in Africa on Loango and Angola. As the populations of these regions declined under the pressures of exports, prices remained at an average of £15, and only declined in the 1850s.

Richard Bean, who pioneered the work of estimating slave prices for Africa, used his data on the years up to 1775 to make two interesting arguments. First, by multiplying his price series by the estimated volume of slave exports, and comparing the resultant value to the estimated value of African gold exports, he was able to demonstrate that gold, not slaves, was Africa's most remunerative export from the time of the voyages of discovery until the turn of the eighteenth century.[28] This argument surely stands. Second, and in association with Robert Paul Thomas, he argued that his price data showed that the Atlantic commerce in slaves was a competitive market, and that neither European merchants nor African merchants and prices were able to exert significant monopoly power.[29] They based this argument on the consistency of slave prices along the Western Coast of Africa, on the periodic entry of new African regions into the export commerce in slaves, and on the ability of European merchants to abandon any African port in which excessive taxes or prices formed a restraint on trade. Thus, Bean and Thomas presented an image of a commerce which, if immoral in that it was a traffic in human beings, was nonetheless smooth and orderly in its organization; their analysis contradicted the notion of European merchants defrauding their African counterparts with derisory prices in the form of a few beads, but it also contradicted the notion that African merchants grew rich off the spoils of monopoly.

The argument against high African profits in the slave trade may be faulted, however, on two grounds. First, with regard to its Atlantic portion, European merchants found their mobility restricted because of their need for the quickest possible turnaround in port, to save lives of both crew and cargo, and because of their need for cordial and dependable relations with the merchants they dealt with. I believe that more careful study of slave prices will show that they varied significantly among regions of the coast: merchants went to ports where slaves were available, rather than to where they were cheap. Second, if the selling price of slaves to Europeans was rather uniform, the purchase price of slaves by the African coastal merchants need not have been so. That is, *economic rents of considerable size* may have accrued to some African merchants. Those who were able to acquire slaves at a low price, for instance, because of their ready availability near the coast, were able to sell at the same price as all the others and pocket the difference. Such economic rents are particularly likely to have existed in the Bight of Benin and the Bight of Biafra, where most slaves originated in coastal areas. Again, this windfall profit may have been distributed among a variety of merchants and tax collectors, so that its magnitude and distribution are impossible to reconstruct.

The image resulting from this approach based on imperfect competition and economic rent is quite different from the model of perfect competition: prices were linked in a tight network, but they varied in regional markets according to levels of demand, and according to the economic power of local buyers and sellers. On the other hand, Bean and Thomas ought perhaps to have emphasized another implication of their competitive model: the anarchic entry and departure of participants in the market. The reasons were as much political as economic, but many African sellers of slaves were here today and gone tomorrow; wealthy and powerful at one moment; and destitute, enslaved, or executed the next.

For Senegambia, Curtin has argued in detail that a "political model" centered on the orientation of warfare around political goals explains the pattern of slave exports better than does an "economic model" centered on price responsiveness. The simplest counter to Curtin's political model is that offered by E. Phillip LeVeen, that even if political conditions were the sole determinant of the number of captives, the cost of transporting slaves to the coast and the selling prices of slaves at the coast acted to determine whether captives were sent across the Atlantic.[30] LeVeen's counter is thus consistent with the approach adopted above in analyzing levels of exports from the African coast, but the problem with it is that it does not directly address Curtin's assessment of the motivations and the mechanisms behind capture.

Bean calculated an overall elasticity of slave supply for the Western Coast of Africa – the responsiveness of slave supply to price changes – over the course of a century, and found it to be positive. This convinced him that Africans were in the business of selling slaves for profit; other estimates of supply elasticity have produced similar results.[31] I think the case for this conclusion can be made in a more convincing fashion by considering the issue on a more restricted regional basis, and by attempting to account for institutional changes as part of the analysis.

For the Bight of Benin, the late seventeenth century appears as a time of a stable and elastic supply schedule: prices rose modestly, and each increase in price brought a substantial increase in the quantity of slaves supplied. The period from the 1700s through 1730s was almost the contrary: in this time, prices rose rapidly, and the number of slaves remained almost unchanged. This decline in volume can be explained primarily as a function of declining population, and secondarily as a result of concentration of economic power in the hands of the newly emergent Danhomè. At this point, institutions stabilized, and a stable, elastic supply schedule returned for the period from the 1730s to the 1790s: quantities of slaves exported rose and fell in accord with changes in prices.[32]

The above analysis is based on average slave prices, which are relevant for evaluating the total cost and revenue of the slave trade. In addition,

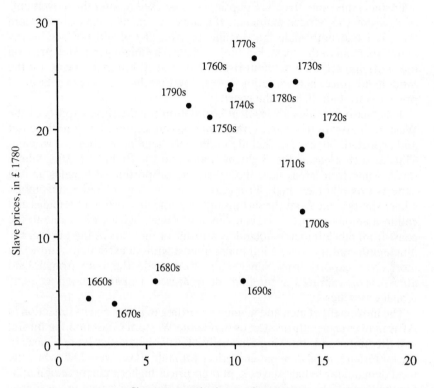

Fig. 5.1. Bight of Benin: quantities and prices of slave exports

more insights into the details of the slave trade are to be obtained by studying prices and quantities of slaves by age and sex. Two major patterns stand
out: one distinguishing female slaves from males, and the other distinguishing children from adults.

As I have suggested above, at the end of the seventeenth century wealthy
Africans developed an increasing interest in female slaves. The proportion
of females among exports fell from 40 to 35 percent. Occidental prices for
young adult women were only about 10 percent lower than prices for males,
yet barely more than half as many women as men made the crossing.
Coastal Africans were willing to pay more for female than for male slaves.
They need only have paid about 10 percent more to have created this
remarkable divergence in demographic flows. Prices for male slaves were
sustained mainly by European demand at the coast; prices for female slaves
were sustained by a geographically dispersed African demand. Slave
markets of the West African coast, in effect, accommodated two price structures at once: that of Occidental purchasers, and that of African purchasers.

97

Further, this same structure of prices can be used to infer the movements of slaves on the African mainland. If a slave merchant some distance from the coast had both male and female captives, he would not necessarily march them all to the coast. For female slaves, he might get a good price on the spot, and sell them without risking the transit. For male slaves, on the other hand, prices in the interior were so low that the only way to get a good price was to send them to the coast.[33]

This factor provides a very neat correlation for the slave exports of the Western Coast. In those areas where slaves were captured near to the coast and exported, the exports included relatively large proportions of women. Thus in such areas as the Bight of Benin and the Bight of Biafra, where slaves came from areas near the coast, the proportion of females among exports was relatively high. From areas such as Angola and Senegambia, where slaves came from the distant interior, the proportion of females and children among exports was relatively low. Hausa slaves, who came to the coast from 500 kilometers inland as a result of the wars at the turn on the nineteenth century, were adult males almost without exception. And while most slave exports from Senegambia were male Bambara from inland areas, slaves captured in the immediate area of Dakar included as many females as males.[34]

The movement of men and women according to prices had its reflection in African marriage patterns. Let us divide the Western Coast into the littoral and the hinterland, thinking especially of Angola and the Ivory Coast. In the hinterland, local demand and prices for male slaves were low, while the local demand for female slaves kept their prices higher than those of males. On the littoral, the export demand for male slaves kept male prices higher than those of females. At the same time, however, the concentration of purchasing power in the hands of slave merchants on the littoral meant that the prices of female slaves were higher there than in the hinterland. Thus prices for both male and female slaves were higher on the littoral than in the hinterland, though the differential was far greater for males.

The hinterland thus exported virtually all its male slaves and perhaps half of its female slaves to the littoral, and developed a high rate of polygyny. Enslavement along the littoral, in contrast, led to the export of a relatively large proportion of women. Thus the littoral was at once buying, raiding, and selling female slaves, but the net result was a lower rate of polygyny than in the hinterland. In sum, most male slaves exported from Angola came from the hinterland, while most female slaves exported from Angola came from the littoral. The drain on the hinterland population took the form of the export of many men and some women. The drain on the littoral population, if dominated by the loss of males, included the export of women in larger proportions than from the hinterland, though this loss was partially mitigated by the import of women from the hinterland.[35]

The changing pattern of child-slave exports is remarkably distinct from the sex ratio of slave exports. In the eighteenth century, children (that is, those below the age of sexual maturity) averaged roughly one-fourth of slave exports, though they were about one-third of African populations. The high mortality of small children, especially with the exposure of long travel, would seem to make this a logical response. Yet in the nineteenth century, children comprised nearly 40 percent of Atlantic slave cargoes – more than their proportion in African populations.

Was there a factor which could simultaneously make child slaves appear more attractive to New World buyers and less attractive to African buyers? The divergence of African and New World slave prices (which followed the abolition of the legal slave trade) was such a factor. In Africa, slave prices fell. There, slave purchasers found little incentive to buy children who would need years of care when one could buy productive adult slaves for a song. In the Americas, however, slave prices rose sharply. The cost of productive adult slaves reached near-prohibitive levels. As a result, purchasers sought to buy child slaves at low prices, in the hope of making a profit over the long run by skimping on the cost of bringing up the children. A strong initial confirmation of this hypothesis arises from child ratios reported by David Eltis. Child ratios were high for Cuba (where the slave trade was illegal) for the whole nineteenth century; child ratios for the trade to Brazil shot up only in the 1830s, when the slave trade became illegal.[36]

In sum, the economic mechanisms of the slave trade and slavery, as reflected in the prices of slaves, put heavy pressures on Africans at all levels of society to condone slavery. These same economic mechanisms guided in a more specific fashion the wide range of roles through which Africans participated in slavery. The persistence of slavery in Africa, however, cannot be explained fully by calculations of costs and benefits: such a level of human exploitation required an ideology to sustain it.

Yielding to temptation: slavery and money

According to a story which is still told today along the lagoons of the republic of Bénin, cowries were obtained by the use of slaves. A slave was thrown into the sea and allowed to drown. Then cowries would grow on the body of the slave, and after a time the body would be dredged up and the cowries collected from it.[37]

The story is both true and untrue. Cowrie shells, of course, were money here and in a wide area of West Africa. The story is untrue in that cowries grow in the Indian Ocean, not in the Atlantic or the lagoons edging it, and untrue also in that slaves were not drowned in order to get them. But the story is true as well as picturesque in its presentation of the sacrifice made in order to gain money in exchange. It is a stark example of the ideology justifying slavery in Africa. Africans seemed to throw away a precious resource, young men and women, in exchange for money – for cash. Further, the slaves who remained in Africa did the work of carrying sacks of cowries inland to the sellers.

I will give particular scrutiny to imported cowries and other moneys in this section, though they were only a portion of African imports in the slave-trade era. Chief among imported goods were textiles: cottons, woolens, velvets, silks, and linens of all descriptions, bleached, dyed, and embroidered. The textiles were mostly of Indian origin until the end of the eighteenth century, and mostly manufactured in Europe thereafter. Next in importance were alcoholic beverages (especially rum, but including a wide variety) and tobacco, mostly grown in Brazil and prepared in rolls. Of lesser but still strategic importance were guns and gunpowder, salt, and iron and copper bars used by smiths. The wide array of remaining goods – shoes, umbrellas, kitchenware, beads, jewellery, sedan chairs and so on – was important to the continuation of the trade, but comprised only a small part of its total value.[38]

The pattern of African imports reveals two contradictory dimensions of the export slave trade: its elite and mass characteristics. On the one hand, the slave trade served the interests of an elite. The slave-trading elite grasped the best cloths and liquor, the most prestigious luxury goods, and most of the firearms. These imported goods served to reflect and to reinforce the dominant positions of monarchs, big men, and great merchants. On the other hand, the slave trade involved all levels of society. The plainer textiles and much of the tobacco and alcoholic beverages passed into the hands of the common people. Some of these commoners had sold one or two slaves themselves; some purchased imports with income they gained otherwise.

The import of money in Africa is of particular interest because it reveals the contrast between the elite and mass dimensions of the slave trade, and because it illustrates the tightness of economic ties among Africa, the Occident, and the Orient. The imported money took the varying forms of Africa's commodity monies – cowrie shells, brass manillas in horseshoe shape, squares of cloth, iron bars, copper wire, brass pans, but also gold dust and silver dollars (Maria Theresa thalers, and Spanish, American, and Latin American dollars of roughly equal value) – but it was money none the less. Large and small squares of imported cloth corresponded to different denominations of currency in Angola, and served as working capital for inland slave merchants. In total, these currency imports ranked relatively high on the list of African imports. In the eighteenth-century Bight of Benin, cowries sometimes amounted to one-third of the value of imports. More generally, money imports may be estimated at from 10 to 15 percent of the value of African imports.[39]

The money supplies of Africa were thus constituted through foreign trade. Africans exported slaves and other goods whose value exceeded that of the goods they imported. They imported money to pay for this export surplus, and added this money to the currency already circulating in their domestic economies. The work of Jan Hogendorn and Marion Johnson has quantified the immense imports of cowries in the Bight of Benin and neighboring regions. These imports led by the end of the eighteenth century to a money supply whose value may have reached £2 million shared among perhaps 8 million people.[40] By the same mechanism, Maria Theresa thalers became widely used as currency across much of Africa during the nineteenth century. Indeed, precisely the same system for constituting the money supply remained in force in twentieth-century Africa. The currencies were now British, French, and Portuguese, but the only means of obtaining them was through export surpluses. Only after World War II did modern central banks gain control of the money supply.

According to certain sorts of monetary reasoning, it may be possible that the addition to the African money supply resulting from the slave trade brought forth a more efficient commercial system and even some new sources of supply of goods and services. As the money supply increased, cash transactions became easier, a larger proportion of output was oriented toward the market, and goods and services flowed more smoothly and over a wider area than before. The sixteenth through the eighteenth centuries along the Western Coast, and the nineteenth century along the Eastern Coast, were times of considerable expansion of money supply and trading activities generally, as a direct result of the slave trade.[41]

On the other hand, and in a remarkable parallel to the European experience of importing large quantities of gold and silver from the Americas (plus African gold), the result of importing so much money into Africa was simply to redistribute the ownership of existing goods and services. In the African case, further, this exchange resulted in the emigration of millions of prime workers, and left behind a declining population and a disordered society. Overall, the imports into Africa allowed first of all for the redistribution of existing wealth, then for the satisfaction of short-term consumer desires, and only lastly for production and creation of new wealth. Some of this was inevitable and natural in the conditions of world trade from the seventeenth through nineteenth centuries. But much of it was a more specific result of the fact that the African slave trade was based on theft and piracy, that is, on the redistribution of wealth already created rather than on the creation of new wealth. So while it seems certain that the slave trade brought an expansion in the African money supply and a displacement of self-sufficient production by production for the market, it is by no means certain that this type of market expansion brought an improvement in African economic welfare.[42]

The desire for money posed the temptation that drew many Africans into the slave trade. There were other things to be gained from selling and holding slaves – imported goods, social prestige, family and political power, a life of ease – but money was an important part of the total, and it crystallizes the crassness of the trade in slaves. Any person could be reduced to a monetary value. African complicity in the slave trade systematically reinforced the primacy of narrow self-interest and of short-term economic calculations. The future in a world with so many reversals could never be certain, so that long-term investment seemed like a poor bet as compared to the possibility of immediate profit and immediate consumption of those profits. The myth of collecting cowries from the cadavers of slaves evokes the crass and cruel mentality of the era. Yet the participants in the slave trade could never escape the humanity of their captives.

Instead, slave raiders, slave merchants, and slave owners devised ways to distance themselves from the fact that they were dealing in bodies for cash. They needed to clothe their greedy motivations and justify the suffering they propagated; they needed to protect themselves against the retribution of men in this world and gods in the next. They lubricated and disguised the flow of slaves with a hundred euphemisms, proverbs, equivocations, and outright lies. European merchants at the coast were told that the slaves had been brought from the far interior, and that each kingdom or ethnic group had a prohibition on enslaving people of their own group: these were half-truths, often stretched very far to preserve the integrity of the sellers of slaves. Slaves brought down the Zaire river by Bobangi merchants were told not that they would be sold, but rather that they were being left for a few days in one village while their owners did business in another. Or, as European and African merchants said to each other about the slaves they shipped off, they would have died otherwise in warfare or sacrifice.[43] Thus did the slave trade influence the ideas and the discourse of African peoples.

By the same token, the slave trade influenced outsiders' perceptions of Africans. One of the most ironic twists is that Europeans came to portray Africans as lacking a money economy, and as knowing no more than simple barter. In the nineteenth and twentieth centuries, such a view fits with European theories of the evolution of civilization, according to which Africans were primitives whose societies had been held at a very simple level. In the eighteenth century, the vision of African barter was simply one more way for slavers to distance themselves from the crass and destructive reality of slavery. While slavery may have done more to impoverish than to enrich Africans over the long run, and while many groups may have sought to escape into self-sufficiency to avoid enslavement, it is impossible to explain African slavery without emphasis on the role of money. Indeed, even among such refugee peoples as the Dogon, who lived in isolated hamlets for protection against raids, elders discreetly sold children and even adults in exchange for cowries.[44]

A world market for forced labor

The Occidental trade of the eighteenth and early nineteenth centuries was so extensive that it drew the African and Oriental markets for slave labor into a web of interactions that may fairly be labelled a world market for forced labor. Captives were drawn from virtually all parts of sub-Saharan Africa, and they were moved within Africa and in all directions beyond the continent, in response to changing prices and levels of demand. No single great market came to dominate the trade, though markets in Cairo, Istanbul, Kilwa, Okeodan (in Nigeria), Mpumbu (at Malebo Pool in Zaire), Rio de Janeiro and elsewhere were major foci of regional trade.[45] The market was rarely smoothly functioning, even in the days of legal slaving: warfare, collusion, trade secrets, abolition, and other restraints on trade prevented the formation of equilibrium prices for slaves. Yet there did emerge a clear intercontinental market for slaves, beginning with the seventeenth-century increase in the volume and prices of slaves in the Occidental trade, expanding across Africa and into the Orient by the end of the eighteenth century, and then gradually undergoing restriction to Africa and portions of the Orient in the nineteenth century.[46] Proof of the existence of such a world market does not require that we locate some single great center for slave marketing at which all slave purchasers were represented – clearly, no such center existed – but only that all regions were linked to each other so that any major change in supply or demand would be felt throughout the market.

For instance, with the dip in the real prices of Atlantic slaves in the late eighteenth century, slaves began moving in larger numbers to North Africa. In particular, slaves from Senegambia who had earlier gone to the New World began to go in larger numbers at this time to Morocco. Similarly, slaves from the Central Sudan began going in larger numbers to Tripoli rather than to the Bights of Benin and Biafra.[47] These interactions of regions were complex rather than simple: thus, the East African slave trade was opened up at a time when the total demand for slave labor had ceased expanding. Slaves brought to the Eastern Coast, however, were sent either to Occidental or Oriental purchasers, according to relative demand. The shipments of slaves from Kilwa and Zanzibar, in turn, affected the prices and quantities of slaves sent from the Horn to Arabia and the Persian Gulf. The links of the slave trade in all the waters surrounding Africa, and throughout the African continent, can be illustrated by stories showing the ways in which changes in supply and demand in each area affected those in the next.[48]

The market for slave labor differed in major respects from markets in such uniform, inanimate commodities as gold and wheat, and the differences showed up in price behavior. To begin with, the quality of slaves varied immensely, not only by age and sex, but also according to their skills and physical characteristics. Prices varied accordingly. Secondly, local variations in supply and demand brought large price fluctuations. Major short-term declines in prices were brought, for instance, either by the arrival of an unusually large supply of slaves in a region, or by the failure of European merchants to show up in a given port. The typical response time in adjusting levels of slave supply and demand was longer than the annual schedule of agricultural commodities, so disequilibria in slave markets tended to persist.[49] Thirdly, transportation costs in moving slaves were relatively high (higher than for gold but lower than for grain, relative to value), thus reinforcing the significance of local markets. Finally, political authorities intervened more heavily in the slave trade than in other markets, either by encouraging and protecting the slave trade, or by restricting it.

The result of these factors is that prices of slaves varied sharply within groups of slaves, over time within a given region, and among regions. Nevertheless, the links among the prices and movements of slaves in the eighteenth and nineteenth centuries are so significant that it is their unity rather than their diversity which should be emphasized. The main trends in the market for slave labor were propagated in relentless ripples sent out from the centers of greatest demand – New World plantations – which sooner or later brought responses in levels of supply and demand from all regions where slavery was to be found.

In the period from 1500 to 1900, the demand of slave purchasers resulted in the emigration of roughly 12 million slaves to the Occident, some six million slaves to the Orient, and the emigration of perhaps another 8 million slaves within Africa. It was the largest migration in human history to that time. Thus, while in the formulations of many economists, capital is a mobile factor of production and labour is a relatively immobile factor of production, the slave trade at its height represented a way of getting around the immobility of labor by making labor cheap enough so that it could be moved for thousands of miles.

The migration of African slave labor should be compared to the largest two migratory movements which succeeded it: those from Asia and from Europe. The Asian emigration was linked to a milder form of forced labor. In the years after the abolition of the slave trade, the desire for cheap labor in areas under Occidental control brought about the recruitment of great numbers of Indian, Chinese, and other workers as contract laborers, dispatched to the New World, to Africa, and to Asian territories and the islands of the Pacific. Roughly 2.5 million men and women came as workers on plantations, railroads, and mines in the period from 1850 to 1920. Most of the survivors stayed on as settlers, but a sizeable minority returned home.[50] A few thousand African contract laborers were brought to the New World at the same time, but the movement never became significant. Contract laborers, who moved from one part of Africa to another under European direction in the late nineteenth century, were, often, slaves with a new label.[51]

The European emigration was larger and is better known. European migrants had come to the New World since Columbus, but not until after 1840 did the stream of European emigrants come to exceed in quantity the cargoes of African slaves. From then until shortly after World War I, nearly 50 million European emigrants filled the cities and countrysides of the Americas. As with the Asian migrants, however, a significant number of European migrants returned home.[52]

The trauma caused by the African migration greatly exceeded that of the Asian and European migrations. This is true even though the African migration represented a smaller proportion of the home population than did the later European migration. The African emigration caused the home population to decline because African death-rates for the whole period were much higher than for Europe after 1840. In addition, the nature of the slave trade brought an additional mortality in capture and transport for which there was no equivalent in Europe or Asia.[53] There were economic as well as demographic differences among these migratory movements. African emigrants were not paid, but their sellers received payments for them; the equivalents in Asia and Europe were the fees paid to labor recruiters, though these were far smaller than the prices of slaves. On the other hand, European migrants to the New World and even Asian contract laborers sent remittances back to their families at home, whereas the families of enslaved Africans received nothing.

Slave supply and demand in the nineteenth century

When slave exports from the continent declined, Africans continued to capture large numbers of slaves. It would be too simplistic to claim that this was merely the continuation of a habit. Instead, the analysis of slavery in this late period reveals that a new logic and a new set of patterns arose to sustain slavery for most of another tumultuous century. The new factors stemmed both from Africa and from the world economy.

The gradual suppression of the export slave trade severed the African system of labor recruitment from the labor systems (both slave and free) of the Occident and the Orient. One clear indication of this break is in the divergence of slave prices across the Atlantic: in 1820 African prices were some 20 percent of New World prices; in 1860 they were less than 10 percent of New World prices, because of the additional costs of transportation and risk in the era of the illegal slave trade.[54] After 1850 for most parts of the continent, and for decades earlier in some regions, Occidental and Oriental slave prices ceased to govern the prices of slaves in Africa.

At the very time when Africa was isolated from the transatlantic *labor* system, the continent was integrated more fully than ever before into the world's *commodity* system. The decline in transportation costs (with the advent of steam shipping and railroads) and the availability of cheap, industrially produced goods increased the value of Africa's transoceanic trade at the end of the nineteenth century to a level well beyond what it had been at the height of the slave exports.[55]

Meanwhile the evolution of African societies (partly in response to these world-economic factors, but also in response to domestic social influences) brought additional new factors into play. New sets of wars broke out, and a new set of large states emerged: the Sokoto Caliphate in the Central Sudan, the Omani Sultanate in Zanzibar, the Chokwe dominions in the southern Savanna, and the Zulu kingdom in South Africa were among the most prominent of these. A wealthy class of aristocrats and merchants emerged, with expensive tastes and the means to satisfy them.[56]

In the matrix of these factors, the African slave trade was transformed and bent to the service of a blossoming *slave mode of production* in many regions of the continent. By this term, I mean a set of institutions and social relations that were united by an economic logic of production, reproduction, and surplus extraction. This slave mode of production (which is discussed more fully in chapter 6) rose to centrality through a modification of earlier African institutions of slavery. In the Savanna and Horn, a slave mode of production had existed for centuries in a marginal sense: it included those sectors of the economy in which palace slaves served monarchs, and in which slaves produced agricultural and artisanal commodities for sale by their masters. Along the Western Coast, millions of slaves, dominantly female, had been held during the seventeenth and eighteenth centuries; most of their production was for households, rather than for the market. The systematic nature of their oppression has too often been ignored, perhaps because most were women. Yet only in the nineteenth century did the organization of production around slavery come to be central to Africa's economic life. And only in the nineteenth century did unmistakable slave classes come into existence. Slaves produced, as before, for the households of their masters and their kings. More than ever before, however, slaves produced goods to be marketed in Africa and abroad. The African demand for slaves, who were to create leisure and commercial profit for their masters, thus displaced Occidental and Oriental demand as the motive force for enslavement in Africa.

Yet there remains an interpretive problem. One of the most remarkable aspects of nineteenth-century African slavery was the continued supply of large numbers of slaves even as the prices of slaves fell sharply. To phrase the problem in price-theory terms: assuming a competitive market, it is expected that, at a given market price for slaves, purchasers are utilizing slaves up to the value of their marginal product, and sellers are providing as many slaves as they can profitably provide, given the costs of procurement. If the price of slaves falls, the incentive to capture and deliver the costliest slaves disappears, and the quantity supplied diminishes.

Since there is no way to measure directly the number of persons enslaved on the African continent in either the eighteenth or the nineteenth century, we can construct no clear test of changing volumes. But the overwhelming qualitative evidence for a great expansion in domestic African slavery during the nineteenth century, plus many direct and second-hand accounts of intensive slave raiding, leave little doubt. The supply of slaves continued at a high level – perhaps equal, perhaps somewhat smaller, and perhaps even larger than in the eighteenth century. If this were simply a result of higher African demand for slaves, prices would have risen rather than fallen. Thus something in the political economy of slave supply caused a contradiction to the simple prediction of the competitive model.[57]

The resolution of this paradox of high slave supply at lower prices lies in the distinction between captive and slave, and in the two-tiered price structure for Africans in captivity. The price of *captives* reflected the cost of capture – which could at times be small indeed – and capture continued as long as the captives could be sold to the profit of the captors. The price of *slaves* reflected their productive value. As long as New World demand dominated the market, the difference between the prices of captives and of slaves was large: the full amount of this difference can be attributed to "costs" of one sort or another. The costs included those of feeding, transporting, and seasoning slaves. They also included costs of taxes, tolls, fees, gifts, and bribes collected by officials or even by religious authorities, the costs of the merchants' services, and simple windfall profit. The latter costs, which had been institutionalized in the structure of the slave trade, were not really necessary to the delivery of slaves. As prices fell, these "costs" gradually disappeared. That is, falling prices eliminated the excess profits of African merchants and state officials, and thereby expanded the number of slaves brought to African markets at any given price.[58]

Yet if these "costs" or excess profits were eliminated by an act of the will in the nineteenth century, why were they not competed out of existence in the eighteenth century? Why should the structure of restrictive practices entailed in the fees and tolls of the slave trade, whose establishment was reflected in the rising prices of the eighteenth century, now be abandoned? The answer I propose is in two parts. First, the nineteenth-century decline in prices put unprecedented pressure on the institutions of slave supply. If costs had not been cut – if merchants had insisted on maintaining their markups and kings had insisted on their tolls – then the volume of slaves traded would indeed have suffered a great decline. Second, by the early nineteenth century an alternative source of profits had emerged: the employment of slave labor. In short, the big men of Africa, faced with a sharp decline in prices, gave up the profits of trading in slaves in order to gain the profits of exploiting slaves. The dominant figures now became identified less as slave merchants and warlords, and more as landowners, slave owners, and merchants trading in commodities other than humans.[59]

In addition to this change in slave supply at the elite level, one may more hesitantly suggest a change at the mass level. Under some circumstances, enslavement may be treated as a communicable disease which, once introduced, tends to spread relentlessly through a cycle of provocation and revenge. When the inhabitants of a village found themselves to be victims of slave raids or kidnapping, it was not uncommon for them to respond in kind against their attackers, or against the people of a third village. When these acts of revenge resulted in captures, it was only a short step to enslaving the captives. Under these conditions, enslavement can be seen as a disease which, once launched on its course, might continue to spread even after the prices of slaves had declined to the point where it became unprofitable.[60]

In addition to these changes in the institutions of slave supply, other factors increased the availability and reduced the cost of slaves in nineteenth-century Africa. First, since slaves were no longer being removed from Africa in such numbers, the African population ceased to decline (though it still required some two decades to bring a newborn child to maturity). Second, to the degree that slaves were now transported a shorter distance (and to African rather than to external destinations), the costs of merchants were reduced. Third, with the expansion of slavery, a growing portion of those enslaved were already in slave status, thus making their socialization easier. Further, while high mortality of captives still remained a factor, it is conceivable that levels of mortality during enslavement declined in this period.[61]

For all of the above reasons, the supply of slaves was maintained even in an era of declining prices. Let us turn next to the demand for slaves: why did slave ownership become more attractive to nineteenth-century Africans? The first factor is straightforward. As New World demand declined and prices fell, the quantity of slaves demanded by African and Middle East purchasers increased. Within Africa, as slaves came to be within the purchasing power of landowners and manufacturers, the commercial utilization of slaves increased. Secondly, the greater availability of slaves led to the development of more effective institutions of production through slave labor. This development was parallel to the development of the New World sugar plantation system by Dutch planters during the middle years of the seventeenth century when slave prices were unusually low. The new institution of African slavery included the supervised slave villages of Nupe, the redefined slave families of Zanzibar, and the agreement to make Calabar slaves immune from being sacrificed at funerals.[62]

A further and very important factor felt in nineteenth-century Africa was an increased demand for commodities that could be produced efficiently by slave labor. Most clearly, demand for African agricultural produce expanded in Europe and elsewhere, and lower shipping costs increased the profitability of the new export trade. Palm oil came first from the Bight of Biafra and then from the whole Western Coast; peanuts came from Senegambia; and cloves came from Zanzibar to India. In Angola after 1850, exports of ivory, beeswax, and rubber arose through a similar dependence on slave labor. Such African developments also had their New World parallels: not only the seventeenth-century increase in the demand for sugar from Brazil and the Caribbean, but also the nineteenth-century expansion in slave-produced cotton from the U.S., sugar from Cuba, and coffee from Brazil. In addition, however, the nineteenth century brought an expansion of domestic African demand for slave produce, notably grain and textiles. Domestic demand grew partly because of actual economic growth, but also because of the redistribution of wealth through slavery: in a sort of feedback mechanism, the growing slave labor sector created demand for more slave produce.[63]

The new slave enterprises, which owed their existence in part to declining slave prices, set up a level of demand for slaves which prevented their prices from falling much further during the balance of the nineteenth century. Prices reported by David Eltis for slave-exporting regions of the Atlantic coast, after reaching a peak of £15 per slave in the 1840s, fell to £10 in the 1850s and fell further thereafter. These prices, which remained well above the prices of slaves sold to Europeans in the seventeenth century, indicate that the level of African demand for slaves had expanded greatly in the intervening century and a half. Abdul Sheriff's series of prices drawn from the Indian Ocean coast are much lower, and they show a decline several decades earlier, during the Napoleonic wars, but the pattern is otherwise similar.[64]

Regional conditions, however, continued to vary, and thereby brought variations in prices and quantities of slaves. For example, observers of the Western Sudan in the late nineteenth century frequently reported mass executions of male captives: even at very low prices, no buyers were to be found, so the female captives were enslaved and the males were eliminated. Martin Klein's studies of the Western Sudan indicate that, at the turn of the twentieth century, most of the slaves in the region were female.[65] This leaves open the possibility that the missing males had died, though it is also possible that there were surpluses of males in areas beyond the borders of his surveys.

Africa's economy in the late nineteenth century relied more significantly on slavery than ever before. This new economic structure had grown logically out of the previous period of heavy involvement in slave exports. But logic was soon to take a new twist. Africa's expanding system of slave production was now in contradiction with the expanding world vision of the European powers which had turned, after a century of anguish, from propagating slavery to prosecuting it. A clash between Africa and Europe was inevitable.

The Europeans who conquered Africa often justified their actions as a campaign against slavery. It is easy to point out the irony that Europeans, a few decades earlier, had themselves been deeply implicated in slavery, and that their involvement helped expand slavery in Africa. Yet one must not refuse to recognize the contribution of those who, for whatever reason, opposed slavery in Africa. Here I want to mention a second and perhaps less obvious irony. In the wake of imperialistic condemnation of slavery and of African life generally, the memory of the African sacrifice to the evolving Atlantic economy was lost. That memory was a casualty of colonization. It was lost not only to the European colonizers and to inhabitants of the New World, but to many of the colonized in Africa.

6

Patterns of slave life

The definition I have used for "slavery" in the analysis so far has been a simplified one: slaves are persons who are held in captivity, and who may be bought and sold. This definition has been sufficient to get us through the previous chapters, which have analyzed the demographic and economic factors that brought about the rise and spread of African slavery, and some of the institutional and ideological factors which helped to keep it going. As we turn now to scrutinize African institutions of slavery in more detail, we must be prepared to turn to a more complex conception of the phenomenon. In this chapter I shall emphasize more fully than before that the conditions of slavery varied greatly from region to region in Africa, and with the passage of time. I shall recount the life stories of a number of individual slaves, then consider the life cycle of slaves in a range of African societies, then turn to discussion of African law and social organization in so far as they were influenced by slavery, and finally assess the influence of slavery on African thought.

The argument in this chapter gives particular attention to the range of experience of slaves, as well as the importance of local factors and the traditions of individual African peoples in conditioning that experience. That is, we shall consider the many Africas in which slaves lived. In the next chapter, by contrast, I will focus on the pressures which tended to create one Africa out of many. I will argue that the wide variance in slave experience was not just a matter of varying individual local traditions, and that many of the variations can be arranged in patterns and explained as historical consequences of the overall rise and decline in the slave trade and slavery.

Lives of slave men and women

African slavery, in the course of the centuries, encompassed the lives of tens of millions of persons. In one sense, however, slavery was not a mass phenomenon but the sum total of the individual lives spent partly or wholly in slavery. While there is no way to present the totality of this experience or

110

even a representative sample of individual slave lives, I have drawn here on the biographies and anecdotes known for a number of slaves, to set forth an impression of the range of their experience.

Perhaps the best-known African slave was Olaudah Equiano, who achieved an education in the West Indies, gained his freedom, and went to England to become a literary and political figure. His book, *Equiano's Travels*, added to the anti-slavery literature of his time. In it, he described the capture by kidnapping of himself and his sister in Igbo country, their repeated sale and his embarcation on a British ship at Badagry.[1]

Equiano was a young boy when he made the Middle Passage, and was in no position to resist. Others, however, rebelled on land and on board ship, as many ships' logs testify. Shipboard rebellions were most common while the ships were anchored off the coast, waiting to complete their cargo. Most such cases were similar to the case of the *Guadeloupe* off Calabar in 1769, where the male slaves gained control of the front deck and killed some of the crew members. They were only put down when the captain, from the rear, fired a cannon into their midst, killing some twenty men. Jean Mettas, in his encyclopaedic review of French slave voyages, notes two cases in which the slaves actually gained control of the vessel, killing or driving off the crew. In the first case, at Ouidah, the slaves actually made it to land and many of them seem to have escaped; in the second case, off Cameroon, a fire on board reached the powder magazine and the ship blew up, killing all on board.[2]

The battles of the slave trade were not only between slaves and masters. The wars among competing kingdoms of the littoral of the Gold Coast and the Slave Coast (as the Bight of Benin was also known), for instance, included heavy tolls and spectacular executions of leading enemies or turncoats. The French official Pruneau de Pommegorge gives a gruesomely detailed description of the week-long execution of the British governor of Cape Coast fort, Testefolle, by the king of Cape Coast.[3]

The other side of the brutality of the slave trade was the wealth it brought, which in turn provided some of its beneficiaries with an elegant life. The *signares* of Guinea, women slave merchants, lived such a life: George Brooks has recounted the life and times of Mãe Correia of Bissau during the nineteenth century.[4]

Nor were human sensibilities fully effaced by the commoditization of humanity. One interesting story of filial piety, though at the royal level, is that of Agõtĩme, a slave wife of Agonglo, king of Danhomè, and mother of prince Gankpe. At Agonglo's death his son Adandozan won the contest to gain the throne; he punctuated his victory over the young Gankpe by selling Agõtĩme into slavery. Years later, in 1818, Gankpe overthrew Adandozan and became king Ghezo. He immediately sent a series of embassies to search the New World, but especially Brazil, in an effort to find his mother. The search failed. A century and a half later, however, Pierre Verger found in Maranhão the traces of the secret cult of the women of the Abomey palace, with a list of names which ended at such a point as to make almost certain that he had found the historical trace of Agōtīme. Judith Gleason has told the tale of Agōtīme in an admirable historical novel.[5]

In the nineteenth century the pace of the Oriental slave trade picked up, and in some cases it involved raiding parties covering vast distances in search of slaves. In 1872 Gustav Nachtigal, the German explorer, accompanied such an expedition from Baghirmi which went to the south. Nachtigal describes the day-long battle for the village of Kôli, well defended by thick brambles, but doomed because of the inferiority of the bows and arrows of its defenders when set against the firearms of the attackers. At the end of the day resistance was broken. Many of the men had been killed, and the rest were captured. The women were taken but the children, worthless to the captors, were left behind. The remaining casualties were among the Baghirmi raiders themselves as they struggled for control of the captives.[6]

At much the same time, David Livingstone told stories of the horrific death-rates of slaves making the long march from Lake Malawi to the coast. If Livingstone opposed the enslavement of Africans, he also felt that, once enslaved, they became hopelessly degraded. Thus, only in special cases did he attempt to come to the aid of slaves. One such case was that of a young woman whom he determined, by her bearing, to be of royal blood. In her case he was able to obtain her release.[7]

While the toll in the East African slave trade was heavy, many survived it. Perhaps the best available description of an East African slave caravan comes from Swema, a Yao girl from what is now north-western Mozambique who made the journey while perhaps ten years old. In a narrative of her story published by French missionaies, Swema told of being enslaved by a Yao creditor and sold to a passing Arab (i.e. Swahili) merchant for three meters of American cloth. Her father had died some years before, her mother had become impoverished, and her three siblings had also died. After Swema was enslaved, her mother decided to accompany the caravan. Her mother did not survive the trip to the coast: she carried a load of ivory as long as she was able, and when she was unable to carry it, her Swahili captors refused to feed her, and drove her away from the caravan. After the loss of her mother, Swema ate little and could no longer walk. But the caravan leader, expecting to receive a *piastre* for her from his patron upon arrival in Zanzibar, had her carried by another slave. Swema arrived with the rest of the caravan at Kilwa on the coast, and after a few days was shipped on a small and tightly packed *dhow* to Zanzibar. There the owner of the caravan concluded that she was a loss, and ordered that she be taken to the cemetery. Swema was indeed buried alive, but a young man discovered her and delivered her to the Spiritains' mission.[8]

At the end of the nineteenth century, the biographies of slaves turn less on the slave trade and more on the fate of slaves in African society. In the cases of those slaves destined to be victims of human sacrifice to the honor of past kings in Danhomè or Benin, or executed en masse in the Western

Sudan, their fate was most unhappy.[9] At the other end of the scale was Jaja, born in Igbo country and enslaved as a boy, who grew up to be head of a great trading house in the Ijo port of Bonny, and subsequently founded his own state of Opobo. It was his prominence and his success which induced the British, in 1887, to capture him and exile him to the West Indies. Only in recent times has it come to light that, late in life, Jaja regained contact with his family, an aristocratic lineage from Amaigbo, so that it may be said he not only rose in status but that he also carried the high status of his birth into slavery.[10]

More representative of the lives of slaves in this period, however, is the story of Adukwe as told to Claire Robertson. Adukwe, born in about 1890 in the interior of the Gold Coast, was brought to the coast and made a slave in Accra. She told her life story while in her nineties: it was a life not greatly unlike that of other women in Accra, except that she developed remarkable self-reliance to make up for the fact that she had no other family. Another well-known woman's story of the colonial era, that of Baba of Karo, shows the life of slave women from the viewpoint of the master's daughter.[11]

Stages of the life-course

Orlando Patterson, in his magisterial survey of slavery in human society, took as his organizing principle the notion that slavery meant social death.[12] The slave, though necessarily a living, breathing being, had no right to participate in society except as the proxy of a free person: the slave was socially dead.

This useful concept of social death may be extended, to permit an analysis of the life-course of slaves. Birth, childhood, maturity, old age, death: these normal stages of the life-course applied to slaves as much as to anyone else. Yet in addition to these *physical* stages of slave lives, our analysis must account for the stages of the slave's *social* existence. Thus, if upon enslavement a person died a social death, that person experienced by the same token a birth into slave status. Similarly, for those enslaved after birth, the process of socialization ("seasoning," as it was called in the New World) was equivalent to the childhood socialization of those born into slavery. At the other end of the cycle, the slave might die a natural death, or might die at the hand of his or her master. On the brighter side, a freed slave is reborn as a member of society, yet in that moment also dies as a slave. Or if a slave were sold, it was in a sense death and rebirth: the slave began the cycle anew with socialization at the hand of a new master. With this dual meaning of the life-course in mind, let us review some aspects of each stage of the slave's life.

Those born into slavery, in many African societies, benefited from more protections than those brought in as captives. They could not be sold or killed; after a couple more generations, their descendants might lose slave status altogether. Such advantages, where they existed, were not always

113

sufficient to encourage slave women to have children: Robert Harms reports remarkably low birth-rates among Bobangi slaves on the Zaire river, though this may be in part a result of poor health conditions along the river.[13]

Were slave children of any value? Stanley Engerman has noted that this issue may be resolved by whether slave infants had a positive price, and he argued that slave children born in the New World did have a positive price.[14] For Africa, this same issue must be resolved with regard to the difference between captives and slaves. Children born into slave status may have been expected to bring some small reward, on the average, to their owners. But for captured infants the opposite seems to have been the case: when women were captured, their children were generally left behind, or if they were sold with their children, the infants added nothing to their price.[15] Gustav Nachtigal, reporting on an 1872 slave raid south of Baghirmi, noted that the captors made no special effort to collect infants; at the same time, he noted that the women, once they knew their capture to be inevitable, killed their infants.[16] This might have been to protect them from life under slavery, but more likely it was to hurry a death which their mothers knew to be inevitable.

Those born into slavery were brought up with the understanding that they were inferior beings. Their natural parents sought to give them love and protection, yet they were subject as well to the whim of their masters and of the whole master class, however that should be defined. They differed from their captured parents in native language and in early socialization. Sometimes this meant that they had higher social status, but not always. The Hausa slaves on the *rinji* or slave villages remained in slave status as long as their masters could keep them there.[17]

For those captured at any age, they were by that act "born" into slavery, and were treated as infants within the confines of their new status. Those who were enslaved as children were in effect assigned a kin status. Terminology was often kept ambiguous: a slave might be referred to as "sister" or "daughter" one day, but could be sold the next. Each captive, after enslavement, had to go through a process of socialization or seasoning before he or she could become a slave of any value. The slave had to learn the language of the masters, just as a child had to learn to speak, though in some cases the special and liminal status of the slave was emphasized linguistically as the slave learned a language or dialect spoken only among slaves and between masters and slaves. The slave had to accept orders, either voluntarily or under threat of sanction. Few persons could be made into good slaves unless they were far enough away from home that they had no hope of escape or rescue. Seasoning was naturally more difficult to achieve for older slaves than for the young, but an adult male slave *could* still be valuable if, for instance, he had skills in construction, metal work, or weaving. Women slaves were generally expected to be more docile than men, though stories of female obstinacy are not lacking.[18]

For free Africans, passage to maturity was generally marked by rites of initiation. Males were often initiated in ceremonies involving circumcision; female circumcision too was widely practiced. With the physical initiation went moral training and social recognition. For slaves, however, initiation was often of the crudest and roughest sort: the initiation of many female slaves was the sexual initiation at the hands of their masters.[19]

At best, once the slave reached chronological and social maturity, he or she could be accorded full participation in the host society, given acceptance of the proposed social role, and acceptance as well of a fictive kinship position which could never be as well grounded as biological kinship. At worst, the slave could be the object of physical and social degradation, and could be executed as a sacrifice or a bearer of messages to the next world.

The work life of slaves in Africa was limited only by the range of tasks to be performed: domestic labor, agricultural labor, manufacture and craft work, commerce, transport, government and military activities, all included the work of slaves. In addition to work for the master, slaves commonly had to find time to cultivate their own little plot of land to feed themselves. Since the slaves of Africa were in majority female, we should address women's work to begin with.

The laborious tasks of fetching firewood and water, of pounding grain into meal or yams into *foofoo*, of washing clothes and of sweeping floors and yards, kept many women busy in domestic work alone. In addition, women did much of the agricultural labor in many parts of the continent, especially in the times when men were in short supply. This was particularly true for Loango and Angola, but it was also true for some coastal areas of West Africa. In East Africa, the sexual division of labor which gave men the work with cattle and women the work on the farms predated the great expansion of slave exports. To the degree that women in particular were exported from this region, self-sufficiency in food production became more difficult.

Women also participated in craft production and services, including porterage. In urban areas and along trade routes, female slaves were put to work as petty traders. Women spun cotton while men wove in the Western Sudan. The great indigo dye works of nineteenth-century Kano drew on the labor of many female slaves. In the extreme cases, some women slaves rose to positions of power and influence: the most notorious cases are those of the royal palace in Danhomè, and a related group, the Amazons, the female soldiers of nineteenth-century Danhomè.[20]

But in Africa, as in the New World, women's work was first in the fields, then in menial domestic work, and only a very few female slaves achieved other occupations. Male slaves had a greater variety of occupations, and a greater chance of having interesting work.

Male slaves too did a great amount of agricultural work, as is shown on the *rinji* of the Sokoto Caliphate and in other areas of the Savanna. In coastal areas, the work of male slaves is documented for the nineteenth century in the production of peanuts in Senegambia, of palm oil from the Gold Coast to Cameroon, and of coffee in Angola.[21]

Men were also employed as transport workers, mostly as porters but also as canoemen. While the work of canoemen required skills in boat-handling, the work of porters mostly required endurance, as they carried loads of some 25 to 40 kilograms for distances of 25 kilometers per day. Slave craftsmen included those skilled in construction, basketry, weaving, dyeing, metal work, and so forth.

Certain slaves rose in the trust of their masters to higher positions. Reports of slave soldiery are common for the Western and Central Sudan. Slave officials, in addition, presented certain advantages to heads of government: they were dependent on their owners, they had no relatives to rely on or pass secrets to, and for these reasons their ambitions were limited. In the Oyo empire the *ilari* formed a whole caste of slave officials, easily identified by their half-shaven heads and their black costume.[22]

But the meaning of this upward mobility and of the power of individual slaves should not be distorted. In one sense, it did represent a finite chance that certain slaves might rise above their menial position to one of power and influence. More important, however, was the obverse side of this message: these slaves could be allowed to rise only because many more were held in utter subjection. They could be trusted because they were absolutely dependent on their patrons, and they could be sent back to the fields, the mines, or to the executioner for any reason whatever or no reason at all.

Family life for slaves meant, in some cases, life within slave families; more often it meant the lives of slaves within families dominated by their masters. The widespread African demand for slave women, especially as it had developed by the eighteenth and nineteenth centuries, reflected a demand by African men for women who would become subordinate members of their families. They could perform domestic labor and produce children. In addition they were desired by masters for sexual exploitation and as conspicuous indications of wealth.

Claude Meillassoux has argued that the specifically sexual aspect of female slavery in Africa has been exaggerated. Claiming that female slaves had few children in any case, he emphasized instead that women were valued as productive workers who did not have the same power as men to revolt, because of both their physical frailty and their socialization to submissiveness.[23] Meillassoux's emphasis on the importance of female slaves in production is an important contribution, but the sexual aspect of female slavery is not to be dismissed. The immense harems kept by African big men all over the continent leave no doubt as to this fact; even if they were a small proportion of the population, their power and visibility meant that their values would be communicated to the wider society. The proportion of female slaves held in great harems was never large, but by a sort of trickle-down effect lesser men sought to emulate the great, and women slaves suffered as a result.[24]

Slave families as autonomous organizations developed in situations where slaves had become a distinct social class. This was most prominently the case in Muslim societies of the Central and Western Sudan, where slaves lived apart in their own villages, producing for their masters under overseers. In many cases these slave villages were dominantly male, so that the class aspect of this life was clearer than its family aspect. In other cases, as along the coast of West Africa during the nineteenth century, slave families effectively became collateral lineages, claiming ancestry from the founder or the ancestor of their masters.

Once slaves came to develop the identity of a social class, their ritual and ideological life developed increasing autonomy. Slaves, not being full members of society, did not benefit from the rituals of initiation that were so important in recognizing the passage of Africans to adulthood, nor from the rituals of marriage or death. Since slaves benefited little from the celebration of African religions, as a group they were relatively open to conversion to Islam and to Christianity. Conversion to Islam, for instance, might mean that one could escape from the status of slavery and join the society of one's former masters; more likely it meant that one's children would be free rather than slave. The conversion to Christianity in the nineteenth century and earlier was different, in that few African rulers were Christian: conversion to Christianity thus meant forming or joining a new community outside the confines of the old. Christian missionaries did find that large portions of their flocks of converts were slaves seeking to escape slave status.

Slaves resisted their degradation not only morally, through religion, but physically. Free persons resisted capture. Those captured and shipped to the New World revolted with predictable regularity, and revolts of slaves in Africa took place wherever they were gathered in large numbers: for instance, a wave of slave revolts rippled along the West African coast in the 1850s.[25] On an individual level, slaves ran away, sometimes in an attempt to reach home, sometimes to start a new existence on their own, and sometimes as an act of defiance before returning to their masters. As in the New World, slaves were widely condemned by their masters for malingering. The low fertility of slave women in many settings fed speculation that they were aborting births. While demographers have expressed skepticism about the significance of such voluntary abortions, historians have noted the beliefs that such abortions occurred: for instance, Gabriel Debien for St.-Dominigue and Robert Harms for the Bobangi of the Zaire valley. In the later days of slavery, as slaves had become an identifiable social grouping, they entered into collective negotiations with their masters, for example with the demonstrations of Calabar slaves in the 1850s to end human sacrifice.[26] As slavery came to an end with the European conquests in Africa, slaves individually and collectively renegotiated the conditions of their servitude with their masters.

The end of the slave life cycle, for those who lived long enough, was retirement and reduction of the work load to one normal for an old person. At death, however, slaves again met up with the absence of family ties. In societies where the funeral was often the most important ritual, the moral deprivation of slaves was made particularly clear. With the proper celebration of a funeral, the deceased became an ancestor and was guaranteed a continuing participation in the family. Slaves were generally denied funerals – in some areas they could not even be buried – and thus lost the opportunity to become ancestors, as well as being denied the outpouring of affection from family and friends which accompanies proper African funerals.

All too often, slaves died as part of the funeral of another person, when they were executed as sacrifices. Such sacrifices took place at the state level: Danhomè and Benin are best known for their execution of slaves in celebration of the royal ancestors. They took place at funerals of major dignitaries, and at times even ordinary families found themselves called upon by religious authorities to make human sacrifices.[27]

Another end, or sharp turn, in the life course of a slave was to be sold or captured again, and to go once more through the process of transportation, socialization, and starting a new life. A more fortunate end to a slave life, of course, was to gain freedom. Freedom came from manumission, as when Muslim masters freed female slaves who bore them children; from self-purchase, when slaves were able to pay their masters an agreed-upon price; and from successful escape.[28]

Slavery in law and the social order

What appeared to individual slaves as the tragedy of their own life experience must have appeared to their masters as the natural operation of law and the social order. That is, slavery reinforced the social order among many African peoples; at the same time, institutions of slavery provided a tool for corrupting or transforming the social order. By the social order, I mean the structures of kinship, status, and seniority in each African society. In kinship, slavery became written into the rules of marriage and the patterns of lineage structure. In status, slavery encouraged the differentiation within societies which produced social classes, occupational castes, and hierarchies of lineages. In seniority, the pervasive chronological categories of child, adult, and elder – usually distinguished by ritual initiations – were transformed by the placement of most slaves at the lowest level of seniority.

The Tofin fisherfolk of Bénin provide a straightforward example of slavery reinforcing the social order. Their men purchased adult women slaves, and adopted them as wives with full rights within the society, though as immigrants they did not have any family except their adopted family to fall back on. The Tofin lineage structure was reinforced, at the cost of a minor increase in the social distance between husbands and wives.[29]

More commonly, slave women were kept as concubines by their masters, and the women's subordination significantly reinforced the dominance of leading men. In general, the expansion of slaveholding did more to corrupt, subvert, and otherwise transform kinship systems than it did to reinforce them. This corruption of the kinship system is perhaps most obvious for the case of marriage in societies with matrilineal descent systems. According to the normal rules of this system, a man's own sons are members of his wife's lineage, not his own (for his lineage is that of his mother and his sister); and the most closely related male in the next generation, who would inherit his goods and titles at his death, was his sister's son. The relationship between a man and his sister's son (or, to proceed in the opposite direction, between a man and his mother's brother) was the key link in questions of inheritance. Despite the logic of this system (you always *know* who your mother is, if not your father), men chafed against it constantly, since they could not pass on land or goods to their own sons. But since a slave woman had no lineage except that of her master, a man's sons by slave wives would be in his own lineage – or in no lineage at all. Thus for a man to marry his female slave provided more than the advantages of his personal power over her. It also gave him new control – not to be shared with his brothers or elders – over the labor of his offspring and the inheritance of his goods, without formally breaking matrilineal descent rules. This corruption of the matrilineal system through slavery took place on a wide scale in Angola, in the matrilineal areas of the Gold Coast, and later among the Yao of Malawi. In large areas of West Central Africa, this process seems to have contributed to the breakup of matrilineages, and to their replacement by a kinship system which was in fact bilateral.[30]

Less obvious, but perhaps nearly as important in practice, was the equivalent corruption of patrilineal social structures. The normal patrilineal rules called for inheritance from father to son through the male line. Daughters, on the other hand, left the lineage of their fathers, as they and their children became full or part members of their husbands' lineages. But if a man married his daughter to his male slave (who was at once in his lineage and yet not of it) then the master's daughter and her progeny would remain within his lineage. The master thus failed to collect a bride price from the family of his son-in-law, but his grandchildren through both male and female lines remained in his own lineage.[31]

Patterns of kinship and marriage among slaves depended heavily on their numerical and sexual proportion in the captor population. Where there were many female but few male slaves, for instance along the Western Coast in the eighteenth century, slaves were attached intimately to the dominant family structures, albeit always in a subordinate position, rather than be allowed to develop their own families. The children of slaves, however, were often distinguished from the fully free members of their lineages; in effect they became identifiable, slave-descended fractions or branches of the masters' lineages. In this situation, the male slaves had a greater chance for social integration and social mobility. Since these male slaves were not large enough in number to represent a threatening group, they might marry free women of the family, and their children would be free.

In the opposite case, where there were more male than female slaves, the male slaves were unlikely to marry. In societies valuing polygyny, free men took many of the scarce female slaves as wives and concubines, and found little reason to share them with slave men. As a result the slave men found themselves living in a barracks situation: on their own in slave villages, without families, and without descendants.[32]

Under conditions where the numbers of female and male slaves were equal, it was more likely that slave men would marry slave women. The slaves generally lived apart from their masters – as in the slave villages of the Savanna – and they and their progeny came to form a well-defined slave class.[33] In kinship terms, however, they might still be counted as members of the masters' families, in that their own lineages were accounted as branches of the lineage of their owners.

In both systems – where slaves lived with and were married to masters, and where they lived apart and married each other – the masters defined the slaves as part of their "family." And in both systems, the "family" contained within it the essence of a class system.

The expansion of slavery confused African structures of seniority as well as those of kinship. Age groups, separated by initiations, distinguished relations among the stages of life. While slaves too fitted the chronological stages of life of free persons, the fact that they did not have the formal status of adults meant that young persons who were free had authority over slaves far greater than they might otherwise have expected. As a result, seniority functioned not simply in terms of age, but also in terms of social status. For instance, a free person with many slaves might be in practice "older" than a free person of the same age who held no slaves.[34]

Slavery changed African structures of social class even more than it changed those of kinship and seniority. In short, classes of slaves and of slave owners emerged. I do not propose to argue that African societies were homogeneous and undifferentiated prior to the expansion of slavery. Instead, I want to emphasize the specific sorts of hierarchy in social status and economic function brought about by slavery. I believe these social structures are most clearly explained through the term *slave mode of production*.

Where *slavery* refers to the presence of persons held in slave status, a *slave mode of production* refers to an organized set of social roles and economic relations based on slavery; a socio-economic system which sustains and reproduces itself from generation to generation. Karl Marx coined the term in his studies of the ancient Greek and Roman economies; Paul Lovejoy utilizes the same term and a modified concept in his survey of African slavery. Lovejoy, in turn, drew significantly on the writings of Emmanuel Teray.[35]

120

The advantage of using the term *slave mode of production* (rather than referring more neutrally to *slave production*) is that it emphasizes the organized and integrated nature of the social systems to which it is applied. It draws attention to the expansive and transformative power of slavery in nineteenth-century Africa, and calls out for a fuller analysis of its role in African societies.[36]

At the same time, adopting the term also requires applying it carefully. The collection and export of slaves, no matter how numerous, did not in itself qualify as a slave mode of production. The settling of large numbers of slaves to work in agricultural production did not qualify as a slave mode of production if the result, after a generation, was the freeing of the descendants of all the slaves. Claude Meillassoux has emphasized two further conditions that must be satisfied before one can identify a slave mode of production. First, he noted that slaves rarely reproduced themselves biologically, because of the hard conditions under which they lived. Even less did they reproduce themselves socially, since some of them and their offspring were freed. Therefore, an economic system based on a slave mode of production must include reproduction of the social order through recruitment of new slaves. For instance, identification of a slave mode of production on nineteenth-century Zanzibar is incomplete until the economic system is defined to include the communities from which the slaves were obtained. Second, if a social system relying on the exploitation of slaves changed so rapidly that it did not reproduce itself with some stability, it cannot qualify as a slave mode of production. Thus, the warrior regime of Samori Toure in the late nineteenth-century Western Sudan, though it relied heavily on slaves, underwent too much tumultuous change to be treated as a slave mode of production.[37]

There were two major variants of the slave mode of production in Africa. One is what Meillassoux has called *aristocratic slavery*, in which slaves produced agricultural and artisanal goods for the king and his retinue, or for an entire class of aristocrats. The masters were thus relieved from any manual labor. The other is what Meillassoux calls *mercantile slavery*, in which the slaves produce goods sold on the market by their owners. In both these cases, the slaves spend almost all their time working for the benefit of their masters, and have little time left for themselves.[38]

In Meillassoux's schematic set of African classes, the aristocrats are a class of leisure and warfare, who are served by their slaves. Because of the limits on agricultural productivity, a large number of slaves was required in order to relieve the masters of all work. But comparing this case to that of a self-sustaining class of serfs who gave a portion of their crop to their lords, Meillassoux found that the number of serfs required would be more than twice the number of slaves required. Peasants in these "aristocratic societies" were dragooned into much of the work in the wars and raids recruiting new slaves. They had to hand over their captives as tribute, in exchange for protection. In *mercantile society*, merchant classes sold slave produce as well as slaves, and they usually bought rather than captured new slaves. Peasants collaborated with the great merchants, selling their produce to them, and buying some slaves from them.[39]

The formation of slave classes was primarily a phenomenon of nineteenth-century Africa, when the institution of slavery was widespread, but when the export trade had diminished. The establishment of slave colonies for peanut production in Senegambia typifies this short-lived but important type of African slavery.[40] Slave families lived in the farms: their lineages might be linked formally to those of the masters, but they were in reality separate families. In a situation where the key labor was that of the male slave, masters emphasized providing male slaves with wives in order to stabilize them and tie them to their place in society. There was a certain tendency for the system to evolve toward serfdom in succeeding generations, with the families bound now to the land rather than to the person of the landowner.[41]

In this section I have provided both generalities and specifics. The point is that there was a wide range of legal conditions and social structures in African slavery. I have focused on the slave mode of production, not to suggest that it functioned in a uniform way, but to offer the reminder that, for some areas and some times in Africa, slavery functioned as a coherent and self-reproducing socio-economic system.

Slavery and African thought

Among the people of Angola, as on other parts of the coast, it was rumored that the whites were cannibals, carrying off their captives in order to eat them. More chillingly, because it showed the circularity of the system, the Angolans heard that Portuguese red wine, sold in exchange for slaves, was made of slave blood. Similarly, it was said that the bones of dead slaves were ground up to make the gunpowder used to capture new victims.[42]

The pervasiveness of slavery in African life brought its impact on African thought. Of course, it will be next to impossible to reconstruct the thought of eighteenth-century Africans in any detail. Still, I do not think we should leave the topic of patterns in slave life without considering, even speculatively, the mind set created by the life of slaves. We may turn for some help to recent studies on African systems of thought and on the ideology of African slavery.[43] I shall attempt to combine some of the evidence from such studies with the picture I have presented so far of slavery's influence on Africa, and speculate on changing patterns of thought. Few of my hypotheses can be documented, and in any case the regional variations in culture and conditions surely generated a great variety of ideas. My point, nevertheless, is to assert that the experience of slavery must have wrought changes in African thought, and to embark on some speculation as to what those changed ideas might have been.

First, to consider Africa at the time of the greatest extent of slavery and the slave trade, we must imagine a situation in which everybody knew the value, as a captive, of everyone he or she met. What seems to a twentieth-century person as normal response – to refuse, when possible, to put a money value on a person – was replaced in Africa with a conscious and unconscious commodification of anyone encountered. People were forced to think of how much they could get for selling a neighbor, or how much they would pay to ransom a loved one.[44]

A related judgment was reinforced systematically by slavery. Africans were exposed daily to temptation. The sum one could gain from the sale of a slave was very large, in comparison to one's daily earnings. One had only to bend the rules a little more than usual to steal a young girl from the next village, or to blink, in exchange for sufficient payment, as she was brought through your village. Or again, why not make the accusations against an unpopular person in town serious enough to guarantee his enslavement?[45]

The widespread African belief in fate as a specified deity, the belief that one's fate has been set by the gods and that free will is nonexistent, and the common practice of consulting diviners before undertaking any important action, have all been reinforced by the insecurity of centuries of the slave trade. The areas known by anthropologists as those where recourse to diviners is most fervent – the central Sudanic areas of Chad and Central African Republic – are places where the slave trade was particularly intense and devastating in the nineteenth century.[46]

The experience of sudden turns of fate tended systematically to undermine efforts in long-term investment. Life was so unsure, since wealth was here today, gone tomorrow, that there was little point in investing in any long-term future. Thus it was not only the scarcity of capital that restricted the level of African investment in production and commerce, but the high level of insecurity and the belief that such insecurity was in the order of things.

Life's pleasures had to be seized while the opportunity presented itself. The strong had to act while they were the strongest. Thus did slavery serve to reinforce male supremacy in Africa. This is not to argue that slavery created male supremacy in Africa. But, for example, the sharp increase in the number of slave concubines and wives in the era of slave exports, many of them in positions of utter dependence on their men, certainly served to degrade all wives and to drive them toward the position of the slaves. The concept of patriarchy underwent redefinition. If before it had meant that community leadership resided with the senior male – the patriarch – and was maintained by a consensus of the community, now the patriarch's position was defined more by raw power than by seniority, and his power was maintained as much by the threat of enslavement as by community consensus.[47]

Thus African slavery and the slave trade exemplify sharply the contrast between individual gain and social advantage. The sale of a slave had an airtight logic from the viewpoint of the captor and the merchant. But when all the individual decisions were aggregated, the result was a net loss for the society. This was all the more true since the major slave captors often became objects of revenge at the hands of their victims, or objects of cupidity on the part of competitors. Fortunes built up through the slave trade, therefore, while often spectacular, tended to be short lived.[48]

The defenders of the slave trade – those who defended it while it continued and those who now believe it to have been advantageous or at least inevitable for Africans – argue that the slave trade brought Africans into contact with the outside world, and particularly into contact with Europeans, so that they gained in technology, in exposure to new ideas, and in superior imported goods. To phrase the impact of the slave trade in this way is to elide smoothly but gracelessly the suffering and the anguish involved in such contact.

A Nigerian student of my acquaintance once wrote, as part of a history exam, a far more subtle and graceful statement of the same outlook. As he said, "The slave trade taught us how to conduct business." That is, it is a recognition that Africans did indeed learn a great deal about commercial practice and about available goods through the slave trade. At the same time, his formulation suggests that when it is through the slave trade that one learns to do business, one begins with the nastiest side of business. Or, to turn that idea on its head, perhaps he was suggesting that the slave trade is after all a fair representation of the modern business world.

To use a more contemporary terminology, slavery was corruption: it involved theft, bribery, and exercise of brute force as well as ruses. Slavery thus may be seen as one source of precolonial origins for modern corruption. The whole story on corruption involves weaving together flaws inherent in African society, the influence of the slave trade, the influence of colonial rule, and the pressures of the mid-twentieth century.[49]

Slavery meant different things to different Africans. It tended to develop contrasting ideas at once: the ideal of hierarchy and centralization, on the part of those who benefited from state power and from slavery; the opposition to hierarchy and centralization in the minds of those who stood to lose from slavery.

Even for those who saw themselves as winners in the rough-and-tumble life of participation in slavery and the slave trade, the outlook was not entirely positive. Thus it is that the Bobangi slave traders of the Zaire river, according to Robert Harms, viewed life as a zero-sum game.[50] One could gain only at the expense of one's neighbor. In fact, given the overall conditions of demographic decline in the region, one could say that to view society as a zero-sum game was more optimistic than cynical. One had to steal from one's neighbors to avoid falling behind, and not simply to get ahead.

The commoditization of humanity, the zero-sum game of life, the ruthlessness of political and social life and the endless presence of temptation combined to force Africans to take a short-range view of economic conditions. The slave trade required merchants to have a time perspective of as much as two to three years, the time required from capture to sale and back, or the time for an Atlantic slave ship's voyage, but not much longer than that. Wars, displacements, and changing politics made it difficult to plan construction, open new fields.

I have chosen to focus on the negative, narrowing, and discouraging effects which slavery may have had on African thought. Perhaps there was another side as well. There must have been, among the slaves, valiant determination to defend their families, struggles to achieve some autonomy, or efforts to overcome on a spiritual plane the hopelessness of their material existence. Still, I am left with the impression that they had to live each day as if it were their last.

7

Transformations of slavery and society, 1650–1900

In the preceding chapter we have seen the wide range of institutions, experiences, and attitudes which made up African slavery. The editors of a major volume of studies on African slavery, Igor Kopytoff and Suzanne Miers, found the range to be so great that they placed the term "slavery" in quotes, and argued that the various forms of servility had too little in common with one another to be placed under a single label.[1] I shall not attempt to contradict their conclusion that the individual genius of the many African societies led to the creation of a kaleidoscopic array of African conditions of servility. Nor do I claim that slavery by itself explains African history or economic life. The income from the export of slaves, for instance, rarely exceeded 10 percent of the domestic product of African economies. The value of goods produced by slaves in African societies, even during the nineteenth century, was rarely a majority of the total output.[2] These proportions suggest that slavery, while widespread, fell short of dominating the daily life of the average African. (Other factors – climate, food crops, political innovations, religious beliefs – caused major developments in African history, but those stories are told in other books.)

I do claim, however, that the influence of slavery, working systematically over a long period of time, led to the transformation of African societies. More precisely, a single force – the New World demand for slaves – conditioned the development and differentiation of slavery throughout African society. The variety of patterns of slavery in Africa resulted not simply from the unique characteristics of African societies, but also from the changing impact of that single force over time and across the regions of the continent.

The explanation I offer for slavery's transformation of African life relies on three types of explanatory images. I have labelled them mechanical, organic, and societal.[3] By a mechanical explanation I mean, for example, the demographic principles I applied in chapters 3 and 4, and the price theory applied in chapters 2 and 5. In these cases one sets a given logic, and allows for the quantitative change of variables within that logic, such as the increased quantity supplied and the decreased quantity demanded that

126

usually result from higher prices for a commodity. The organic image, secondly, relies on analogies to the changes of a living organism. These include birth, maturation, and death for the individual organism, or evolution of a type of organism over the course of generations. One such example is the cycle, found in several African regions, of a rise in slave exports, followed by a declining population, followed by a regional withdrawal from slave exports. Both the mechanical and organic images reflect changes which take place automatically, in response to impersonal forces, and regardless of the wills of the actors. Mechanical images portray the stability of a given logic; organic images reflect the evolution of a given logic.

In some cases I will add societal images. These concentrate on cases where human consciousness undergoes qualitative changes that cannot be explained through the simpler mechanical or organic models. In particular, through the process of *emulation*, one person *decides* to do as another does, rather than be induced unconsciously to change. The invention and spread of new devices for increasing the capture of slaves (under pressure of slave demand), or the development of a new sexual division of labor (under pressure of a shortage of males), are cases where I will offer an explanation of change in a societal image. These are cases where a new logic is adopted in place of the old.

In this chapter I assemble the evidence and arguments of the previous chapters into an overview of slavery and the transformation of African society. The chapter recapitulates much of what I have said before, in order to reveal the patterns and the pace of social change. I have organized it as a chronological narrative, but with explanations of the main changes. Wherever possible, I use the simple, mechanical explanations of changes in prices and demographic structures. For more complex changes, I turn to organic and, ultimately, to societal images of change.

For succeeding periods, the narrative distinguishes the impact of slavery and the slave trade on the sub-continental zones of the Western Coast, the Savanna and Horn, and the Eastern Coast. Within each period, I focus first on the sub-continental zone which was most seriously affected, or where the most important changes were taking place; then I provide some discussion of themes for the remaining areas of the continent.

The era of the Oriental trade, to 1650

In the period before the Atlantic slave trade, slavery was of no more importance in Africa than in most other places in the world. Virtually nowhere on the continent was there a strong enough political power or a sufficiently well-developed market for slave produce to have justified the enslavement of people on a large scale. The possible exception to this rule was in portions of the Savanna and Horn, where both domestic slavery and slave exports were at the highest levels of development on the continent.

Much of this development of slavery was in response to the external demand for slaves. A modest but long-standing slave trade sent perhaps as many as 10,000 slaves per year, mostly female, from sub-Saharan Africa into the Orient. At the same time, Middle Eastern demand for slaves drew on captives from the Caucasus, the Black Sea, and to a lesser degree from Europe. In Africa, the loss of this number of slaves was enough to depopulate restricted areas of the Savanna and to leave the adjoining source societies with sex ratios perhaps as high as 115 men per 100 women. This in itself provided some incentive for holding slave men in isolated villages where they could produce agricultural surpluses which might provision palaces or be sold on the market. At the same time, the trade in females provided an occasion for some women to be drawn into the service of African leaders.[4]

In addition, there are indications for Mali, Songhai, and Borno that the scope of slavery expanded even beyond what can be explained by the export trade, and that a domestic slave economy, based on slave villages and perhaps slave manufacture, had already begun to spring up. This early version of the slave mode of production is described best for Songhai: according to J. P. Olivier de Sardan, it was the needs of the monarchy rather than the demands of foreign trade which had caused slavery to expand. The justifications for enslavement, and the institutions of slavery, were those given by Muslim law and ideology, so we may label this as Muslim slavery in Africa. But in the same period slavery seems to have grown to a considerable extent in Ethiopia, not only among the Muslims but also among the Christians there.[5]

This sort of aristocratic slavery could not, I think, have sprung up by itself, but only in association with an export trade in slaves. The development of the means to capture and socialize large numbers of slaves was costly. Slave prices had to be high to make such coercion worth the effort. In societies which had few slaves to begin with, aristocrats were too few to hold many slaves and too weak to force peasants to do the work of collecting many slaves through raids. Similarly, mercantile slavery was obviated by the absence of enough money to buy slave produce.[6] But when export demand built up the number of captures, the increased focus on slaves permitted the perfection of institutions of capture, of seasoning, and of exploitation. Then, even if export demand died out, the structures for maintaining aristocratic or mercantile slavery remained in place. To restate the analysis: I have argued that mechanical pressures – higher prices and greater flows of trade in the export market – were prerequisites to the societal changes which expanded slave supply sufficiently for domestic slavery to develop.

Societies of the Western Coast of Africa, in these early times, held slaves in small numbers. Such persons were enslaved as prisoners of war, and perhaps for debt. They were mainly held within family units or by monarchs. Some, however, were used for market production, as is indicated by the willingness of peoples from the Gold Coast to buy slaves (which the Portuguese purchased in Benin kingdom) in return for gold. Certain of the slaves were used in gold production.[7]

Europeans, in their early ventures along the coast, sometimes landed to capture isolated Africans or even whole villages. In fact such escapades continued throughout the history of the slave trade, but they were rapidly superseded in importance by a system of working through African buyers. In the early days of the Atlantic slave trade, from the mid-fifteenth to the mid-seventeenth centuries, Europeans purchased small though steadily growing numbers of African slaves, which went to the Atlantic islands, Europe, and America. The ups and downs of establishing such relationships are reflected in the turbulent Portuguese relationships in Jolof, Benin, Kongo, and Angola. In Kongo the Portuguese established their closest alliance in all of Africa, but their involvement in the slave trade led to the progressive dismemberment of the kingdom. The Portuguese, as their link with Kongo weakened, moved south to establish a base in Angola, initially in hopes of obtaining silver but soon with a concentration on the slave trade. This and other histories of early involvement in slave exports provided an insight into the fate which was later to overtake all of the Western Coast.[8] In general, however, the growth of slave exports was a simple response to levels of European demand.

Supremacy of the Occidental trade, 1650–90

The steady growth in the Occidental slave trade from its fifteenth-century beginnings brought it, in about 1650, to the same annual volume as the Oriental trade. For the next two centuries, the Occidental trade dominated the commerce in African slaves. From the moment of its emergence to its dominance, the Occidental slave trade began to affect social conditions in Western Africa generally, no longer just in isolated areas of the coast.

Although the growth in the Occidental slave trade was steady and gradual, averaging a 2 percent increase per year, its seventeenth-century eclipse of the Oriental trade was accompanied by some dramatic new developments. The northern European powers had joined the struggle for maritime power, and now the Dutch, English, and French, not to mention the Danes, Swedes, and Brandenburgers, plied the seas in search of colonies, booty, commerce, and slaves. New maritime power relationships and technology combined with improved efficiency in plantation operation and with changes in European demand. The result was a rapid expansion in the New World sugar plantations and an equivalent increase in demand for African labor.[9]

Gradually and systematically, if not consciously, Africans made institutional changes which led to a more regular stream of slave deliveries. Overall, that is, Africans decided to supply slaves to meet the new European demand: this conclusion is supported by the fact that the number

129

of slaves exported in 1690 was nearly double that of 1640, but the price of slaves had not increased. In the previous forty years, the volume of slave exports had grown while prices fell.[10]

It would be naive, however, to assume that slave exports expanded as a result of an easily formed African consensus. This decision to participate in the slave trade was contested. The documents do tell us most clearly of the monarchs who opposed the slave trade, as in Jolof, and of the slaves who rebelled against their condition, but one must presume that there was a broader discussion of the opportunities and dangers inherent in expanding the slave trade. Overall the opportunists – those determined to profit in the short run from slavery – won out, but it is surely the case that the dimensions and conditions of the slave trade were affected by those critical of it.

Warfare became more frequent and more deadly in the areas contributing the largest number of slaves: the growth in warring activity can be traced clearly for the Bight of Benin and the Gold Coast; Angola's earlier domination of slave exports is reflected in mid-century warfare there.[11]

With this steady expansion of the slave trade, the African market for female slaves came into existence. As the sale of slaves to Europeans caused many young women to pass through the hands of slave traders, these merchants gradually developed a desire to hold on to some of them. For those men who avoided slavery and remained in Africa, the potential reward of this new demographic imbalance was multiple wives, female servants, and a position as beneficiary of the developing system of "family slavery." So the bifurcated price system in the Atlantic slave trade expanded in the seventeenth century: European prices for men became slightly higher than for women (reflecting higher male productivity in a situation where men could be controlled), and African prices for women became higher than for men (reflecting their sexuality, their slightly greater productivity in domestic labor under conditions of a restricted market for slave produce, and the difficulty of controlling men under African conditions). As a result, most male captives went to the Europeans, and over half of the women went to the Africans, with the difference that the male fraction of slave exports grew as slaves were drawn from further inland.[12]

All of these seventeenth-century changes are best described by the "societal" image: the development of New World plantations, the expansion of African slave supply, the development of African demand for female slaves, all were cases of the development of a new logic and new social institutions. This new logic, once set in place, dominated the Western Coast for nearly two centuries.

The seventeenth-century period of irrevocable commitment to the slave trade along the Western Coast was not accompanied by any such dramatic change in other areas of the continent. The Savanna and Horn, where the slave trade and political affairs had been rather constant for most of a century, was to retain a similar continuity for most of another century. The Eastern Coast of Africa, where key battles were fought in this period among the Portuguese and local Swahili dynasties, was not yet drawn into a large-scale slave trade.[13]

The social impact of the Atlantic slave trade, 1690–1740

By the turn of the eighteenth century, slave exports had reached the level where further expansion was more difficult to achieve and brought significant social changes in its wake. New methods of enslavement continued to develop. While African leaders almost uniformly denied that they went to war in order to capture slaves, the intensity of warfare continued to grow, feeding the increasing demands of slave merchants at the coast. Kidnapping became more attractive to adventurers, despite the dangers involved, as the rewards for selling slaves improved. In addition, African justice systems came more and more to punish the convicted with enslavement; it may also be true that witchcraft accusations, punishable by enslavement, become more frequent with time. These new institutions may be thought of in organic terms: once the commitment to slave exports had been taken earlier, the maturation of the system of slave supply led to the perfection of new techniques both for collecting slaves and for profiting from them.

The most dramatic evidence of the pressure of the slave trade on the Western Coast of Africa was the increase in slave prices. With increased European demand and European competition for markets, prices of African slaves were bound to go up. But average slave prices in the 1730s were roughly four times higher than they had been in the 1690s, an increase which far exceeded any growth in demand. This price increase was accompanied by an actual decline in the volume of slaves exported from the Bight of Benin, the main exporting region, but by increases in exports from other regions such as the Gold Coast. The main reasons for this remarkable price increase, therefore, lay on the African rather than the European side. Those reasons included, first, the scarcity of potential slaves as African populations began to decline; second, a related scarcity of potential slaves as people learned to defend themselves against enslavement more effectively; third, the growth of the African demand for female slaves, which drew them off the export market; fourth, the increase in fees, tolls, and administrative costs imposed on the slave trade by officials; and fifth, the growing margin of profit retained by the expanding class of slave merchants. Let us consider these one by one.

According to Richard Bean's figures, the prime cost of slaves on the African coast went from a low average of some three pounds sterling for a prime male in 1690 (this was just over one quarter of the annual per capita income for England in that period) to an average of nearly twenty pounds sterling in 1740 (almost twice the level of English annual per capita income).[14] Along the Gold Coast, this expansion of the slave trade coincided with an increased import of muskets. Consumer goods, especially textiles, became important in the imports received for the sale of slaves. In addition, slaves were sold for money, in its many African forms: cowrie shells, iron bars, copper bracelets, squares of cloth, and gold.[15]

The decline of the population, while it did not become general until after 1730, had become serious before 1700 in the Bight of Benin, the greatest exporter of slaves in this period. Since it now became more difficult to obtain slaves, they cost more. For the source populations who lost more slaves than they gained, the opportunity cost of having young men and women disappear rose as more and more of them were gone.

In those cases where enslavement was by warfare, this was a time of major population movement. In the Bight of Benin, people fled to hilltops, to marshes, across rivers, and for long distances to escape the fighting. Further west, and inland from Asante, the great market and manufacturing center of Begho declined in this period to a small village, its population having been carried off or having otherwise escaped.[16] This development led not only to the physical displacement of African populations, but to the accentuation of ideological differences. For the captors, those monarchies who succeeded in profiting and expanding at the expense of their neighbors, the dominant values came to be centered on hierarchy, centralization, and the glorification of wealth. For the source populations, on the other hand, a contrasting ideology developed, in which the values of self-sufficiency, an egalitarian opposition to authority, and a willingness to live without great accumulations of wealth were dominant.[17]

As the African demand for female slaves rose, and as the intensity of the export trade grew, the ratio of men to women on the Western Coast declined steadily. This sexual disproportion was concentrated in the slave societies (that is, the captors and their domestic slaves), where it led to major social changes. First, the shortage of men pushed women into taking up new areas of work. In areas where women had traditionally participated in agriculture, their role expanded to that of near total domination of agricultural labor: such was the case in Central Africa, and to a lesser degree in the Bight of Biafra and the Gold Coast. An exception to this rule may be noted for the Aja peoples of the Bight of Benin. There women traditionally did less agricultural labor than men, and the shortage of men pushed women more into commerce than into cultivation.[18]

The shortage of men also brought pressure for changes in marriage patterns. Twentieth-century Africans sustained a system of polygynous marriage by causing men to postpone marriage until their late twenties, while women married at puberty: by narrowing the range of marriageable age for men, they artificially created a situation in which there were more marriageable women than men, and polygyny thrived. Perhaps this same situation prevailed on the Western Coast before the slave trade. But in the era of slave exports there was an unmistakable shortage of marriageable men: those men who remained in Africa were able to have multiple wives, without having to postpone their age of marriage.

While polygyny became a status within the reach of most African men, the wealthy and powerful partook of its benefits to the fullest: the very nature of the slave trade was such as to encourage the establishment of large harems by monarchs and merchants alike. The result was not only to reflect and actually increase the power of these big men, it served to demean and diminish women in general and the institution of marriage in particular.

African states, large and small, grew and benefited from their ability to control access to markets, and to increase the taxes and dues paid by merchants. The rise of the Imbangala state of Kasanje in the Angolan interior represents such a case, as does that of Asante. The kingdoms of Ardra and Hueda on the Bight of Benin profited greatly from slave exports, only to suffer conquest by Danhomè between 1724 and 1727.[19] We have already discussed the other side of this equation: the development of an anti-authoritarian ideology among those peoples required by circumstances to defend themselves regularly against wars and slave raids.

Profits from the slave trade went not only to monarchs, but to slave merchants. The increase in slave prices went largely into their coffers. A new and prosperous class of slave merchants arose in the eighteenth century to assume a leading role in those societies participating actively in slave exports.[20] These merchants were the instruments through which Africa made its mistaken exchange: slaves for cash. This exchange, while highly profitable and beneficial in the short run to those who made the trade, was a most unequal exchange for African society as a whole. Although Africans imported a wide range of goods in exchange for slaves, it is worth re-emphasizing the exchange of slaves for money.

Perhaps the best way to make this point clear is with the example of the Gold Coast, which from the fifteenth century had been the major African focus of European merchants because of its important gold mines. In fact, the exports of gold from this region were greater in value than the entire Atlantic slave trade as late as 1700. But by 1730 the direction of trade had changed, and the Gold Coast was now exporting slaves and *importing gold*. Was this not a case of carrying coals to Newcastle? The answer to the riddle lies in the fact that gold dust was money on the Gold Coast, and that the prices of slaves had risen so high that people could not resist selling large numbers of slaves. In return, they demanded cash. Slaves who had previously mined gold were now sold abroad, gold mining declined since its profitability was exceeded by the slave trade, and the source of money became external rather than domestic.[21] The logic, at an individual level, was flawless; at a social level it verged on the disastrous.

For the Gold Coast, not only was gold production undercut by the new focus on slave exports, but the accompanying warfare and political centralization brought massive social change. The political economy shifted from its town-centered, artisanal emphasis – which Ray Kea has described in such detail for the seventeenth century – to a system of dispersed settlement and payment of land rents to central authorities. The Benin kingdom, already centralized in earlier days, was able to avoid such a

Map 7.1. African slavery, 1750

dramatic transformation by withdrawing from slave exports, but other areas which joined in the slave trade may have undergone changes parallel to those of the Gold Coast.[22]

In addition to the mechanical changes in price levels, sex ratios, and population sizes, the organic development of the slave-supply system came into evidence in this period. There emerged a broad pattern in which European purchases of slaves built up at one point of the coast until the population began to decline and export quantities along with it. At that point the Europeans sought out new markets. It was virtually always possible to find persons at the coast who would collaborate in the collection and sale of slaves, with the result that institutions of enslavement were set up, and the whole insidious cycle of revenge and retribution turned around in yet another area. In order, this pattern struck the Bight of Benin, Senegambia, the Gold Coast, Loango, the Bight of Biafra, and the Upper Guinea Coast.[23]

Population decline, 1740–90

The middle and late years of the eighteenth century saw an expansion throughout the Western Coast of the trends set in place earlier in the century. The mechanical pressures of prices and demography, within the confines of now-established institutions, worked out their terrible effects on African societies. Population decline became increasingly serious up until about 1790, and then continued at a slightly diminished rate to 1850. Of the regions which entered the slave trade much more actively during the late eighteenth century, two stand out: the Bight of Biafra and Loango. In the Bight of Biafra this corresponded to the expansion of the Aro trading network. The Aro were an Igbo clan whose control of the oracle at Arochukwu gave them a position of religious and judicial leadership. They used this position of strength to develop a trading network drawing slaves from all parts of Igbo country and funneling them to the ports of the Niger delta and the Cross river estuary. For Loango, the expansion of the slave trade resulted from two developments: diversion to the north of slaves collected in the northern hinterland of Angola, and expansion of the Bobangi trade network along the middle Zaire river, which resulted in the export of slaves drawn from as far as the Ubangi river valley.[24]

In addition to these major expansions of the slave trade, each of which initiated a decline in regional population, the slave trade expanded to a lesser degree on other portions of the coast. Along the Upper Guinea Coast, the expanded slave trade was related to the wars of establishment of the Fulbe state in Futa Jallon. In the Gold Coast, slaves were brought to the coast from the hinterland of Asante, especially to the north and the west of the now formidable empire. In the Bight of Benin, the export of Yoruba slaves began to rise, largely as a result of the expanded slave trade by the Oyo empire.[25]

For those areas with strong monarchies, such as Asante, Danhomè, and Oyo, the monarchs were able to amass significant numbers of state slaves, both as servants of the state apparatus and as producers of agricultural and artisanal goods for the palace. But with the departure of so many slaves for the New World, and with their continuing high prices, the market for domestic slave produce did not expand much beyond this state sector.

Other important effects of the slave trade in this period for the Western Coast were the imports of large quantities of money and the development of a substantial shortage of men. The combination of high export volume and high prices of slaves meant that money flowed into the Western Coast as never before. Since African monies were mainly obtained by purchase from outside rather than by manufacture or by coining at home, the sale of slaves increased the size of the money supply several times over during the eighteenth century.[26]

At the same time, the declining ratio of men to women in the African population became more and more general. To the degree that changing sex ratios affected marriage patterns and the domestic division of labor, this was the time when such changes would have been most concentrated.

For the Savanna and Horn, this was largely a time of continuity with the previous period. Slave exports to the Orient continued to influence domestic sex ratios and economic organization to some degree, and the major states of the region were able to capture slaves for use as palace slaves and suppliers of the palace as they had before.

A series of great droughts was recorded for the eighteenth-century Savanna, from east to west, and it may be that these natural phenomena were more influential in determining patterns of social and economic organization than was the slave trade during this time period.[27] The droughts led to periods of great devastation, but these in turn were followed by dramatic economic recoveries. One must imagine that great numbers of people were enslaved as a result of their impoverishment through drought in the early stages of this cycle, and that the opportunities for expansion in the later stages of the cycle caused landowners to seek large numbers of captives who could be called upon to work the land once it had begun to produce again.

This situation foreshadowed a paradox of wealth and deprivation which was to become more prominent in the nineteenth century. The Savanna states, as their power became more concentrated, were able to raid for slaves with such impunity that they reduced the regional population and brought a decline in total regional output. Yet the rulers of the Savanna states were able to protect a thriving domestic market in their heartland: levels of demand in these heartland economies were able to grow, thus calling for production of more goods by slaves. Commercialization and cheap labor thus expanded symbiotically, but at the expense of broader economic welfare.

Along the Eastern Coast slave exports rose in this period in response to new Occidental demand. French planters on the Indian Ocean islands, which are now known as Mauritius and Reunion, sought out slaves from the coast of Mozambique to work their expanding sugar estates; Brazilian merchants sought slaves from Mozambique as the supplies from Angola became more expensive. Initially they tapped into the supply routes used by the Portuguese-allied planters of the Zambezi valley, the *prazeros*. With time the familiar pattern of response to external demand took hold. New groups, in this case the Yao of Malawi, became specialized in collecting and delivering slaves to the coast.[28]

The expansion of the Oriental trade, 1780–1840

The turn of the nineteenth century saw the emergence of some new trends in the slave trade. Most striking among these was the growth in Oriental slave demand at a time when Occidental slave demand was beginning to decline. That is, just as the Occidental trade ceased its growth, was declared illegal, and began to decline, slave exports from the Savanna and Horn and from the Eastern Coast rose sharply, feeding an expanded Oriental demand. The Oriental expansion and the Occidental decline were linked to each other, and to other developments.

The previous level of Occidental demand had kept slave prices relatively high: when Occidental demand for slaves declined, slave prices declined as well, and did so throughout Africa. The timing of the decrease in African slave prices is a matter of some importance, and the evidence on the issue has not been sufficiently researched. It appears, however, that there were two periods of decline in slave prices, as measured on the Atlantic coast of Africa: the first one at the turn of the nineteenth century, and the second one centered on the 1840s.[29] The first decline in prices coincided with an expansion in the Oriental slave trade; the second one brought about an expansion in the African trade.

The changes in volume, direction, and prices in the slave trade show – particularly in this period – that the market for slaves was continental in scope. The decline of slave prices in Africa, caused by decreases in effective Occidental demand for slaves, made slaves easier to buy in Africa and in the Orient.[30] At the same time, and for reasons which need further study, economic growth in the Middle East resulted in an increasing demand for imported slave labor.[31] Thus for the Western and Central Sudan, regions which had been sending significant numbers of male slaves to the Western Coast, there was now an opportunity to send more female slaves across the desert to the north.

The nineteenth-century expansion of Oriental demand for slaves has too often been explained in terms of political change. According to an oft-repeated version of the story, Napoleon Bonaparte landed in Egypt in 1798 and bruised the sleepy old Mamluk order irreparably. After Napoleon's departure, Muhammad Ali arrived in 1803 with orders to re-establish Turkish control, but immediately set up his own independent regime. In 1820 he decided upon the conquest of the Sudan in order to procure slave soldiers for his army, and thereby launched a half-century of great slaving expeditions based on Khartoum.[32] Muhammad Ali's importance is not to be neglected, but the trouble with this version of the story is that it does not account for the rise in the Egyptian slave trade before Napoleon's arrival, nor for the increases in slave exports to other parts of North Africa and to the Arabian peninsula.

Reflections of the growing Oriental demand for slaves are to be found in the history of the Savanna. The late eighteenth century was a time of increased warfare and perhaps a changing mentality in the Western and Central Sudan. Religious leaders in the Central Sudan complained that Muslim rulers of the Habe states (in the north of modern Nigeria) condoned the enslavement of Muslims. Usuman dan Fodio made this one of his charges against the Habe rulers as he proclaimed his *jihad* or holy war against the Habe states in 1804. His victories led to establishment of the

Sokoto Caliphate, and also, perhaps ironically, to a further expansion of slavery and the slave trade in the Central Sudan. Further east, the aggressive expansion of slave trading in Dar Fur, beginning in the late eighteenth century, has been well documented.[33]

In between the Savanna and North Africa lay the Sahara desert. Not only did slaves cross the Sahara, but a surprising number were halted to live out their lives there in servitude. The Sahara is often referred to as a sea: *sahel*, the term for the southern edge of the desert, is the Arabic term for "coast." In the terms of this analogy, the Saharan mountains and oases in which thousands of slaves were held can be seen as equivalents to the Atlantic islands with their plantations. Large numbers of slaves went there to work out their lives in the production of export goods, and few survived. Saharan slaves produced dates and other crops in oases, they mined the salt which was exported to the Savanna, and they performed the most menial work in the pastoral lives dominated by their camel- and goat-owning masters. The Saharan slave trade grew during the nineteenth century as did that of the Savanna and the Orient.[34]

In sum, declining slave prices made it possible for purchasers in Africa and the Orient to buy more slaves. New needs for labor in the Orient caused purchases of slaves to increase. Further, the expansion of enslavement in the Savanna supported the development of expanded institutions of slavery, and African slavery expanded along with exports to the Orient, giving further support to slave prices.

Along the Eastern Coast, the expansion of slave exports resulted from an intimate connection between Occidental and Oriental trades. The demand of French and Brazilian planters had brought a growing supply of slaves from Mozambique from the 1760s. The decline in Occidental prices and levels of demand during the Napoleonic wars permitted Oriental purchasers to divert the supply of slaves northward.

At the end of the Napoleonic wars, a combination of domestic and external factors caused the slave trade of the Eastern Coast to expand further. First, the wars of the *mfecane*, beginning with Shaka's accession to power in the Zulu state in 1816, brought about large-scale migrations of warring groups – including the Ngoni and the Shangaans – northward from South Africa into Mozambique. Each of these, but particularly the Ngoni, captured large numbers of captives who were delivered to the coast. Second, French planters of the Indian Ocean expanded their purchases of slaves for the sugar industry, compensating in part for those lost with the slave rebellion in St.-Domingue. They purchased slaves in Mozambique, in Madagascar, and at other East African ports.[35]

The third great factor in the rise of the Eastern Coast slave trade was the expansion of ties between Zanzibar, Oman, and Gujarat. In 1820 Sayyid Sa'id came to the throne of the Omani emirate of the Arabian peninsula, and began emphasizing ties with his nominal colony in Zanzibar. Among the attractions of the region was that it was a major outlet for ivory, for which the market in India was expanding by leaps and bounds: white East African ivory was less brittle when carved and of more permanent color than Indian ivory. (European use of ivory in piano keys and billiard balls was also expanding.) By 1835 Sayyid Sa'id had moved his capital to Zanzibar, and there he and his successors presided over a remarkable commercial empire for nearly forty years. Ivory went to India. Slaves went to India, to South Arabia, and the Persian Gulf. Slaves were also brought to Zanzibar to cultivate the clove plantations developed by the Omanis, which made Zanzibar and Pemba the world center for clove production. Slaves were also settled on the coast opposite the islands, and grew grains.[36]

Omani and Swahili merchants opened up major trade routes leading across modern Tanzania to Lake Tanganyika, to Lake Malawi, and into Zaire. They and leaders from inland peoples who became associated with them – Mirambo of the Nyamwezi was the most important of these – not only opened trade routes, they formed states, and sent back large quantities of ivory and slaves.[37]

In contrast to the expanding Oriental trade, the Occidental trade in this period underwent fluctuation and some decline. The wars of the French Revolution and the French empire interfered with the slave trade from 1792 to 1815: France abolished and then reinstituted slavery. A development of more lasting significance was the illegalization of the slave trade by the British and by other powers. Britain made seaborne slave trade illegal for its subjects in 1808, and most British merchants respected the law immediately. (Some British merchants, however, profited indirectly from the slave trade for decades thereafter.) Britain subsequently pressured other powers to sign anti-slave trade treaties, and outfitted a fleet to enforce the treaties by capturing slave ships and delivering the captives to Sierra Leone, where they were liberated.[38]

How are we to explain the British decision to abolish the slave trade? Clearly we must rely on what I have called a societal image: the new law reflected a new logic, adopted in response to new conditions. Historian Eric Williams, unsatisfied with the notion that this change was entirely an act of the human will, sought to find unconscious causes as well. He argued that the evolution of slavery and capitalism were clearly linked, and that the needs of capitalism, after a certain stage, called for the end to slavery. The debate on his thesis continues to range over both the conscious and unconscious causes of British abolition (or, as I have phrased it, over mechanical, organic, and societal interpretations of the British abolition of the slave trade).[39]

Laws, treaties, and the British fleet were not enough, however, to overcome the effects of high New World demand for slaves. The level of slave exports was to rebound, though under different conditions. French, Spanish, and Brazilian traders purchased slaves north of the equator, but such trade was illegal after 1818. The high risks and losses of this illegal trade forced merchants to buy African slaves cheap and sell them dear, thus adding to the spread between rising New World prices and falling African prices. Only south of the equator were Brazilian and Portuguese merchants able to trade legally in slaves, and then only to 1830.

Supremacy of the African trade, 1830–60

African demand for slaves increased during the eighteenth and nineteenth centuries in response to the factors discussed above: greater exposure to slavery through the export slave trade, the expansion of demand for female slaves in particular, the growth in royal slave holdings, and the expansion of domestic and foreign markets for slave produce: grains, palm oil, peanuts, cloves, and textiles, for instance. After 1850 the African purchases of slaves exceeded the volume of slave exports to the Occident and the Orient combined.

The decline in slave prices, as Oriental and Occidental purchasers dropped out of the market, served only to make slaves more attractive to potential African purchasers. On the other hand, these lower prices of slaves meant lower profitability in the slave trade. Thus, the number of Africans enslaved might have been expected to decline. But the capturing of slaves continued at a high level, as a result of a new logic.

The merchants, warlords, and monarchs who dominated the capture of slaves also dominated the exploitation of slaves within the continent. They now faced a relatively conscious choice: whether to be merchants or planters. That is, whether to collect their profits as earnings on the slave trade or as earnings on the sale of slave produce. In the first case, they maintained high taxes and tolls on the movement and marketing of captives; in the second case they sought low prices on the slaves they purchased, and marketed slave-produced crops and manufactures at free-market or (when possible) monopolistic prices. Overall, one may say that Africa's big men made the transition from being merchants to planters. They acquiesced in the decline in slave prices. They allowed the profits of slave merchants to be bargained down to a minimum, and enabled the profits of slave owners to rise. (A further factor was that the costs of delivering slaves within Africa were lower than for the longer voyages of exported slaves.) In short, the profits in slave trading declined, but with the result that the number of Africans enslaved remained high to the end of the nineteenth century.

To list but a few of the areas which underwent extensive enslavement in the years after 1830: the Yoruba-speaking lands of Nigeria and Bénin; the eastern fringes of the Sokoto Caliphate, especially Adamawa; the large area of northern Angola and southern Zaire dominated by the Chokwe; the Central Sudanic areas raided by the states of Dar Fur, Wadai, Baghirmi, and by lesser adventurers; and large areas of the Western Sudan drawn into the wars of al-hajj Umar and Samori Touré.[40]

The transatlantic slave trade continued on a clandestine and increasingly restricted basis, into the 1870s. The high profitability of slavery in Cuba and

Map 7.2. African slavery, 1850

Brazil combined with the scarcity of slave imports to drive New World slave prices to unprecedented heights. Most of the increase in prices, however, went to Atlantic merchants rather than African suppliers, as compensation for the high risk and high cost of the illegal Middle Passage. African export prices hit occasional peaks in the 1830s and 1840s, and otherwise declined.[41]

The conditions of the clandestine export trade required the development of new methods. Along the Upper Guinea Coast, the Bight of Benin, and the Zaire estuary, exporters learned to mass large quantities of slaves in their barracoons, and on a given signal march them or send them by canoe to the rendezvous at which they were loaded on the slave ship. A slave cargo was now embarked in a matter of hours rather than over a period of weeks. Payment was now made often in cash – silver dollars – rather than in laboriously bargained assortments of imports. African sellers then bought imports at leisure, with cash.[42]

These new methods of slave export attest to the flexibility of slave supply, and they give some insight into the changes in enslavement which were taking place at the same time. The men who played the role of slave merchants while exporting slaves also played other economic roles: owners of slave plantations and merchants dealing in import goods and in slave produce. Their ability to marshal large numbers of slaves at short notice and their increasing use of cash reflected the new conditions of the slave trade and the new importance of production by slave labor.

Slave society in Africa, 1850–1900

The last half of the nineteenth century was the period in which slavery expanded to its greatest extent in Africa. If there is any time when one can speak of African societies being organized around a slave mode of production, this was it. For the Western Sudan, many accounts show the majority of the population to have been in slave status. Even for East Africa, great numbers of people were enslaved in this period.[43]

Many of the changes in this era can be accounted for in terms of mechanical images. With the virtual end of slave exports from the continent, the demographic drain ended and the population began to grow again, though the mortality caused by continued enslavement slowed the rate of growth. Further, since both men and women stopped leaving Africa in large numbers, the sex ratios tended to equalize as new generations came to maturity. In economic affairs the prices for slaves fell, and in consequence the quantity of slaves demanded rose. Additional changes resulted from the decline in the cost of ocean transportation, notably because of the early importance of steam in African shipping. In particular, cheaper transport combined with growing industrial demand to create higher levels of demand for such agricultural exports as palm oil, peanuts, and cloves. These changes in sex ratio, population growth, and agricultural demand brought pressures for institutional change.

For instance, the equalization of sex ratios brought changes in marriage patterns. In areas of the Western Coast where there had been fewer adult males than females, the men now found women less available than before. The easy polygyny of the slave-export days was gone. The younger men found it harder than ever to compete with older men for wives. Men's age at marriage increased, and the age difference between husbands and wives also increased.

Under these pressures, African societies and their leaders devised a series of innovations, affecting kinship, marriage, commerce, and production.[44] In marriage, for instance, leading men of the Western Coast found ways to hold on to large numbers of women even as the sex ratio returned to equality. In economic affairs, the powerful men of Africa allowed the profits of enslavement to decline, thus increasing the number of persons enslaved at any given price. They increased their demand for slaves, at any given price, to utilize them in producing goods for export markets. To do this, they had to develop new ways to hold slaves.

The size of African slaveholdings in this period increased, so that one can begin to use the term "plantation" in referring to them. The exploitation of slaves for the maximum of their labor became more serious than ever. Masters sought to increase the productivity of their slaves, not so much by making them more efficient, but by making them work longer hours, to the point where slaves had no time for themselves.

Out of these changed conditions developed an expanded African leisure class. This class had slave servants in its homes, and slave workers in its fields and workshops. The number of slaves required to liberate a whole master class from manual labor was large indeed, but a number of societies achieved this level of slaveholding in the late nineteenth century. Slaves produced the agricultural and artisanal goods to satisfy the consumption needs of their masters, and produced a surplus sold on domestic and export markets. The wealth of the master class thus became a factor itself: domestic demand reinforced export demand in the expansion of the slave mode of production.[45]

The result was magnificent cities and brilliant courts. Kano and Sinsani became bustling commercial centers. Abeche in Wadai became the largest city in North Central Africa. The court of the Mangbetu king in northeastern Zaire was quite literally brilliant, shining with burnished copper and dazzling the visitor in the king's presence. This court, as many others, was sustained in this period by the labor of slaves.[46]

In a significant change from earlier times, most of the wealth of this expanded leisure class came from the production and sale of agricultural and artisanal commodities, and no longer from the sale of slaves. In one sense the slave owners were now involved in the creation of wealth, where their predecessors had confiscated wealth created by others. Yet enslavement continued unabated. Indeed, Martin Klein has argued that sales of slaves on the African market remained an important source of commercial profit in the Western Sudan until nearly the end of the nineteenth century.[47]

The concentration of wealth in the centers of power was offset by the increasing poverty of the inhabitants of marginal areas. As the Sokoto Caliphate city of Zaria prospered in the nineteenth century, the remains of the previous dynasty and its loyal followers eked out a precarious existence in distant hills. Even more precarious was the life of those along the frontier of the old and new states, who were sure to suffer in raids from one side or the other.[48] The growth of the slave production system indicates the growth in *market* demand within Africa. On the other hand, the *total* level of demand (met by market and subsistence production) was most likely decreasing through this period, given the cost of slavery to the source peoples. Overall, the effect of the expansion of African slavery was further redistribution of wealth, though now with a return to growth in population.

143

The timing with which the slave mode of production expanded varied from region to region. On the Gold Coast, for instance, the transition took place relatively early. Export demand for slaves virtually ended by 1810, and slave prices presumably fell sharply. A substantial local demand grew up, using male and female slaves as agricultural laborers in the production of palm oil, kola, yams, and later cocoa. Asante slaves also worked in gold mining, as porters, in administration, and even as fishers. In the Bight of Benin, the transition was slowed because slave exports continued on a large scale until the 1840s, thus keeping slave prices high. Even before the end of the slave trade, however, planters were buying male slaves for work in producing palm oil and later palm kernels.[49]

In the Bight of Biafra, where oil palms grew in greatest profusion and production costs were lowest, a similar phenomenon had already taken place. Before the end of slave exports in the 1830s, palm oil exports had already risen to a high level, and slave labor became quite important in this production. This transformation is best documented for Old Calabar, where diaries of the kings and descriptions of slave revolts in the 1850s make clear both the importance and the novelty of large-scale slave-labor agricultural production. Further to the west, the remarkable expansion of peanut production in the Senegambia owed much to the settling of slaves in new areas. On a smaller scale and in later years, immigrant Portuguese in Angola set up coffee plantations relying on slave labor.[50]

The expanded system of slave labor, set in place by the mid-nineteenth century, matured rapidly during the next half century. The initial enthusiasm of slave masters led to rapid growth and extreme exploitation of their slave populations. Such enthusiastic expansionism soon met its limit, however, in a wave of slave conspiracies and revolts.

The concentration of increased numbers of slaves in common residences, along with their work in commodity production, developed a growing sense of class identity among them. The old ideology of family links no longer prevented them from acting independently or as a group. Nupe slaves ran away in large numbers. Authorities in Danhomè barely succeeded in averting a major rising of Yoruba slaves in 1855. Rebellious slaves dominated the Niger delta capital of Itsekiri from 1848 to 1851, and carried on political demonstrations in Calabar from 1850 to 1852. In Zanzibar, a revolt broke out in the 1820s, in the early years of the slave plantations.[51]

The emergence of increasingly coherent slave classes presented a challenge to the masters. African slave owners, while they held the power of life or death over their slaves, never achieved a degree of control over their slaves' lives equal to that of New World plantation owners. This was largely because of the limits on African kings' power to enforce slavery: African monarchies lacked the administrative technology, the military might, and the wealth which New World states had utilized in maintaining control over slaves. In turn, the ability of African slaves to escape, to rebel, and especially to go slow was greater than that in the Americas.

As a result, the slave owners had to institute reforms in order to preserve and strengthen their new system. In Calabar they conceded immunity from execution to slaves. In Danhomè they simply slowed the expansion of slave plantations. In Zanzibar they emphasized the establishment of nuclear families, allowing slave men and women to marry. Slaves were increasingly allowed to have their own plots of land, and given more time to work them. Rather than owe all their produce to the master, some slaves were required to give a specified quantity of produce to him.[52]

Thus did the system evolve into one with a fuller set of rules to hold it together. Slave classes constituted themselves and gained recognition from masters in revised codifications of rights and duties. Slave families grew stronger and more self-sufficient. They still had to accept the masters' notion of "family slavery," but henceforth it hung on the slim thread of the notion that the slave family was a collateral – or subordinate – branch of the master family.[53]

Slave owners, once they began to focus their search for wealth on exploiting slaves in agricultural and artisanal work (rather than on the slave trade), began to shift their attention toward assuring their ownership of valuable land. In the areas of intensive slave labor, there are many indications of active competition for land from the mid-nineteenth century. In areas where land was legally held as private property – as is the case under Muslim law – this took the form of numerous purchases, sales, and disputes over deeds and contracts. In areas where land was legally held collectively, as by a lineage or by the state, there developed disputes over the rights to use lands, claims to permanent usufruct, and attempts to legalize private property. The disputes between those favoring the individual and collective versions of land law continued into the twentieth century.[54]

The system continued to evolve. In some areas, as replacement slaves became more difficult to obtain, the conditions of slaves were eased further. Slaves were required to pay the master a certain proportion of their produce (rather than a fixed amount), thus making it far easier for slaves to sustain themselves and bring up a family. To this degree, slavery tended to evolve into serfdom.[55]

The evolution of the slave mode of production was, however, anything but smooth. Great fluctuations in slave supply, and occasionally in slave demand, caused prices to vary sharply from region to region and over time. The mid-nineteenth century was a most difficult time for the African populations of the Savanna and Horn and of the Eastern Coast. These areas were exporting large numbers of slaves at the same time as they were building up domestic slave populations. Levels of mortality in raiding and transporting were often high (distances were long), and these factors combined with the predominant loss of females to cause a reduction in the population of portions of the modern Sudan Republic, the Central African Republic, and Mozambique. For the Western Sudan, wars among the major states and

145

against French invaders continued for decades, resulting as much in endless raids and counter-raids as in the construction of a slave society.[56]

For some areas of the Western Coast, the jockeying for position among European and African powers compromised the ability of African states to consolidate their slave system. Thus leaders of the Fante states in the Gold Coast and the Egba state in the Bight of Benin criticized slavery in order to maintain ties to the British. They made an invidious comparison between themselves and their respective enemies, Asante and Danhomè. The latter, in turn, were put in the position of defending slavery and taking a hard line against the Europeans. In response, the Europeans (at the time of the colonial conquest) put more effort into ending slavery in Asante and Danhomè than in most other areas.[57]

In spite of such variability, the slave mode of production prospered in the late nineteenth century. The attractiveness of this political economy of African slavery, in the eyes of the proprietary class, was made clear by their determination to protect it. When Egyptian rulers of the Sudan attempted, in alliance with the British, to end the slave trade, the region erupted in 1880 in religious revolution. Muhammad Hassan proclaimed himself the Mahdi, the expected one. Once the British and Egyptians were expelled, the recently expanded slave labor system prospered until the British returned as conquerors in 1898. The slave system of production lasted in the Sokoto Caliphate until 1900, it lasted in Dar Fur and in Dar al-Kuti until 1911, and it was phased out in Ethiopia only after World War I, as the kingdom sought international recognition.[58]

African slave society, though it grew dramatically and seemed in some ways to be setting the solid foundation of an enduring social order, was a historical dead end. It was doomed to fail, and rapidly so, both from external pressures and from internal opposition. Its short-run success in expansion led it into the long-term contradictions of insufficient slave supply and European determination to end the slave trade. If slaves were oppressed too tightly, they revolted; if the regime became too liberal, the slaves became serfs rather than slaves. If African slave owners sought accommodation with European powers, they had to end or sharply restrict the slave trade to get signatures on a treaty. If they refused to accommodate the new European threat, they faced conquest and the forcible end to the slave trade. Some of the contradictions in this rapidly evolving system were revealed in the evident loss of life at the end of the century: witchcraft accusations, human sacrifice, and execution of captives demonstrated the dissonance of the political economy of slavery.

But if African slave society was ephemeral, it was not lacking in vitality during the time it existed; nor has it failed to convey a heritage to the present day. A class of slave merchants rose and fell. There also arose a class of landowners and merchants whose wealth was based on the exploitation of slave labor. Classes of slaves constituted themselves, only to change their identity within a generation or two into serfs, peasants, or townspeople. European colonial governments, seeking to set up new labor systems, could scarcely think of alternatives to slavery. The nineteenth-century rise of a slave society represented an enormous change for the Western Coast, an equally enormous change for the Eastern Coast, and a lesser change for the Savanna and Horn.

Social change in precolonial Africa

European conquerors of Africa were happy to argue, at the turn of the twentieth century, that they had taken over benighted societies which had stagnated for all eternity, and which awaited the inventive minds of westerners in order to benefit from progress and change. If Africans were skeptical about such European optimism, if they seemed to prefer conti-nuity and "tradition" to change, it was perhaps because the promise of progress had brought too much change and too little advance during two centuries of intensive slave trade.

The great strength and malleability of African cultures has been demon-strated time and again. The slave trade was no more able to crush them than was colonial rule. But to mistake the survival of African cultures for stagnation would be to falsify the historical record. The pressures of the slave trade brought a range of tragically interconnected transformations into the lives of Africans.

The slave trade drew down the populations of large areas of the Western Coast, yet expanded the quantities and the uses of money. With the allure of imported goods and the brutality of capture, slave traders broke down barriers isolating Africans in their communities. Merchants and warlords spread the tentacles of their influence into almost every corner of the continent. By the nineteenth century, much of the continent was milita-rized; great kingdoms and powerful warlords rose and fell, their fates linked to fluctuations in the slave trade. If some Africans responded to the temptations of slavery by reaching out to the wider world, others found ingenious ways to reaffirm their autonomy. They fled the slave raiders, or battled them to a standstill from well-constructed fortifications. They developed ideologies of self-sufficiency and principled opposition to paying tribute. Yet there was no real escape. Even in egalitarian communities, the temptation to profit from the sale of captives or culprits kept the slave trade alive. And with each major twist in slavery, the demographic and social relations between African men and women underwent change, often reinforcing the patriarchal authority of senior men. Changes in the world market for forced labor tended to make labor expensive in eighteenth-century Africa, and cheap in nineteenth-century Africa.

Finally, slavery in Africa expanded from an institution of modest importance to a focus of the social order. The slave trade to the Occident and the Orient, by causing expansion in African systems of slave supply, introduced more Africans to the use of slaves, and thereafter caused the

147

expansion of slavery in Africa. Nineteenth-century African slavery represented a step into capitalism on the continent. The preceding export slave trade had linked Africa to the mercantile capitalism of the New World slave plantations. Now, slave merchants and warlords brought the labor, brutally displaced as before, into aristocratically dominated market economies all across the African continent. In addition to producing for growing domestic markets, African slavery opened expanding links to the industrial capitalism of Europe by providing such raw materials as peanuts and palm oil.[59]

All these changes in precolonial African society may be seen through the lens of the slave trade. They are not the only changes which took place, and conceivably not even the most important changes. (Other types of change can be seen through considering ecological changes, cultural interactions among Africans, changing nutrition and disease environments, and so forth.) But the particular importance of the changes brought by slavery is that, not only do they verify a succession of transformations in African life, but they demonstrate that those changes were part and parcel of the transformation of the modern world as a whole.

8

The end of slavery

The abolition of slavery in Africa was not a simple act, but a process extending over more than a century. The central events in the abolition of African slavery took place with the European conquests and during the first generation of European rule, from 1890 to 1920. These crucial events of African abolition will appear more understandable, however, if they are set in the context of a previous century of abolitionism in thought and in practice.

The beginnings of anti-slavery, 1760–1808

The beginning of the end for slavery took place in the New World, before slavery reached its full extent in Africa. The great 1760 rebellion of the Coromantyn slaves in Jamaica may be seen as having heralded the changes to come.[1] The slaves achieved a remarkably wide unity, and the effectiveness of their revolt made their masters fear not only for their lives, but for the institution of slavery. The slaves, clearly, opposed slavery quite strongly in practice, though we do not know how they enunciated the principle of their unity.

At about the same time, a principled opposition to slavery began to develop in some Christian communities. David Brion Davis has suggested, as a crucial step in this evolution, the tour of the Pennsylvania Quaker, John Woolman, from Delaware to the Carolinas, and the reflections he published in 1754. Woolman concluded that no Quaker could hold a slave without compromising himself in the eyes of God, since he could not overcome the temptation to use the power he held over his slave. Such a belief spread rapidly among Quakers in America and Europe, and was then adopted by other religious groups.[2]

Among the reasons why this change in religious belief was possible was the contemporaneous development of a democratic tradition of human rights, as it was set forth in the 1688 reaffirmation of the English constitution, the American Declaration of Independence in 1776, and the French Declaration of the Rights of Man and of the Citizen in 1789. This political thought, further, formed part of the philosophical movement of the Enlightenment, in which ideas of human perfectability, progress, and movement toward greater human unity were fundamental.

These three trends – slave opposition to their conditions, religious opposition to slavery, and democratic political thought – combined in the events of the Haitian revolution. When the French revolution broke out in 1789, the planters of St.-Domingue first supported it. As budding capitalists, they opposed feudal restrictions and privilege, and hoped to reduce monarchical restrictions on their activity. Later they became more cautious and combined forces with the colonial administration. The free mulattos of the colony – an artisan and small farmer class – entered the revolution as democrats, hoping for enfranchisement. Bloody tests between the mulattos and the white planters began early in 1791. Only later in the same year did the slaves take advantage of the fighting to enter the field themselves. They were united by a demand for liberation and were soon to be led by Toussaint l'Ouverture, who rapidly distinguished himself as a general and a statesman.[3]

The events of the revolution in France were such that the National Convention in 1794 abolished slavery, with great popular celebration, for slavery was seen not only as the shackling of black slaves, but also as the imposition of feudal privilege against popular liberty in general. The revolution continued in St.-Domingue, with many transformations and reverses, including the reconquest of the island in 1802 by Napoleon and the capture and exile of Toussaint l'Ouverture. At the same time, Napoleon reimposed slavery in Guadeloupe. When word reached St.-Domingue, the black population – embattled but free for the previous eight years – rose up and expelled the French definitively, and declared the republic of Haiti on the first day of 1804. The half a million black inhabitants of Haiti represented half of the population of the Caribbean and one-sixth of the slave population of the entire New World. Their challenge to slavery was thus a truly imposing threat.

Eugene Genovese, the historian of American slavery, has argued that slave revolts in general underwent a transformation at this time, from rebellions against being held in the status of slavery to revolutions aimed at the destruction of the institution of slavery.[4] The difference between the uprisings of 1760 in Jamaica and 1791 in St.-Domingue was thus more than the difference between failure and success. The slave movement for abolition became a significant arm of the Atlantic movement of democratic revolution, and deserves a place of distinction along with the democratic revolutionary movements of the United States, Spanish America, and Europe.

Several northern American states abolished slavery in the wake of the American revolution. More prominent on the world scene was the British anti-slavery movement, which began before the outbreak of the Haitian revolution, and achieved its first great success shortly after Haitian independence. In a long and impassioned parliamentary campaign – the first in Britain to be focused on a broadly based letter-writing campaign – the publicist Thomas Clarkson and the parliamentarian William Wilberforce persevered until, in 1807, Parliament declared the oceanic slave trade illegal for all British subjects.[5]

The campaign was on the verge of success as early as 1792. Indeed, it seemed so likely that the British would abolish the slave trade in that year that the Danish government abolished it in anticipation of the British decision. But the course of the revolution in France alarmed British leaders so much that they became reluctant to undertake any changes. Thus the Danes were alone for sixteen years as the unwitting precursors of the humanitarian tradition. The United States followed the British, abolishing the slave trade in 1808, and the other nations of Europe were gradually brought into line.[6]

In the early days of their campaign, Clarkson and his colleagues struck upon two vital images which have been enshrined ever since in the iconography of slavery. The first was a small medallion picturing a black man, on his knees and in chains, raising his hands and his eyes in prayer, with the caption, "Am I not a Man and a Brother?" The anti-slavery committee approved the design of this medallion in October of 1787, and Josiah Wedgwood, the famous ceramicist, began reproducing and distributing them. This image made a strong statement, for it called into question the very institution of slavery as well as the trade in slaves.

The second key image was created in July of 1789. From the architectural drawings of the slave ship *Brookes*, the committee made up a diagram showing the placement of 450 slaves on board, in which they appear jammed head to toe and elbow to elbow, in virtually every available space: 200 copies were printed and distributed. The diagram was not entirely accurate in its placement of the slaves, but that mattered little.[7] The *Brookes* immediately became a stunning piece of anti-slave-trade propaganda. This image focused on the slave trade – on the Middle Passage. It was thus focused more narrowly than Wedgwood's medallion, but no other image has ever equalled its effectiveness in conveying the inhumanity of the slave trade. Clarkson carried copies of this poster to France, then in the early stages of its revolution, where again they were received with great enthusiasm. The *Brookes* became the image *de rigueur* of the Middle Passage. In fact one may criticize subsequent writers on the slave trade for relying so heavily on this image, rather than following Clarkson's example and seeking out new information on the slave trade.[8]

The beginning of the humanitarian campaign against the slave trade brought an immediate response from its defenders. Liverpool merchants arranged testimony before Parliament to defend slavery as socially inevitable and economically mandatory. Two veteran slave traders, William Norris and Archibald Dalzel, were active in this campaign. Norris published a book in 1789 on his experiences in West Africa; Dalzel published his

Plate 8.1. "Am I not a Man and a Brother?" (jasperware medallion, 1787)

History of Dahomy in 1793, in the heat of the campaign. A great deal of Dalzel's book is simply taken from Norris, and it includes descriptions of brutality in the course of the slave trade similar to those with which Pruneau de Pommegorge, across the Channel, was condemning the slave trade.[9] But for Dalzel the meaning of these facts was that brutality was inherent in African life, and that European purchases of slaves saved the enslaved from death – or a miserable life – in Africa.

In the United States, the abolition of slavery was debated at the Constitutional Convention, but the debate ended in 1787 with slavery being enshrined in the Constitution in the article which defined a slave as three-fifths of a person for purposes of counting the population in determining the allocation of seats in the House of Representatives. Slavery was officially abolished in French territories from 1794 to 1802. In practice, the benefits of abolition extended mainly to St.-Domingue and Guadeloupe, and only in small measure to other French colonies. The reinstitution of slavery in Guadeloupe in 1802 and the independence of Haiti in 1804 did not, however, bring to an end the impact of democratic revolutions on New World slavery.

152

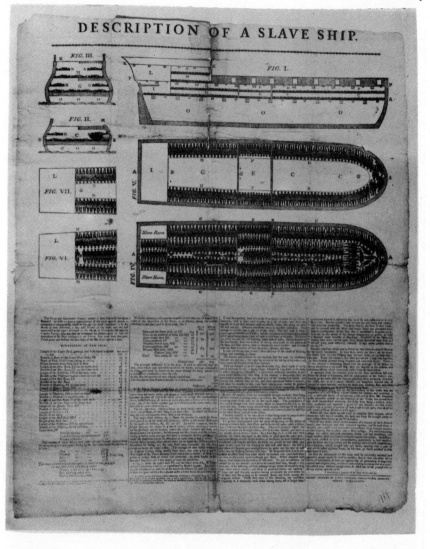

Plate 8.2 Partial plan of the ship *Brookes* (copper engraving by James Phillips, 1789)

The abolition of New World slavery, 1792–1888

As the Spanish territories in the Americas rebelled and gained their independence, some abolished slavery outright (Chile in 1823 and Mexico in 1829, for instance). In most cases, independence led to laws restricting slavery, yet requiring slaves still to provide service to their masters. Adult slaves served out their life terms, while the children were spared from

153

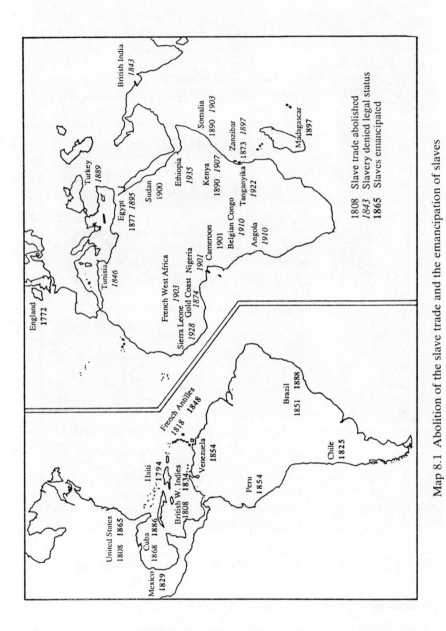

Map 8.1 Abolition of the slave trade and the emancipation of slaves

slavery, as was to be the case for Africa later. Only in the 1850s did such countries as Argentina, Peru, and Bolivia abolish slavery completely.[10]

In the territories remaining under slavery, a black abolitionist movement began to form, led by free blacks who saw their only individual and collective chance for advancement in the general abolition of slavery. Haiti, as a black-ruled state where slavery had been abolished, formed an essential link in this movement. The black abolitionists, small in number, poorly financed and often widely separated, nonetheless led a relentless, imaginative, and ultimately influential campaign. In this campaign they were usually allied with the larger and better financed organizations of white abolitionists. The activities of the abolitionist movements included resettlement schemes: in Haiti, in Sierra Leone (beginning as early as 1787), and in Liberia (beginning in 1821).[11]

The British anti-slavery squadron, set up officially soon after 1808, only began to be active after 1820, once anti-slave-trade treaties had been signed with France, Spain, and Portugal. The squadron captured slavers at sea, then deposited the recaptives in Sierra Leone. A smaller American squadron did likewise at Monrovia in Liberia, and the French followed suit after 1848 in Libreville, Gabon. The colony at Sierra Leone became numerically and politically significant. The black abolitionist movement, therefore, included activists in the United States, in the West Indies, in Mexico and Brazil, in England and in West Africa, with a level of movement and communication among these areas which is perhaps surprising.[12]

With time the British humanitarian movement began to attack not only the slave trade, but slavery itself. Josiah Wedgwood's medallion, "Am I not a Man and a Brother?", now regained its relevance to the campaign. A fitting real-life parallel to the image came to light in the case of Henry Williams, a Jamaican slave nearly flogged to death in 1829 for attending a Methodist chapel. This case became notorious in England. The protest against Williams' treatment effectively linked the Enlightenment vision of human equality with the nonconformist Protestant vision of freedom of worship. The result was an effective statement of the immorality of slavery. In 1831 Jamaican slaves rose up in revolt, under Christian leadership, and the repression of that revolt was visited especially upon Christian slaves.[13] The moral dilemma had become unmistakably clear.

The abolitionist movement in Britain, led now by Thomas Fowell Buxton, was able in 1833 to achieve a law announcing the abolition of slavery, which was thus one of the reforms forced by popular opinion on a retreating aristocracy in the wake of the great Reform Bill of 1832. The slaves, meanwhile, were not yet freed, but were required to work for their masters as apprentices. Finally in 1838 a second Emancipation Act freed the slaves in British territories unconditionally.[14]

The French movement for abolition, halted first by Napoleon and then by the heritage of his defeat, became active again after the July revolution in 1830, under the leadership of Victor Schoelcher. But as the French revolution had slowed the British abolition of the slave trade, so too did British pressure on the French slow the French abolition of slavery. British insistence on the right to visit French ships on the high seas, in search of slave cargoes, offended French national sensibilities. So it was necessary to await the next outburst of popular enthusiasm for republican and human rights – the 1848 revolution – for slavery to be abolished in all French territories, and for their newly freed inhabitants to become citizens of France.[15]

At the same time the scope of slavery was contracting in some areas, it was growing in others. In addition to the three New World bastions of slavery – the United States, Cuba, and Brazil – slavery was growing in Africa. In the United States, the unprecedented growth of cotton production brought the westward migration of over a million slaves and the extension of slavery to new territories. Among these was Texas, where American settlers won independence from Mexico in 1836 in order, in part, to reinstitute slavery. American shipbuilders in Maryland, Rhode Island, and Massachusetts constructed ships used in the illegal slave trade to Cuba and Puerto Rico, and often sailed the ships under Spanish and Portuguese flags. In Cuba a dramatic expansion in sugar production, using the most modern and industrially efficient means available, led to the importation of 700,000 slaves in the nineteenth century. In Brazil the expansion of coffee production in the south brought a dual migration of slaves – from Bahia in the north, where sugar production was stagnating, and from Angola, Loango, and Mozambique – totalling another million slaves displaced.[16] Along the Western Coast of Africa, slavery expanded quantitatively and became more rigorous in response to the new conditions brought, in part, by the reduction of slave exports across the Atlantic. In the Savanna and Horn, both slave exports and domestic slavery expanded, in response to increased Oriental demand and an expanded domestic market for slave produce. Along the Eastern Coast, slave exports continued, after their sudden increase, at a high level, and domestic slavery began to expand rapidly.

Abraham Lincoln foreshadowed the abolition of slavery in the United States with his 1863 Emancipation Proclamation; full emancipation came with the end of the Civil War and the passage of the thirteenth amendment to the Constitution in 1865. With this, the United States joined more actively in the international campaign against the slave trade, including in its action the recognition of the republic of Liberia, which had declared its existence in 1847. The black abolitionist leader Frederick Douglass was later appointed American consul general in Haiti.

The end of the American Civil War was soon followed by a war for independence in Cuba which might, if it had been successful, have ended slavery. But victory in the Ten Years' War went to Spain and its allies among the great planters. Slavery in Cuba was finally abolished by stages in the 1880s, as a result of domestic pressures from slaves and from free republicans, and as a result of pressures on Spain from Britain.[17]

Brazil, having gained its independence from Portugal by 1822, and being governed by a constitutional monarchy with a functioning, elective legislature, remained remarkably resistant to external pressures for abolition. Slave owners had political power and slaves did not. Imports of slaves in large numbers continued until 1850, when Brazil finally signed a treaty with Britain abolishing the slave trade in the southern hemisphere. Slave imports still continued, though on a small scale, until nearly 1870. In 1888, finally, Brazilian slaves were granted their liberty.[18]

Thus ended nearly four centuries of New World slavery. The freed slaves embraced their emancipation enthusiastically. They dreamed of new lives, perhaps as independent farmers or artisans: "forty acres and a mule" was their slogan in the United States. Most ex-slaves, however, were soon disappointed. They found their new lives constrained by remnants of the slave system, and also by new limits imposed in the name of "free" labor under a developing racist ideology. The experience of ex-slaves in the New World – the succession of hope, frustration, and melancholy – was to be re-enacted in later years as African slaves gained their freedom.[19]

The abolition of the African slave trade, 1830–1900

After 1888, slavery and the slave trade were restricted to the African continent and to parts of the Orient. The story of slavery's extinction in these remaining areas may be broken into three topics: the abolition of the surviving export slave trade, the abolition of the slave trade on the African continent, and the freeing of the slaves. The European powers worked energetically on the first two, to suppress slave exports and also to halt the slave trade within Africa. In a remarkable contrast, however, European officials often opposed actively the emancipation of African slaves. Large numbers of the slaves, for their part, declared their freedom whenever the opportunity arose. Because of these differences, it is best for us to review the abolition of the African slave trade first, and then to turn to the emancipation of slaves in Africa.

By treaty action the British and, later, other European powers restricted the export of slaves. Treaties and naval patrols in Sierra Leone and on the Gold Coast halted slave exports by 1820, and treaties in the Bight of Biafra from the 1830s had the effect of halting slave exports. Britain's 1851 occupation of Lagos island brought to an end the export slave trade from that major port. Treaties with Zanzibar from the 1820s restricted the destinations of slave exports, but did not reduce the number. Then in 1873 the British induced the sultan of Zanzibar to abolish the slave trade in his domains, with the result that slave exports ended, but also that the sultan lost control over all his mainland territories, where slavery survived another thirty years.[20]

On the African mainland, European colonial powers halted the slave trade once they gained control: the British along the Gold Coast from the 1830s, the French in Algeria from about 1850. Tunisia and Egypt abolished

Plate 8.3. "Gang of captives met at Mbame's on their way to Tette"

the open slave trade in the 1870s as part of an attempt to gain European recognition. In 1874 the British sent in an army which defeated the Asante kingdom, and thereafter abolished the slave trade in British dominions on the Gold Coast.[21]

Christian missionaries in Africa campaigned against the slave trade, and in some cases speeded the involvement of European states in halting it. With David Livingstone's anti-slave-trade publicity emerged a new and powerful anti-slavery image. Livingstone's condemnation of the Central African slave trade became known to the world with the publication of his first travel narrative in 1858. His second voyage, centering on Mozambique, led him to an even stronger condemnation of the slave trade. His narrative of that voyage, published in 1865, included a lithograph of an African slave caravan, entitled "Gang of captives met at Mbame's on their way to Tette." A later such illustration, published in Livingstone's last journals in 1875, presents the new image in even more forceful terms: it shows the execution of a captive unable to keep up with the caravan, under a sky filled with vultures. This illustration of the cruelties and hardships of the slave trade within Africa now gave European abolitionists an image which drew them into the African continent as none had before.[22]

The influence of Christian missionaries in condemning the slave trade went far beyond that of Livingstone. German missions in the Gold Coast from the 1850s, Scottish missions in Malawi from the 1870s, and French missions in Tanzania, Uganda, and Zaire from the 1870s led active critiques of the slave trade, often at considerable risk of retaliation by slave merchants and their allies.[23]

As of 1880, however, enslavement continued without interruption in most areas of Africa. European and African governments were reluctant to take on the task of suppressing slavery, because of the entrenched power of slave merchants and slave owners, but also because of their own desire for cheap labor. Thus British and German officials in Togo and the Gold Coast, competing in the 1880s for control of Salaga, the greatest slave market of the region, allowed the slave trade to continue, recruited and even purchased slaves for military and other service, and even collected taxes on the slave trade.[24]

From 1880, the abolition of the slave trade was caught up inextricably in the accelerating European conquest of Africa. The initial French military advance up the Senegal valley and into the upper Niger basin brought the abolition of the slave trade in its wake. But during the decades of severe fighting between the French and their enemies – al-hajj Umar up to 1863, his successors until 1879, and Samori Touré until 1898 – the number of persons enslaved in the area increased until the moment French conquests were consolidated, and the French themselves took large numbers of slaves.[25]

Meanwhile the travels of Henry Morton Stanley in Central Africa began to fix attention on that region. Stanley's transcontinental expedition began near Dar es Salaam in 1874 and successfully descended the course of the Zaire river to the Atlantic three years later. Soon thereafter, he linked up with the ambitious King Leopold II of Belgium to form the International African Association, dedicated to exploration, trade, and anti-slavery activity in Africa. At much the same time, Savorgnan de Brazza launched expeditions into the interior from Gabon, and then moved to the Congo on the north side of the Zaire river, claiming these areas for France.[26]

The first International African Congress, held in Brussels in 1882, bound the powers to free trade and the abolition of slavery in Africa. The second such congress, held in Berlin in 1885, ended up setting down ground rules for the recognition of European occupation in Africa: signed treaties and "effective occupation" were the keys. The Berlin congress enabled Leopold to declare the vast Congo river basin as the Congo Free State, under his own personal rule rather than that of Belgium. The "effective occupation" of this huge tract of land, however, made for strange bedfellows. Stanley appointed, as governor of the eastern part of Congo Free State, Tippu Tip, who until that time had been the leading figure in organizing the export of slaves and ivory from the region. The alliance did not last: in 1890 Tippu Tip led one final great caravan east to Zanzibar and retired. The restriction of the slave trade came only after another ten years of conquest, mutinies, and finally establishment of a stable administration.[27]

On the other side of the river, the French pushed rapidly up the Congo as far as Bangui, and only then encountered difficulties in gaining control, in areas raided by or dominated by the rulers of Borno and Baghirmi. It took three successive French assaults to defeat Rabih, the warlord of Sudanese origin who gained control of Borno in 1890. The final expedition, in 1900, included columns sent from the Niger, from the Zaire, and across the Sahara. Further south, the slave-trading principality of Dar al-Kuti did not come under French control until 1914.[28]

In East Africa, slavery had never grown much in the major highland states, and Buganda renounced the slave trade in its 1890 agreement with Britain. The missionary campaign against the slave trade was more prominent here than elsewhere on the continent. The Scottish missionaries in Malawi, the White Fathers in Tanganyika and Uganda (under the leadership of Cardinal Lavigerie), and the London Missionary Society all preceded European government agents into East Africa, and their campaigns against the slave trade had the effect of speeding European occupation. To the north, the British conquest of Sudan, completed in 1898, destroyed the Mahdist regime and soon ended slave raiding in the region.[29]

The occupation of West Africa was almost completed by 1900, following the French conquest of Danhomè and of Samori, and the British annexation of Asante, of southern Nigeria, and the military defeat of the Sokoto Caliphate. Remaining were the Portuguese possessions below the equator. Portuguese forces extended their control over larger regions of Angola and Mozambique, but only under substantial pressure from British authorities did they act to interdict the slave trade.

Thus, in the period between 1880 and 1900, large-scale enslavement of Africans was brought to an end as a result of European conquests. The newly established state power could not tolerate enslavement, and with the repression of any significant military opposition, slave raiding ended. Even in Ethiopia, the only large unconquered area, the state acted to suppress large-scale enslavement because it threatened the independence of the country.[30]

Enslavement continued, of course, on a smaller scale. Kidnapping, witchcraft accusations, and sale of oneself or one's kin could still go on without the authorities being able to know or do anything about it. At the same time, the colonial conquests permitted slaves to escape, to gain manumission, or to renegotiate their service, so that more people were freed from slavery than were enslaved from this point. To generalize for tropical Africa as a whole: just as the export slave trade from Africa was finished by 1880, the slave trade within Africa was finished by 1900. Of course there were many smaller Africas within this one great Africa, and the timing and the means of abolishing the slave trade varied significantly from region to region.

The end of slavery in Africa, 1890–1930

While New World countries celebrate the anniversaries of the emancipation of slaves, most African countries cannot do so: there was rarely a definitive, official decision to liberate slaves.[31] Nor did there ever develop for African slavery an image of oppression which attracted the attention of abolitionists the world over (that is, no parallel to the illustrations of the *Brookes*, of the West Indian slave in prayer, or of Livingstone's image of the caravan of slaves destined for export). African slaves were too often forgotten by humanitarians who assumed that their oppression was minimal or (worse yet) unavoidable. Further, the end of slavery in Africa is tied up inextricably with the rise of new forms of labor coercion under European colonial rule. As a result, African slavery ended through a protracted process rather than as a discrete event; it ended not with a bang, but with a whimper.

If the slave trade in Africa was suppressed mainly through the actions of European conquerors, the actual freeing of slaves was primarily an achievement of the slaves themselves. Slaves liberated themselves by escape frequently, even before the colonial conquest. At the moment of conquest, much larger numbers of slaves took the opportunity to escape, and were sometimes given encouragement to do so by the invaders. Thus the French General Dodds was so determined to bring utter destruction to the kingdom of Danhomè that he fragmented it into its constituent provinces and encouraged slaves to take their freedom. No proclamation emancipated slaves officially, but a large number of slaves declared their freedom and many left the areas where they had been held.

When the British took Lagos in 1851 to end slave exports, hundreds of fugitive slaves began to take refuge under the British flag each year. The administration hardly knew what to do with them, but eventually recruited a core of these ex-slaves into the West African Frontier Force, a colonial army. After the British defeat of Asante in 1874, thousands of slaves escaped their masters and came to seek their futures in British-ruled towns and at mission stations. Similarly, the Scottish missions in Malawi began by receiving large numbers of fugitive slaves, but reversed the policy after a few years in order to gain the approval of local rulers. The French conquest of the Western Sudan from 1880 to 1900 brought as much enslavement by the French army as it did liberation of slaves: the French tended to encourage the flight of the slaves of their enemies. In areas under French control, the military actively discouraged the escape of slaves, and settled the escapees into "liberty villages" where they lived and worked under conditions much like those in slave villages. Similarly, a few years later the British conquerors of the Sokoto Caliphate rapidly came to an understanding with the old elite, and acted directly and indirectly to prevent slaves from liberating themselves. Paul Lovejoy has labelled this policy an "imperialist justification of Islamic slavery."[32]

Why were the new colonial governments reluctant to emancipate the slaves of Africa? Frederick Cooper has scrutinized this question closely for Zanzibar and coastal Kenya, and shows that the end of slavery is tied up with the particular conception of "free labor" the British there sought to impose on Africans.[33] At one level, many colonial officials seemed genuinely convinced that the status of the slave in Africa was not one of significant inferiority. At the same time, they recognized that emancipation of slaves would bring significant social upheaval. As a result, they are open to the charge of moral inconsistency or of social prejudice against slaves. The desire to run inexpensive colonial governments and to utilize African labor cheaply further encouraged them to wink at slavery. In the case of colonial northern Nigeria, the government headed by Lord Lugard sought explicitly to ally with the ruling class, and therefore sought to strengthen rather than weaken the position of that class.[34]

Ex-slaves in Africa sought, whenever possible, to settle down as independent peasants or artisans. Defining their own economic welfare was more important to them than providing wage labor to European or African employers. European officials, frustrated with the difficulty of obtaining sufficient labor at low rates, condemned slaves and peasants alike as lazy, violent, and lacking in economic motivation. Thus the moral imperative of emancipating slaves from the cruelty of their masters' grasp came to be tempered by the economic imperative of requiring African slaves, ex-slaves, and peasants to perform work recognized as valuable by the colonial overlords. The result was the continuation of slavery or of "apprenticeship," the levying of taxes, the imposition of forced labor, and other devices to induce people to work in the wage-labor sector of the economy.[35]

The gradualism of emancipation resulted not simply from European ambiguity about freeing slaves, but also from the entrenched interests of the slave owners. As I argued in chapter 5, many African societies in the nineteenth century had changed from emphasis on slave exports to utilizing slaves for domestic production. Profits came less from exporting slaves than from exploiting them. Thus, while merchants' and monarchs' resistance to the abolition of the slave trade was severe, the slave owners' opposition to the emancipation of slaves was overwhelming. Colonial rulers would indeed have had to provoke social revolution to emancipate slaves. In some areas, such as the Gold Coast and in many of the colonial towns, slaves were indeed emancipated, and the social revolution proceeded quickly. In most cases, the colonial rulers avoided emancipation.[36]

The abolition of slavery came about, therefore, through a series of processes stretched over more than a generation. The first of these, the immediate self-enfranchisement of slaves, has been discussed above. A second mechanism was through movements of slaves, after several years of colonial rule, to emancipate themselves *en masse*. The best-documented such case is that of the Banamba slaves of the upper Niger who, after producing grain under French direction for more than a decade, and after a couple of false starts, announced their departure and left for home in large groups in 1905. French officials protested initially, but had to accept the *fait accompli*. Similar movements have been documented in several parts of Africa.[37]

As the colonial powers began to set up formal systems of rule, they were faced with the conflict between their reluctance to abolish slavery and their inability to give slavery legal recognition. One common approach was to set up dual legal systems, with European law being applicable in certain situations and Muslim or "customary" law being applicable in other cases.[38]

Internal and external pressures against slavery continued to mount. Where slaves constituted organizable groups, they were able to enter negotiations with their masters for the amelioration of their conditions. The masters, anxious to avoid losing complete control over their slaves, often agreed to new terms, for instance changing the relationship to one of tenancy.

The same sort of renegotiation could, of course, take place on an individual level. One sharp distinction, however, separated male from female slaves: the greater mobility of the males. Men had more chance of finding employment in towns or with European governments and merchants, and they were less likely to be restrained from leaving by obligations to family and children. Women, on the other hand, to the degree that they had children by non-slave men or children they would be unable to take with them, had a greater tendency to stay put, and in staying found it hard to escape slave status.[39]

External pressure against the continuation of slavery continued to be felt from missionary and other humanitarian groups. If French missionaries, for instance, were reluctant to criticize French governments, they did not mind criticizing the lax attitudes of Liberia or of the Germans in Kamerun. British anti-slavery activists, by criticizing Portuguese activities in Angola, implicitly caused the same standards to be held up to British colonies.[40]

Thus, eventually, most colonial administrations adopted a law of decree setting a date after which no person could be born into slavery. The dates and the details of these laws varied remarkably from colony to colony. Thus slaves were declared free in 1874 in the Gold Coast, but only in 1928 was slavery abolished by law in Sierra Leone. In addition, legal or administrative procedures were set up by which slaves could sue for freedom, especially on the basis of mistreatment, or set a price for the purchase of their freedom.[41]

In the last decades of slavery, under colonial rule, masters could no longer punish or sell slaves as in days of old. Slaves did indeed become, more than ever, part of the family. Certain of their disabilities continued: their lack of kin, their responsibility for the heaviest and most unpleasant work, and the requirement that they be deferential to free persons. But under these conditions it is not hard to see how the official ethnologists writing about African societies in the early twentieth century concluded that African slavery was a mild form of social oppression.[42] Their mistake was to project backwards in time what they saw before them, on the assumption that African societies were incapable of rapid social change.

In 1933 the International African Institute, led by Lord Lugard, expressed its pleasure that the League of Nations had made permanent its commission (first established in 1926) to collect information on any surviving instances of slavery. For Lugard, this symbolized the end of "slavery in all its forms" – the term was taken from the 1882 Brussels agreement – in Africa. The remaining doubts concerned Ethiopia and Liberia, but the governments of these countries, anxious to preserve their status as recognized members of the League of Nations, took what measures they could to ensure the demise of slavery.[43]

The heritage of slavery

What is the heritage of African slavery and the slave trade, after its rise and fall over three centuries? We know that African societies have remained vital and durable even in the most adverse situations, but it is unreasonable to think that they should have remained unaffected. Could it be true that the corrosive effects of three centuries of commerce in humans, with its temptations, its inbuilt opportunism, its reduction of humans to a cash value, its cycles of revenge, and its inevitable physical brutality, have built lasting flaws into African patterns of thought and action? This question should be posed with delicacy but with persistence. We may never arrive at a consensus on the impact of slavery on African thought, but we will learn from studying the question. To conclude this chapter, I have chosen two aspects of the heritage of slavery for discussion: the development of racist ideology in Occidental minds, and the continuity of colonial African labor systems with certain traditions of slavery.

Racist ideology existed among Europeans and non-Europeans before the nineteenth century: of this there is no doubt. The extent of racism and the means of justifying it, however, changed significantly with time. In the earliest days of European-African contact, racist ideas consisted of simple cultural arrogance – ethnocentrism, as we call it today. With the initial expansion of African slavery, racism came also (in the minds of white slave owners) to justify the master–slave relationship as the natural order of things: Africans were inherently social underlings, the commanded rather than the commanders.[44]

In the eighteenth century, the Enlightenment spread the notion of human progress and evolution toward perfectability, but also, by the same logic, the notion of human backwardness. As evolutionary schemes began to be set, Africans were placed at the bottom of the hierarchy, and a new element was added to racism. This newly strengthened racism grew further during the nineteenth century, feeding on four types of new phenomena. First was the determined campaign of slave owners to preserve their ownership of slaves by proving the slaves were not fit for freedom. Second, even those humanitarians who had supported emancipation turned against the ex-slaves upon finding how little interest they had in providing wage labor with which to keep the plantation economies thriving.[45] Third, the rise of nationalism (in Europe and elsewhere) encouraged the classification and analysis of humans into national (and also racial) groups, rather than as individuals or in groups based on political structures or on occupation. Those earlier seen as central European peasants now became identified as Germans and Poles; subjects of the Austrian king were now identified as Bohemians or Hungarians. Fourth, the scientific classification of plants and animals into species on an evolutionary scale encouraged some scientists to rank groups within the human species in a similar way. The technical superiority of Europeans over non-Europeans in this period, when linked to categorizations of people in national and racial terms, could only reinforce racism. European racism had become, by the mid-nineteenth century, a specialized ideology.[46]

But for all this prior development, nothing approached the depth and the virulence in racist ideology which exploded at the end of the nineteenth century.[47] Never before had it led to the physical segregation of blacks from whites, nor to the systematic removal of blacks from positions of influence.

The Morant Bay events of 1865 in Jamaica marked a turning-point in British thought. In these events, the British governor provoked and then crushed a revolt of blacks, led by the churchman Paul Bogle, who were demanding equal access to land and the judicial system. Soon thereafter, the British government dissolved the legislature of Jamaica and of other colonies, and disenfranchised the British West Indian population under the system of crown colony government.[48] Thus, the strongest form of racism was reserved for black ex-slaves, rather than for slaves.

The threat posed to established orders by millions of freed slaves, the need felt by economic leaders to obtain their labor for the dominant economic system – these factors led, I think, to the development of an ideology which would hold black people in submission where chains had ceased to restrain them.[49] The case for modern racism as the heritage of slavery relies on the amazing temporal coincidence of the restrictions imposed on black people on all shores of the Atlantic at the end of the nineteenth century. Black Americans gained political rights from the national government in the 1860s, and lost them to state and local governments beginning in the 1870s; black office holders fell rapidly from power. Soon followed the Jim Crow laws of the 1890s, segregating housing, schooling, and all public facilities. In the British West Indies, well-placed black teachers and administrators found themselves removed from power in the 1880s. In British West Africa Samuel Ajayi Crowther, Anglican Bishop of the Niger since 1875, was humiliated and stripped of his powers by young English clergymen in 1890. Black civil servants and merchants in Sierra Leone, the Gold Coast, and Lagos found themselves on the defensive. Racial segregation in housing was now implemented ostensibly for reasons of health: the French administration segregated Dakar in 1914 after an outbreak of plague. Still in the 1890s, the black leaders of Luanda now found their press restricted and their access to good positions in the Portuguese administration limited. In South Africa the segregation of the labor force began as the diamond and gold mines expanded.[50]

The coincidence of these developments surely means that local or national explanations of them, no matter how detailed, are insufficient. Some international force or collection of forces brought about similar changes in a variety of areas. The best candidate for that force, I argue, is the end of slavery at the end of the nineteenth century and the ideological reaction to it. This ideological response, regardless of the conscious motivation of its developers, had the effect of preserving black people as an underpaid and overworked labor force by replacing the physical and proprietary restraints of slavery with the ideological restraints of the doctrine of inherent black inferiority. In each case, blacks not only performed an extra workload with inferior compensation, but by doing so they also served to weaken the bargaining power and lower the compensation of all laborers.

In addition to racism, a second form of the heritage of slavery is to be found in the labor systems of colonial Africa. The colonial states established by European conquerors sought to organize labor for transportation, for public works , and for agricultural and industrial production.[51] In the early colonial days, thousands upon thousands of Africans were required by governments to act as porters, carrying burdens for long distances with little compensation. As we have seen, the colonial states often tolerated slavery, though they did not actively support it as had their predecessors. Yet they inherited the remains of the system of slavery, and they relied on coerced labor in their own way. This system was not slavery, for it no longer involved purchase or ownership of slaves. There are, however, a number of parallels and continuities linking the two systems.

At a general level, the new system shared with the old that it was coercive. Chiefs were called upon to recruit workers for porterage, road work, construction projects. Especially in the first half of the colonial era, much of this work went unpaid. The French used the term "corvée" for this sort of work, and aptly so, for it was exactly the same as the old demands made on French peasants by the kings of France. At other times the work of recruits was paid for, but usually at a level below the value of what the recruits could have produced if left on their own. The only way to obtain recruits who would accept such wages was, again, through coercion. One type of coercion was political: chiefly administrative harangues, threats of arrest, and other reprisals. The other type of coercion was economic: taxation. In most colonies, colonial subjects were required to pay a head tax, which had to be paid in official colonial money. As a result, every family was constrained to earn enough to acquit the tax. The combination of these factors is the root of the famous and quaintly ridiculous controversy over the "backward-sloping labor-supply curve" of African workers, also known as the "target worker" thesis. As wages rose, workers spent less time working for colonial cash. Colonial officials argued that such a reaction was in the *nature* of African attitudes toward work.[52] In fact it resulted from the *conditions* of African workers. When low wages rose a bit, African employees worked shorter hours, paid their taxes, and returned to work on their own farms for which the benefits were greater. This reaction, far from being aberrant or culturally conditioned, is a logical and general response of the underpaid and overworked. If wages had been raised substantially – above the level achievable in other types of work – the labor supply curve would have turned around and sloped upward. But for colonial rulers and entrepreneurs, as for precolonial slaveholders, labor had to be cheap. Thus the slave labor and colonial labor systems shared the characteristic that, whenever possible, the workers would withdraw from it and simply work less hours or less days, and put the extra effort into their own households.

Colonial labor systems also resembled slavery in that they required a great deal of migration, especially by young men. In some cases the very routes of migration were the same, as with the movement of Savanna workers into coastal regions of the Gold Coast, the Ivory Coast, Senegal, and Nigeria. As late as the 1930s, the French government recruited men from the Savannas of what is now the Central African Republic, brought them down the Zaire river to Brazzaville, and then walked them the 300 kilometers to Mayombe – exactly the old route of slave exports – to work in the rain forest in construction of the Congo-Ocean railroad, and to die in large numbers as they did so.[53] In other cases migrants were sent in new directions, as toward the mines of Central and Southern Africa. The substantial inequalities in colonial sex ratios – few women in the towns, few men in the countryside – echoed the uneven sex ratios of the previous century.

Beyond these similarities, there are even direct links between slave labor supply and colonial labor systems. The Gaza state in Mozambique, for instance, became involved during the nineteenth century in raiding for or otherwise recruiting slaves – mostly male – who were sold at the coast and sent to Madagascar and the Mascarene islands. At the very moment this export trade was being suppressed, a new demand for labor sprang up in the 1870s in the diamond mines at Kimberley. The Gaza rulers, recruiting in similar fashion, redirected their recruits to South Africa. The differences were that now the recruits collected a wage and were allowed eventually to return, instead of facing permanent exile; the chiefs now collected a recruitment fee in place of a selling price for their recruits.[54] In sum, labor in colonial Africa was not slavery, at least not after the first generation of colonial rule. But the colonial labor system was a direct offspring of slavery, and the family resemblances remained evident.

Slavery has now been abolished in Africa for nearly three generations. Yet its great extent in earlier days, and the repeated and tumultuous social changes which it brought about over a three-century period, cannot be ignored as factors influential in African life today. Effects of slavery still mark the social and economic realities of modern Africa, and the ideas of Africans and non-Africans alike.

9

The world and Africa

Africa is at once the most romantic and the most tragic of
continents. . . . There are those, nevertheless, who would write
universal history and leave out Africa.

W. E. B. DuBois, *The Negro*

In 1915 W. E. B. DuBois, the black American scholar and publicist,
published a sketch of "the general history of the Negro race." This slim
volume, *The Negro*, appeared during the flood-tide of European imperial
conquest and racial discrimination, in the midst of World War I. DuBois'
interpretation was remarkable for its time in that it presented Africans as
participants – not just as bystanders or victims – in the development of the
modern world. He returned to this theme repeatedly during his long life.
Thus in 1946, after another world war, he published *The World and Africa*.[1]

The problem of the world and Africa, for DuBois, was not just oppression of Africans, but also neglect of Africa's place in the world. He
proposed to rethink history, and to recognize African life as an integral part
of the human experience. An acknowledgment of Africa's role in world
history, DuBois thought, would help to end the political exclusion,
economic oppression, and cultural denigration of black people which had
been reinforced by slavery, racism, and colonial rule. Yet the task of
rethinking history would not be easy. In practice, DuBois was able to hold
forth the vision of a new world history, and he was able to outline some
African chapters to add to existing history, but he could get no further.[2]

DuBois' task remains before us. The problem of the world and Africa
retains its importance, and not only for black people. It is, for the moment,
the most outstanding case of the yawning gap which exists between rich and
poor, between north and south, between creditors and debtors, and
between the hungry and the obese. It is the problem of the origins and the
propagation of inequalities among the regions of the world.

The twentieth century has been a time of unique contradiction: inequalities in wealth and power among humans have grown to unprecedented
levels, and yet the demand for social equality has advanced even more

168

rapidly. The United Nations – to take but one example – is an embodiment of this contradiction. It was founded and initially directed by the great powers, yet its existence is predicated on the principle of equality among nations. The organs of the United Nations, in turn, have sought actively to reduce inequalities among people of all nations and races, of both sexes, and of all economic levels.[3] As we enter the twenty-first century, the desire to achieve human equality – and the conflicts arising from the pursuit of that desire – will surely be central to the course of human events.

Can we learn to live together as equals? To do so, we will need a vision of history appropriate to the twenty-first century. That is, if we are to envision a future without inequality, we cannot succeed without reconsidering our past. How are we to prepare for existence as one broad community if our history is restricted to stories of separate races and separate nations, each closed off within its own world? How are we to prepare for decisions by consensus if our history is dominated by tales of the powerful imposing their wills on the weak? We need an approach to world history recognizing and respecting the identities and traditions of various communities, yet emphasizing their interactions and their commonality.

Such an approach to history will differ in important respects from earlier conceptions. The old stories of the rise and fall of great empires, or of the flowering and decay of great civilizations, are too reliant on the belief in the independent inspiration by the heroes of those cultures to be helpful for today's purposes.[4] The interpretations of modern history which portray it in terms of the rise of the west (or of the "modernization" of economy and society) succeed in unifying a great deal of historical material in a straightforward framework, but they are too reliant on diffusionism, and too certain of unidirectional causality from the strong to the weak.[5] The notion of modern history as the story of a single great world-system has the advantage of centering on the world and not just on Europe, but it ends up being too focused on the system as a whole and not enough on its constituent parts.[6]

To succeed in clarifying the problem of the world and Africa, the historian's approach must focus on interactions among communities, and on transformations of communities through interaction. The drama of human history, in this case, is no longer limited to the speeches and actions of great men under the spotlight at center stage. Lights now illuminate the entire stage: the players move and interact, and the narrative emerges out of the lives and speeches of figures in many subplots. The relationships among the players, and not just the characters of the heroes, give the story its meaning. My interpretation of the tragedy and sacrifice of slavery is intended to fit into such a vision of world history.

African slavery in world history

The rise and fall of African slavery was an important development in modern history. Slavery was linked, in greater or lesser degree, to all the other great modern changes: industrialization, the rise of the capitalist and wage-earning classes, the scientific revolution, the rise of nations and nationalism, the emergence of war and social revolution on an unprecedented scale, rapid population growth, huge migrations, the dramatic expansion in education, and changing social roles for men, women, and children. Slavery was especially important in defining Africa's place in the modern world, and it also helped to define history in each of the other continents.

To integrate slavery into world history is to develop a deeper understanding of modern social change. The history of industrialization, taken by itself, appears as a European success story, leading to growth, progress, and even liberation from drudgery. Yet in Africa these same forces brought declining population, not growth. The interpretation of growth in the modern world economy must be revised to include the experience of Africa, as that vast continent was linked through slavery to New World plantations and European industry.

Beyond growth and decline, the changes in Africa and the Americas took the form of transformations in society. In the Americas, the land was physically transformed by the work of slaves. At the same time, the ideas of Europe and especially of the Americas were transformed by the development of racial discrimination and its justification. Within Africa, the changing sexual balance resulting from slave exports led to pressures for a new sexual division of labor and new patterns of marriage.

Further, the growth, decline and transformations took place because of interactions among regions, not simply as elaborations of local trends. Historians have too often fallen prey to the error of offering parochial explanations for global phenomena. A striking example is the literature on the rise of racism in the United States. This literature, while complex and sophisticated, has been flawed by the implicit assumption that American racism could be understood by an analysis limited to the borders of the United States, when, in fact, the movement of peoples and ideas all over the Atlantic are what gave racism its shape.[7] Within Africa, similarly, the expansion of slavery and the development of a multitude of specific institutions of servility cannot be explained (as anthropologists first attempted) as the evolution of institutions within each ethnic group, but as responses to economic and demographic pressures felt throughout the Atlantic basin.

Finally, these patterns in the history of slavery form part of the main line of development in modern history. Can one imagine what an interpretation of the rise of the modern world would be like if it left out the formation of new social classes, or if it left out the influence of Christianity? These examples may give an idea of the distortion brought to history by leaving out the experience and the influence of slavery.[8]

Africa has not fared well in this great transformation.[9] Estimated populations of the continents demonstrate Africa's declining share of the world population. In 1600 the tropical African population was perhaps 50 million, or 30 percent of the combined population of the New World, Europe, the Middle East, and Africa. By 1800 the population of Africa had fallen to 20 percent of the total. By 1900 tropical Africa's population had grown to perhaps 70 million, but it had fallen to little more than 10 percent of the greater region. On the other hand, accounting for persons of African descent in the New World and the Middle East, one may argue that the African population remained over 15 percent of the total in 1900.[10]

Africa's proportion of the world population declined for three related reasons: absolute loss through emigration, absolute loss through slavery-related mortality, and relative loss because African death-rates remained high while others dropped. The conditions of slavery reinforced this proportionate decline through the nineteenth century. The absolute loss through emigration from Africa reached a cumulative total of about 18 million persons over three centuries, and I have estimated the absolute loss through slavery-related mortality as a cumulative total of some 4 million persons. The continued high level of African mortality cost at least as many lives as did the direct effects of enslavement. The continuation of this high level of mortality resulted partly, though not entirely, from the perpetuation of enslavement and the displacement it brought. Taken together, these three factors left tropical Africa with an 1850 population of little more than half what it would have been in the absence of slavery and the slave trade. (In the twentieth century the African population has grown in absolute terms, and has regained some lost ground in proportionate terms.[11]) In addition to population change, economic transformation has been the main focus of my analysis of slavery in world history. The 10 million immigrants to the Occident and the 5 million immigrants to the Orient brought their strength, their skills, their habits, and their outlooks to work for their masters. So did the 15 million persons enslaved within the African continent. Historians of world economic growth have tended to leave these massive changes in African demography and economy out of their discussions.

The slaves who reached the New World, on the other hand, have received some recognition in analyses of Atlantic economic growth. There the discussion has centered on the Williams thesis.[12] Eric Williams, in summarizing the world-historical impact of slavery, concentrated on the issue of profits. He argued that British profits from slavery and the slave trade were high, and that they contributed significantly to the success of English industrialization. Williams' description remains unchallenged: West Indian planters and Liverpool merchants sat at the peak of their economic order in the eighteenth century; in the nineteenth century they were displaced by industrialists using wage labor. In his analysis, Williams attempted to show that Britain was transformed economically and then politically through its interactions with the West Indian colonies.

Williams' recent critics have argued, in contrast, that rates of profit in the slave trade and on slave plantations were not unusually high. As a result, they maintain, the wealth of slave owners comprised only a small proportion of the capital of English industrialists. In further contradiction to Williams, his critics have argued that the British campaign against slavery was not led by rising industrialists, and that slavery continued to be profitable into the nineteenth century.[13] These studies have generally been careful, though it is remarkable to what a degree they have remained focused on links between Britain and its West Indian colonies in the eighteenth and early nineteenth centuries. The implication of these studies would seem to be that slavery, while lamentable, was insignificant in determining the course of the world economy.

Such a conclusion – minimizing the impact of slavery – runs counter to common sense, as I see it. Too much energy went into perpetuating slavery, and too much went into destroying it, to permit us to set it at the margins of history. More recently, other scholars have come to the support of the Williams thesis.[14] We should be prepared, however, to acknowledge that the Williams thesis – the attempt to link slavery and capitalism – may not stand in its original form. Our response, then, should be to reformulate the Williams thesis rather than dismiss it.

The most logical reformulation of the Williams thesis, I think, is to state its analysis in terms of productivity rather than profitability, and to state its geographical scope as the whole Atlantic basin rather than as Britain and her West Indian colonies. The debate on profitability has centered on the net earnings of planters, merchants, and industrialists, after their costs are paid. If we focus instead on the productivity of human labor, our study will center on the quantities of goods and services produced by slave laborers, as compared with the quantities produced by all other laborers. The analysis of profitability focuses on the owners and on Europe; the analysis of productivity focuses on the laborers and on the Americas and Africa.

What portion of New World agricultural production from 1500 to 1850 was by slave labor? What was the contribution of slaves to building the cities of Mexico, Lima, Havana, Salvador, Cartagena, New Orleans, Philadelphia, or New York? What portion of land clearing and of artisanal work was performed by slaves? Answers to these questions would certainly show that the economic growth of the New World was based disproportionately on slave labor. The 15 percent of today's New World population which is of African ancestry understates the contribution of slave labor in the early days, because so many slaves died early and left no progeny other than the work they had completed. (It was only with the end of the slave trade that European immigrants, whose descendants now predominate in New World populations, came to outnumber African immigrants to the Americas.)

Europe too relied on slave labor. Slaves in Europe worked for their masters; Europeans bought sugar, tobacco, gold, coffee, and textiles produced by slave labor; European merchants and planters repatriated profits from ventures relying on slave labor. As the late Marion Johnson has suggested, the increase in eighteenth-century British textile exports to West

Africa, to pay for increasingly expensive slaves, was a factor in the industrialization of British cotton production.[15]

This expanded and reformulated Williams thesis should be applied not just to the Occident, but to the African and Oriental regions of slave exploitation. All these areas were tied into a single great and diverse system for the supply and exploitation of slave labor. In the Orient, where slaves were dominantly female, the work of slaves was more in household production than in market production. That is, the value of their work, while important in social reproduction, was not generally measured in terms of profit. Even in the Orient, economies went through their own reorganization in the eighteenth and nineteenth centuries: slaves participated, for instance, in the nineteenth-century transformation of Egypt. In sub-Saharan Africa, more importantly, a growing portion of economic production and reproduction came to be the responsibility of slaves.

Migration, heavy loss of life, and modified population structures were the demographic effects of slavery. The economic effects of slavery included large quantities of slave-produced goods, and the redistribution of wealth and productive power from slave to master and from Africa to the Occident and the Orient. Together these demographic and economic effects of slavery brought a major restructuring of the relationships among the continents, and within the continents.

The social changes brought by slavery followed, in a large part, from the demographic and economic changes. Changes in the African sex ratio put pressures on institutions of marriage, child rearing, and the division of labor. Similarly, the shortage of women in New World slave societies influenced family structures. Refugee societies developed in Africa. Plantation societies developed in the New World and maroon societies developed at their fringes; mulatto populations emerged from the voluntary and involuntary unions of white and black. Africa developed systems for the enslavement of millions. In all areas of this slave world there evolved methods for seasoning slaves, as well as places for slaves in artificial kinship systems and structures to ensure that their exploitation was profitable to their masters. With the abolition of slavery, the freed slaves developed peasant societies where none had existed in the Caribbean and Brazil; they returned to peasant life in Africa; and they became tenant farmers in the United States. In all areas, the ex-slaves migrated in numbers to the growing cities of the early twentieth century.

Slavery left a legacy in the ideas and culture of all the people who experienced it. In the Occident, ideas of the nature of race and of racial hierarchy developed out of the experience of slavery. But slavery also became a metaphor for all types of social oppression, and ideas of human rights developed as the logical antithesis to slavery. Christian views of slavery changed from justifying it to condemning it. Islam and African religions underwent similar changes, finally condemning slavery where they had earlier justified it. But just as the development of slavery was most

173

extreme in the Occident, so has the renunciation of slavery there been most vigorous. In Africa and the Orient, by contrast, societies tended to absorb slaves and thereby to diminish and deny the significance of slavery.

The tragedy of African slavery reached its denouement with the European conquest of the continent at the end of the nineteenth century. The cycle of enslavement, oppression, and death finally relented. Slaves gained their freedom in Africa and abroad, but in an atmosphere of racial discrimination that pressured them to renounce their African heritage and to adopt the culture of their rulers. The worst was over, though the experience had been more exhausting than cathartic.

By the same token, African sacrifice had ceased. The demanding gods of Africa, of Islam, and Christianity, the idols of the market-place, the greedy merchants, planters, and monarchs – all those who had gathered and consumed the bodies and souls of slaves sacrificed in their names – seemed at last satisfied. The plentiful fruits of the sacrifice have since enriched the world.

The results of slave labor are still seen in the farms and cities of Europe, the Americas, Africa, and the Orient. The passage of time, of course, makes it increasingly difficult to identify which work was done by slaves, so that their contribution becomes confounded in the work of humanity generally. This much is inevitable. Whether we remember or forget their contribution, however, is a matter of our own choice.

The response to past injustice

How are we to respond to the injustice of slavery? Since this book is more an investigation of social science than of morality, I have focused on explaining the transformations and interactions of societies brought about by the experience of modern slavery, rather than on judging them. At the same time, the issue of morality is central to slavery, and I cannot conclude without addressing it. We are all implicated as beneficiaries in a social and economic system constructed in significant part through the exploitation of slaves. What is our response to that heritage?

We can do nothing to change the past. Yet our actions today are often based on our understanding of the lessons of the past. In these last few words, therefore, let me turn from interpreting the history of slavery to discussing today's response to that history. While it would be beyond my task as a historian to dictate how today's society should respond to the heritage of slavery, I can address a preliminary issue: to outline the various patterns of response to past injustice from which we have to choose. I have labelled them the doctrines of charity, of reparations, of familial self-help, and of remembrance.

The doctrine of charity, the best-known of these patterns of response, is not one I would include as a reaction to injustice. Charity is a response to misfortune rather than to injustice. One party gives to another out of pity and empathy, but not out of guilt or responsibility. The recent great campaigns to collect international aid for African famine victims, by groups of private citizens, by governments, and by international bodies, qualify as charity. For our purposes here, I seek doctrines in which the respondents share in responsibility for the injustice.

Frantz Fanon offered such a doctrine and in a sharp tone. In the heady days of the success of the Algerian revolution and of decolonization, he set forth a demand for reparations.[16] He called the exploitation of colonialism unjust, and demanded reparations and restitution from the exploiters to the exploited. This demand, sometimes ignored and sometimes ridiculed, retains its relevance in this day of north-south negotiations.

The doctrine of reparations as a solution is based on the presumption that the parties in conflict are distinct, independent, and contradictory. The offending party admits guilt, accepts responsibility, and makes restitution. The payments of the Federal Republic of Germany to Israel, in the years after World War II, were examples of reparations made in restitution for the death of millions of Jews at the hands of the Nazi government; the heirs of the Nazi state paid reparations to the heirs of the Jewish tradition.[17]

For the case of slavery, the victims included the slaves themselves, those who died in the course of enslavement, and the African populations set into turmoil by slavery; any reparations would be paid by the heirs of slave owners to the heirs of the slaves and their families.

The practical problem with making reparations of this sort is that it is difficult, after so many generations, to distinguish the parties. Who were the beneficiaries of the exploitation? Who are the current heirs of those beneficiaries? Who were the exploited, and who are the current heirs of the exploited? It would not seem appropriate, for instance, if a great transfer of wealth to Africa were to fall into the hands of the descendants of the slave merchants rather than the descendants of the slaves. On the other hand, one may argue that while some Africans have suffered more than others, African society as a whole suffered as a result of slavery.

So it is not likely that a clear and specific formula for reparations for slave-trade damages could be proposed, much less implemented. But the idea of reparations is important because of a key concept it brings with it: it serves effectively to deny the notion that the current poverty and weakness of Africa is a result of its inherent qualities. For these are the two theses among which the north-south negotiators must choose: that the relative wealth of nations is a function of their individual skill and good fortune in managing their resources, quite independent of each other; or that the relative wealth of nations is a function also of earlier transfers of wealth among nations, some voluntary and some involuntary. In the latter case, almost necessarily, some recognition of those past relations is allowed to affect the terms of current agreements.

For a second doctrine of response to injustice, we may turn to the response of a family to injustice in its midst. This leads us to a different logic. We may consider the case of women demanding an end to injustice at the hands of men, and to inequality which makes them inferior to men. Strongly as women may feel the need for change, the vehemence of their demands is limited by the fact of their unity with men in the family. Women's demands, while sometimes asking compensation, have tended to be for an end to inequality. This is the distinction between a grant to an alien party – as recompense for an injury – and aid to one's kin. A grant to an alien is recompense paid out of guilt, or it is charity paid out of pity for acts of God. Aid to kin is support given to one of one's own who has suffered injury for whatever reason, but especially when the family bears some responsibility for the injury.

Thus at the end of World War II, the United States contributed vast sums of money to the economic reconstruction of war-devastated western Europe. This contribution, laid down in the Marshall Plan of 1947–54, served American political aims by maintaining moderate European governments in power against left-wing oppositions. In moral terms, however, the Marshall Plan reflected the feeling of many Americans that they should assist the lands of their ancestry out of respect for the memory of their ancestors. The wartime contributions of Canada and Australia to Britain are only two of the many examples of support from colonies to the mother country, which fit into the logic of family self-help.[18]

Within this logic, is there not a basis for Americans and Europeans to provide support for African members of the Atlantic family? The contributions would not be based on responsibility for specific acts, as in the case of reparations, but on current need. Still, the past injustice provides the motivation for the current contribution. It appears that past contributions are better remembered when they are voluntary than when they are involuntary. For the contributions of Afro-Americans to the development of the Americas are certainly of great importance. It is not only the direct descendants of African immigrants who might reasonably make such contributions, for other Americans too have benefited from the contribution of immigrants from Africa as elsewhere.

A third response to past injustice, especially that which has occurred within a community, is the doctrine of remembrance. This view has been enunciated eloquently by the Jewish writer Elie Wiesel in the attempt to respond to the horror and the injustice of the extermination of Jews in this century. In his words: "Let us remember, again and again. For at the end that is all they wanted – to be remembered: their names, their faces, their silent songs, their secret triumphs, their struggle, and their death, one as awesome as the other."[19] Since nothing can be done physically to retrieve those who were lost in the holocaust of World War II, Wiesel argues that the propagation of their memory will at least set a moral standard for their descendants today: "Tales of despair ultimately mean tales against despair."[20]

For the case of African slaves, in turn, one may argue that the response to their sacrifice is to honor their memory and thereby ensure that no such sacrifice will be made again.

Appendix 1

Slave prices

This appendix reproduces data on slave prices published by several scholars. All of the prices listed refer to slaves purchased on the Atlantic coast of Africa, though they differ in a number of other particulars: whether for prime or average slaves, whether at constant or current prices, whether in British pounds sterling or in Maria Theresa dollars, and so forth. The note for each column describes the dimensions of the prices given.

Figure 1.2 (in chapter 1) displays most of these prices in graphical form. For that graphical display I have applied conversion figures to the raw data in this appendix, so that all could be presented in terms of British pounds sterling of 1780. In addition, for the Manning curve in figure 1.2, certain other adjustments were made for the seventeenth century.

Note that the real value of slaves leaving Africa is best estimated by the c.i.f. (cost, insurance, freight) cost of goods exchanged for slaves (i.e. including costs of shipping to Africa). Estimates in columns 1, 2, 3, 5, and 6, however, are as f.o.b. (free on board) cost of goods exchanged for slaves (also known as prime cost), because of the difficulty of estimating shipping costs.

1 Bean. F.o.b. cost of goods imported to the Western Coast of Africa in exchange for slaves, in 1601 pounds sterling per prime male slave.[1]
2 LeVeen. F.o.b. cost of goods imported to the Western Coast of Africa in exchange for slaves, in current dollars per average slave.[2]
3 Miller. Prices of slaves at Luanda, f.o.b. reported in milreis and converted to current pounds by Miller.[3] These figures refer to prime slaves to 1750, and to the midpoint of the range thereafter.
4 Curtin. C.i.f. cost of goods imported to St. Louis in exchange for slaves, in current pounds sterling per average slave; Curtin lists these as f.o.b. costs of slaves exported from St. Louis.[4]
5 Eltis I. F.o.b. cost of goods imported to the Western Coast of Africa in exchange for slaves, in Maria Theresa dollars of 1821–3 per prime male slave.[5] (The exchange rate was roughly $MT 4.80 = £1.)
6 Eltis II. F.o.b. cost of goods imported to the Western Coast of Africa in exchange for slaves, in current pounds sterling per average slave.[6]
7 Manning. C.i.f. cost of goods imported to the Western Coast of Africa in exchange for slaves, in 1913 pounds sterling per average slave.[7]

Appendix 1

	(1) Bean W. Coast f.o.b. 1601 £	(2) LeVeen W. Coast f.o.b. current $	(3) Miller Luanda f.o.b. current £	(4) Curtin St. Louis c.i.f. current £	(5) Eltis I W. Coast f.o.b. 1823 $	(6) Eltis II W. Coast f.o.b. current £	(7) Manning W. Coast c.i.f. 1913 £
Date							
1600			9.2				
1610			16.1				
1620	10.84		16.1				
1630			16.1				
1640	3.91		10.8				7.3
1650	6.72						7.9
1655	11.38						
1660							4.4
1665	3.29						
1670	3						3.5
1675	1.76						
1680	3.67		5.9	8.15		3.5	4.9
1685	3.74						
1690	3.22			5.19			5.8
1695	4.24						
1700	5.43		6.2				12.7
1705	10.24						
1710	11.21		9.8	9.71			16.2
1715	11.75						
1720	12.77		11.3	5.61			17.0
1725	11.89						
1730	13.37		11.3	14.38			23.0
1735	17.65						
1740	18.92		14.1				18.9
1745	11.13						
1750	14.26		14.1				18.2
1755	12.52						
1760	14.07		11.8	18.27			22.1
1765	16.54						
1770	17.76		13.5	17.9			22.6
1775	15.96						
1780		80.0	14.9	27.14		22.1	24.0
1790		95.0	17.7	27.52			28.5
1800		95.0	15.8				28.5
1810		74.3	17				22.2
1815					26.2		
1820		72.0	15.8	32.79	33.3	9.9	18.0
1825					51.9		
1830		62.0	33.9	34.33	37.5		15.5
1835					50.9		
1840		57.6		22.32	32.1		14.4
1845					66.8		
1850		52.0		28.52	43.2		13.0
1855					38.2		
1860		48.0			38.2		12.0
1865							

Appendix 2

The demographic simulation

The computer program for simulating the demography of African slavery consists of some thirty pages of source code, written in the Pascal language. Most of the program consists of documentation of the calculations and procedures for printing out the results in appropriate form. The essence of the program, however, is the projection of populations forward in time, and the projection of enslavement, enslavement-related mortality, and migration as it affects these populations. The terminology used in this appendix is the same as that in chapters 3 and 4 of the text.

The data and assumptions of the simulation may be thought of as being divided into three sections. First are the data and assumptions on African populations. The simulation begins with an African regional population divided into source and captor groups, each divided by sex and by one-year age groups (from zero or birth to 80+). The source population is set initially as exactly three times as large as the captor population. The age and sex distributions of these two populations are those given in the Coale and Demeny model south population, level 4, with an annual growth rate of five per thousand or 0.5 percent.[1] The initial data on African populations thus give population size, age, and sex distribution, and levels of age-specific mortality and fertility which reproduce a population with an expectation of life at birth of 27.5 years, growing at a rate of five per thousand.

Second are the data and assumptions on enslavement. These include an enslavement schedule (giving the proportion of the source population enslaved each year), a schedule for the level of mortality upon capture in Africa, a partition schedule (determining the proportion of captives to be exported, and the proportion to remain in Africa), and a schedule for the level of mortality on leaving Africa (i.e. the Middle Passage or the Saharan crossing). Each of these schedules of migration and mortality is written in age-specific and sex-specific terms. For instance, the enslavement schedule assumes the proportion of young adults captured is much higher than the proportion of old people captured; overall, a typical year's enslavement in the simulation resulted in the capture of roughly one percent of the source population.

Third are the data and assumptions on the conditions of the slave populations created during the simulation. These are the domestics and exports populations. The enslavement discussed above determines the immigration into the domestics and export populations; levels of mortality and fertility for these slave populations must then be assumed. In most simulation runs, slave mortality was assumed to be slightly higher than that for free Africans, and slave fertility was assumed to be slightly lower.

With this initial data, the simulation cycles through forty, one-year periods. In each period, it performs the following calculations: the births and deaths (by age) in each population; the enslavement of members of the source population; mortality of the captives; partition of the captives into those directed toward domestic and export markets; integration of domestic captives into the domestic slave population; additional mortality of the export captives; integration of export captives into the export slave population.

After forty years (enough time for the impact of enslavement to work itself thoroughly through each population), the program reports on the details of the resulting populations: their size, age, and sex composition, growth rates, the ratio of slave exports to African regional population, and the cumulative total of persons enslaved.

Because the number of variables in the simulation is large, a sensitivity analysis was performed to show how the results responded to changes in variables or groups of variables. This sensitivity analysis showed that the relationships among the variables were linear rather than complex, and it showed that the most significant variables in the simulation were the levels of fertility, and the size and sex composition of the captive populations.[2]

Results of simulations for the Western Coast showed stable relationships among three key variables: E, the export ratio (current slave exports as a fraction of the African regional population); G, the growth rate of the African regional population; and S, the adult sex ratio (men per 100 women) in the slave society population. Linear approximations to these relationships used were as follows:

$$G = 0.005 - 2.5\,E$$
$$S = 1 - 83\,E$$

Equivalent relationships for simulations of slave exports from the Savanna and Horn were as follows:

$$G = 0.005 - 3.1\,E$$
$$S = 1 + 56\,E$$

Once the export ratio (E) was estimated for each decennial period from 1700 to 1870 (for the Western Coast), the growth rate and sex ratio could also be calculated. For 1870, populations were estimated by projecting backward from the colonial population estimates of 1931. A high estimate of the 1870 population was calculated by assuming a constant low annual growth rate from 1870 to 1931 (0.0049); a low estimate was calculated by assuming a higher growth rate (0.011). Prior to 1870, both high and low estimates of populations were assumed to have intrinsic growth rates of 0.005. The export ratio (E) for the 1860s was calculated as slave exports for the 1860s as a portion of the 1870 population (both high and low estimates). This permitted calculation of high and low estimates of G and S for the 1860s. The 1860 populations were calculated by projecting the 1870 populations back ten years at the growth rates calculated for the 1860s. Export ratios were then calculated for the 1850s, and the process was repeated back to 1700.

For the Savanna and Horn and for the Eastern Coast, this procedure was modified slightly to account for slave exports after 1870. Populations were projected back from 1931 to 1890. The high population for 1890 was estimated by projecting back the 1931 population at a growth rate of 0.002; the low population for 1890 was estimated with a growth rate of 0.015. Prior to 1890, both high and low populations were assumed to have intrinsic growth rates of 0.005. Estimates of E, G, S, and previous populations were then derived according to the same procedure as for the Western Coast, though with some adjustments for changing the sex ratio of exports from the Eastern Coast.

Notes

Prologue: Tragedy and sacrifice in the history of slavery

1 James Hutton, ed. and trans., *Aristotle's Poetics* (New York, 1982), 50–1.
2 Luc de Heusch, *Sacrifice in Africa: A Structuralist Approach*, trans. Linda O'Brien and Alice Morton (Bloomington Ind., 1985).
3 Hutton, *Aristotle's Poetics*, 58.
4 Walter Kaufmann, *Tragedy and Philosophy* (New York, 1968), 317–20.
5 De Heusch, *Sacrifice in Africa*; M. F. C. Bourdillon and Meyer Fortes, eds., *Sacrifice* (London, 1980). Academic economists speak not of *sacrifice* but of the *cost* of investment and production. In contrast, practicing members of business communities – personally and emotionally involved in their enterprises – have often portrayed their ventures as sacrifices.
6 David Eltis's magisterial study of the nineteenth-century Atlantic slave trade has demonstrated in exceptional detail and clarity the contribution of slavery to New World economic growth, and it has the additional merit of addressing African aspects of slavery in detail. Nevertheless, since his approach centers on the calculations of slave owners, he underestimates the cost and the waste involved in the slave system: Eltis, *Economic Growth and the Ending of the Transatlantic Slave Trade* (New York, 1987).

1 The political economy of slavery in Africa

1 David Brion Davis, *Slavery and Human Progress* (Oxford, 1984).
2 Edward Reynolds, *Stand the Storm: A History of the Atlantic Slave Trade* (London, 1985); François Renault and Serge Daget, *Les Traites négrières en Afrique* (Paris, 1985); Albert Wirz, *Sklaverei und kapitalistische Weltsystem* (Frankfurt-on-Main, 1984); Paul E. Lovejoy, *Transformations in Slavery: A History of Slavery in Africa* (Cambridge, 1983); James Rawley, *The Transatlantic Slave Trade: A History* (New York, 1981); C. Duncan Rice, *The Rise and Fall of Black Slavery* (New York, 1975); Basil Davidson, *Black Mother: The Years of the African Slave Trade* (Boston, 1961); Daniel P. Mannix and Malcolm Cowley, *Black Cargoes: A History of the Atlantic Slave Trade, 1518–1865* (New York, 1962).
3 An invaluable tool for the researcher and for the student as well is the remarkably thorough and well-organized set of bibliographies on slavery and the slave trade prepared by Joseph C. Miller. For the period up to 1982 these are published in a single volume: Miller, *Slavery, A Worldwide Bibliography, 1900–1982* (White Plains, N.Y., 1985). For subsequent years they are published as annual bibliographies in the journal *Slavery and Abolition*.
4 Philip D. Curtin, *The Atlantic Slave Trade: A Census* (Madison, 1969); Paul E. Lovejoy, "The volume of the Atlantic slave trade: a synthesis," *Journal of African History*, 23, 4

(1982), 473–501; Ralph A. Austen, "The trans-Saharan slave trade: a tentative census" in Henry A. Gemery and Jan S. Hogendorn, eds., *The Uncommon Market: Essays in the Economic History of the Atlantic Slave Trade* (New York, 1979), 23–76; "The Islamic Red Sea slave trade: an effort at quantification," *Proceedings of the Fifth International Conference on Ethiopian Studies* (Chicago, 1979), 443–67; G. M. LaRue, "The export trade of Dar Fur, ca. 1785 to 1875" in G. Liesegang, H. Pasch, and A. Jones, eds., *Figuring African trade* (Berlin, 1986), 636–68. For a critical view, arguing that these figures for slave exports should be increased, see J. E. Inikori, "Introduction" in Inikori, ed., *Forced Migration* (London, 1982), 19–28.

5 Richard Bean, *The British Trans-Atlantic Slave Trade 1650–1775* (New York, 1975); Eltis, *Transatlantic Slave Trade*; David Tambo, "The Sokoto Caliphate slave trade in the nineteenth century," *International Journal of African Historical Studies* 9, 2 (1976), 187–217; Joseph C. Miller, "Slave prices in the Portuguese southern Atlantic, 1600–1830" in Paul E. Lovejoy, ed., *Africans in Bondage* (Madison, 1986), 43–78; Emmanuel Terray, "Réflexions sur la formation du prix des esclaves à l'intérieur de l'Afrique de l'Ouest précoloniale," *Journal des Africanistes*, 52, 1–2 (1982), 119–44; Manuel Lobo Cabrera, *La Esclavitud en las Canarias Orientales en el Siglo XVI* (Gran Canaria, 1982).

6 For some early and fruitful insights, see Martin Klein, "Slavery, the slave trade, and legitimate commerce in late nineteenth century Africa," *Etudes d'Histoire Africaine*, 2 (1971), 5–28. A study strong in both theory and empirical analysis is Claude Meillassoux, *Anthropologie de l'esclavage: le ventre de fer et d'argent* (Paris, 1986). See also Suzanne Miers and Igor Kopytoff, *Slavery in Africa: Historical and Anthropological Perspectives* (Madison, 1975); Claude Meillassoux, ed., *L'Esclavage en Afrique précoloniale* (Paris, 1957); Claire C. Robertson and Martin Klein, eds., *Women and Slavery in Africa* (Madison, 1983); James L. Watson, ed., *Asian and African Systems of Slavery* (Berkeley, 1980); Herbert S. Klein, *African Slavery in Latin America and the Caribbean* (New York, 1986). On Muslim Africa see Allan G. B. Fisher and Humphrey J. Fisher, *Slavery and Muslim Society in Africa* (London, 1970); and John Ralph Willis, ed., *Slaves and Slavery in Muslim Africa*, 2 vols. (London, 1985). For a detailed study of slavery in an earlier time, see Joseph C. Miller, *Way of Death: Merchant Capitalism and the Angolan Slave Trade, 1730–1830* (Madison, 1988).

7 Paul E. Lovejoy, ed., *The Ideology of Slavery in Africa* (Beverly Hills, 1981); Meillassoux, *Anthropologie de l'esclavage*; David Brion Davis, *The Problem of Slavery in the Age of Revolution, 1770–1823* (Ithaca, 1975); Davis, *Slavery and Human Progress*; Willis, *Slaves and Slavery*, vol. 1.

8 Stanley L. Engerman and Eugene D. Genovese, eds., *Race and Slavery in the Western Hemisphere: Quantitative Studies* (Princeton, 1975); Henry A. Gemery and Jan S. Hogendorn, eds., *The Uncommon Market: Essays in the Economic History of the Atlantic Slave Trade* (New York, 1979); David Eltis and James Walvin, eds., *The Abolition of the Atlantic Slave Trade* (Madison, 1981); Société Française d'Histoire d'Outre-Mer, *La Traite des noirs par l'Atlantique, nouvelles approches* (Paris, 1976).

9 Curtin, *Atlantic Slave Trade*, xvii; Frederick Cooper, "The problem of slavery in African studies," *Journal of African History* 20, 1 (1979), 103–25; B. W. Higman, *Slave Population and Economy in Jamaica 1807–1834* (Cambridge, 1976); Eugene D. Genovese, *Roll, Jordan, Roll: The World the Slaves Made* (New York, 1974).

10 Most of this work is being done by historians trained in the study of Africa. Frederick Cooper, "Islam and cultural hegemony: the ideology of slaveowners on the East African Coast" in Lovejoy, *Ideology of Slavery*, 271–307; Ralph A. Austen, "From the Atlantic to the Indian Ocean: European abolition, the African slave trade, and Asian economic structures" in Eltis and Walvin, *Abolition*, 117–39; J. O. Hunwick, "Black Africans in the Islamic world: an understudied dimension of the black diaspora," *Tarikh*, 5 (1978), 20–40; Willis, *Slaves and Slavery*, vol. 2; and Fisher and Fisher, *Slavery and Muslim Society in*

Africa. See also Ehud R. Toledano, *The Ottoman Slave Trade and its Suppression* (Princeton, 1982); and articles on the Oriental slave trade in *Slavery and Abolition*, 8, 3, (1988).

11 Eric Williams, *Capitalism and Slavery* (Chapel Hill, 1944).

12 Roger Anstey, *The Atlantic Slave Trade and British Abolition, 1760–1810* (Cambridge, 1975); Seymour Drescher, *Econocide: British Slavery in the Era of Abolition* (Pittsburgh, 1977); "The decline thesis of British slavery since *Econocide,*" *Slavery and Abolition*, 7, 1 (1986), 3–24; Stanley L. Engerman, "The slave trade and British capital formation in the eighteenth century: a comment on the Williams thesis," *Business History Review* 46 (1972); 430–43. For a comprehensive collection of recent views on the Williams thesis, see Barbara L. Solow and Stanley L. Engerman, eds., *British Capitalism and Caribbean Slavery: The Legacy of Eric Williams* (Cambridge, 1987).

13 Walter Rodney, "African slavery and other forms of social oppression on the Upper Guinea Coast in the context of the Atlantic slave trade," *Journal of African History*, 7, 3, (1966), 431–43; *How Europe Underdeveloped Africa* (London, 1972).

14 John D. Fage, "Slavery and slave trade in the context of West African history," *Journal of African History*, 10, 3 (1969), 393–404; "The effect of the export slave trade on African populations" in R. P. Ross and R. J. A. Rathbone, eds., *The Population Factor in African Studies* (London, 1975), 15–23. C. C. Wrigley criticized Fage's willingness to accept slavery as a fair price for African state formation. Wrigley, "Historicism in Africa: slavery and state formation," *African Affairs*, 80, 279 (1971), 113–24. Aspects of this controversy have been re-enacted more recently, with David Eltis assuming the role of Fage and Paul Lovejoy playing that of Rodney. Eltis, *Transatlantic Slave Trade*, 64–77; Lovejoy, "The impact of the slave trade on Africa in the eighteenth and nineteenth centuries," *Journal of African History*, 30 (1989), 386–93.

15 David Brion Davis, *The Problem of Slavery in Western Culture* (Ithaca, 1966), 483–93; John Woolman, *The Works of John Woolman* (New York, 1969; first printed 1754, 1762); see also *The Journal of John Woolman* (New York, 1954).

16 Charles Becker, ed., *Mémoire sur le Commerce de la Concession du Sénégal, par Joseph Pruneau (1752)* (Mimeographed, Kaolack, Senegal, 1983); Joseph Pruneau de Pommegorge, *Description de la Nigritie* (Paris, 1789).

17 Archibald Dalzel, *The History of Dahomey, an Inland Kingdom of Africa* (London, 1967; first published 1793); Loren K. Waldman, "An unnoticed aspect of Dalzel's *History of Dahomey [sic],*" *Journal of African History*, 6, 2 (1965), 185–92.

18 Thomas Clarkson, *The History of the Rise, Progress and Accomplishment of the Abolition of the African Slave Trade by the British Parliament*, 2 vols. (London, 1808), vol. 2, 110–14; Marcel Châtillon, "La Diffusion de la gravure du *Brookes*, par la Société des Amis des Noirs, et son impact" in Serge Daget, ed., *De la Traite à l'esclavage: Actes du colloque international sur la traite des Noirs, Nantes 1985*, 2 vols. (Nantes and Paris, 1988).

19 Thomas Fowell Buxton, *The African Slave Trade and its Remedy* (London, 1968, first published 1839–40), 199–201. Buxton noted the severe mortality of the Middle Passage and of New World seasoning, but he did not account for enslavement within Africa nor the attendant mortality.

20 David Livingstone, *Missionary Travels and Researches in South Africa* (London, 1857); David and Charles Livingstone, *Narrative of an Expedition to the Zambesi and its Tributaries* (New York, 1866), 412–13, 481, 483, 497–8, 586–7, 620–3; David Livingstone, *The Last Journals of David Livingstone in Central Africa*, ed. Horace Waller, 2 vols. (London, 1874), vol. 1, 56, 62, 65, 88–9, 97–8; François Renault, *Lavigerie, l'esclavage africain et l'Europe, 1868–1892*, 2 vols. (Paris, 1971); R. W. Beachey, *The Slave Trade of Eastern Africa* (London, 1976).

21 A well-known example is the celebration of the 1897 British conquest of Benin kingdom in modern Nigeria: R. H. S. Bacon, *Benin, City of Blood* (London, 1897).

22 At times, however, Europeans justified slave raids as legitimate suppression of revolts by African states. Frederick Lugard, *The Dual Mandate in British Tropical Africa*, 5th edn (London, 1965), 365–6, 372–6; Michael Mason, "Population density and 'slave raiding' – the case of the middle belt of Nigeria," *Journal of African History*, 10, 4 (1969), 551–64.

23 For examples of the work of official ethnographers on slavery, see Auguste Le Herissé, *L'Ancien Royaume du Dahomey* (Paris, 1911); Louis Tauxier, *Le Noir du Soudan, Pays Mossi et Gourounsi* (Paris, 1912); Northcote W. Thomas, *Anthropological Report on the Ibo-Speaking Peoples of Nigeria; Part IV, Law and Custom of the Ibo of the Asaba District, S. Nigeria* (London, 1914), 111–25; C. K. Meek, *The Northern Tribes of Nigeria*, 2 vols. (London, 1926), vol. 1, 287–93; Capt. R. S. Rattray, *Ashanti Law and Constitution* (Oxford, 1929), 33–46. The largest of the data sets compiled from such sources is the Human Relations Area Files, constructed under the direction of the anthropologist G. P. Murdock. For two studies of slavery based on these files, see Frederic L. Pryor, "A comparative study of slave societies," *Journal of Comparative Economics*, 1 (1977), 25–49; and Orlando Patterson, *Slavery and Social Death* (Cambridge, Mass., 1982).

24 Leaders among these professional anthropologists included Meyer Fortes, E. E. Evans-Pritchard, Max Gluckman, and Marcel Griaule. Two exceptions who gave significant attention to slavery were Melville J. Herskovits, *Dahomey, an Ancient West African Kingdom*, 2 vols. (New York, 1938), and S. F. Nadel, *A Black Byzantium* (Oxford, 1942). Among the later anthropologists who began more detailed studies of slavery were M. G. Smith, Claude Meillassoux, and Igor Kopytoff.

25 Roland Oliver and J. D. Fage, *A Short History of Africa* (Harmondsworth, 1962); Robert Rotberg, *A Political History of Tropical Africa* (New York, 1965), 134–5.

26 Allen F. Isaacman, *Mozambique: The Africanization of a European Institution: The Zambezi Prazos, 1750–1902* (Madison, 1972); Igor Kopytoff and Suzanne Miers, "African 'slavery' as an institution of marginality" in Miers and Kopytoff, *Slavery in Africa*, 3–81.

27 Rodney, *How Europe Underdeveloped Africa*; Samir Amin, *Unequal Development* (New York, 1976), 49–50, 319–26; Claude Meillassoux, "The role of slavery in the economic and social history of Sahelo-Sudanic Africa" in Inikori, *Forced Migration*, 74–99; Immanuel Wallerstein, *The Modern World-System* (New York, 1978), vol. 2; Majhemout Diop, *Histoire des classes sociales dans l'Afrique de l'Ouest* (Paris, 1971).

28 Collective volumes on slavery appearing in the wake of Curtin's census included Engerman and Genovese, *Race and Slavery*; Société française d'histoire d'Outre-Mer, *La Traite des noirs*; Gemery and Hogendorn, *Uncommon Market*; and Willis, *Slaves and Slavery*. For the most detailed published data on the slave trade voyages, see Jean Mettas, *Répertoire des expéditions négrières françaises au XVIIIe siècle*, ed. Serge Daget, 2 vols. (Paris, 1978, 1984). One heated debate arose, in which Curtin responded to Inikori's assertion that his slave export figures were too low. See J. E. Inikori, "Measuring the Atlantic slave trade: an assessment of Curtin and Anstey," *Journal of African History*, 17, 2 (1976), 197–223; Philip D. Curtin, "Measuring the Atlantic slave trade once again," *Journal of African History*, 17, 4 (1976), 595–605; Inikori, "Measuring the Atlantic slave trade," *Journal of African History*, 17, 4 (1976), 607–27.

29 For more on the estimation of slave prices in Africa, see chapter 5 and appendix 1.

30 Eltis, *Transatlantic Slave Trade*, 260–64.

31 For evidence that the extent of slavery in Africa increased during the nineteenth century, see A. J. H. Latham, *Old Calabar, 1600–1891: The Impact of the International Economy upon a Traditional Society* (Oxford, 1973); Frederick Cooper, *Plantation Slavery on the East African Coast* (New Haven, 1977); and Lovejoy, *Transformations in Slavery*.

32 Lovejoy, *The Ideology of Slavery in Africa*; Martin Klein and Paul E. Lovejoy, "Slavery in West Africa," in Gemery and Hogendorn, *Uncommon Market*, 184–98.

33 The "window" technique is used implicitly in many sorts of analysis. For an explicit

discussion of its assumptions, see Patrick Manning, *Slavery, Colonialism, and Economic Growth in Dahomey, 1640–1960* (Cambridge, 1982), 88–9, 115.

34 In fact, the "Africa" of which I speak is limited to tropical Africa, the part of the continent on which enslavement concentrated. This was the majority of the surface and the population of Africa. I do not mean, however, to suggest that the people of northern and southern Africa left out of the analysis for these purposes are otherwise any less African than inhabitants of the tropics.

35 V. Y. Mudimbe, *The Invention of Africa* (Bloomington, Ind., 1987). Mudimbe focuses on the invention of Africa as a result of the colonial experience. The analysis could be extended, though perhaps with different results, to the invention of Africa as a result of slavery as well.

2 Why Africans? The rise of the slave trade to 1700

1 Orlando Patterson, *Slavery and Social Death: A Comparative Study* (Cambridge, Mass., 1982).

2 Ibid., 30, 179; M. I. Finley, ed., *Slavery in Classical Antiquity* (Cambridge, 1960); *Ancient Slavery and Modern Ideology* (London, 1980). On Mesopotamia see, for instance, Bernard J. Siegel, *Slavery during the Third Dynasty of Ur* (Memoirs of the American Anthropological Association, 66, 1947).

3 Martin C. Wilbur, *Slavery in China During the Former Han Dynasty, 206 BC – AD 25* (Chicago, 1943); E. G. Pulleyblank, "The origins and nature of chattel slavery in China," *Journal of the Economic and Social History of the Orient*, 1 (1958), 204–11.

4 Dev Raj Chanana, *Slavery in Ancient India* (New Delhi, 1960).

5 Mark Elvin, *The Pattern of the Chinese Past* (Stanford, 1973), 30–2, 73–4; Olga Lang, *Chinese Family and Society* (New Haven, 1946); Amal Kumar Chattopadhyay, *Slavery in India* (Calcutta, 1959); Ellen S. Unruh, "Slavery in medieval Korea" (Ph.D. dissertation, Columbia University, 1978); Bruno Lasker, *Human Bondage in Southeast Asia* (Chapel Hill, 1950).

6 Berthold Spüler, *History of the Mongols* (Berkeley, 1972), 22–3, 86–7; Richard Hellie, *Slavery in Russia, 1450–1725* (Chicago, 1982).

7 Marc Bloch, *Slavery and Serfdom in the Middle Ages: Selected Essays*, trans. William R. Baer (Berkeley, 1975); H. A. R. Gibb, *Mohammedanism*, 2nd ed. (London, 1953); Ali Abd Elwahed, *Contribution à une théorie sociologique de l'esclavage* (Paris, 1931). An analogous debate rages on the impact of Islam on the status of women: see Lois Beck and Nikki Keddie, eds., *Women in the Muslim World* (Cambridge, Mass., 1978).

8 Harold A. McMichael, *A History of the Arabs in the Sudan*, 2 vols. (Cambridge, 1922); Patterson, *Slavery and Social Death*, 148–59; Andrew Ehrenkreutz, "Strategic implications of the slave trade between Genoa and Mamluk Egypt in the second half of the thirteenth century" in A. L. Udovitch, ed., *The Islamic Middle East, 700–1900: Studies in Economic and Social History* (Princeton, 1981), 335–45; I. M. Lewis, ed., *Islam in Tropical Africa* (London, 1966).

9 Austen, "Trans-Saharan slave trade," 58–65; Jean-Pierre Oliver de Sardan, "Captifs ruraux et esclaves impériaux du Songhay," in Meillassoux, *L'Esclavage en Afrique précoloniale*, 99–134; Lovejoy, *Transformations in Slavery*, 15–18, 28–35.

10 Bloch, *Slavery and Serfdom*; Peter Foote and David M. Wilson, *The Viking Achievement* (London, 1970), 65–78.

11 Charles Verlinden, *L'Esclavage dans l'Europe médiévale* (Bruges, 1955) vol. 1, (Ghent, 1977) vol. 2. In contrast, William D. Phillips has more recently emphasized the Mediterranean tradition of small-scale slavery (in contrast to the large-scale or gang slavery of New World plantations), and has expressed skepticism about the importance of slave labor in the sugar plantations of the medieval Mediterranean: Phillips, *Slavery from Roman Times to the Early Transatlantic Trade* (Minneapolis, 1985).

12 Hellie, *Slavery in Russia*.

13 H. J. Nieboer, *Slavery as an Industrial System* (The Hague, 1910).

14 Charles Verlinden, *Les origines de la civilisation atlantique. De la Renaissance à l'Age des Lumières* (Neuchatel, 1966); Lobo Cabrera, *La Esclavitud en las Canarias Orientales*; A. C. de M. Saunders, *A Social History of Black Slaves and Freedmen in Portugal, 1441–1555* (Cambridge, 1982).

15 Frederick Bowser, *The African Slave in Colonial Peru, 1524–1650* (Stanford, 1973); Colin Palmer, *Slaves of the White God: Blacks in Mexico, 1570–1650* (Cambridge, Mass., 1976); Klein, *African Slavery in Latin America*.

An influential economic model of the demand for slaves is that of Evsey Domar, who focuses on the relative shortage of labor (in comparison to land) as the principal cause of demand for slaves; Domar acknowledged his debt to Nieboer's earlier statement of this view. Domar, "The causes of slavery or serfdom: a hypothesis," *Journal of Economic History*, 30, 1 (1970), 18–32; Nieboer, *Slavery as an Industrial System*; see also Pryor, "Comparative study of slave societies."

16 Sherburne F. Cook and Woodrow Wilson Borah, *Essays in Population History: Mexico and the Caribbean*, 3 vols. (Berkeley, 1971, 1974, 1979); Henry F. Dobyns, "Estimating aboriginal American population: an appraisal of techniques with a new hemispheric estimate," *Current Anthropology*, 7 (1966), 395–416; William N. Deneven, ed., *The Native Population of the Americas in 1492* (Madison, 1976); Noble David Cook, *Demographic Collapse: Indian Peru, 1520–1620* (Cambridge, 1981); Alfred W. Crosby, *The Columbian Exchange: Biological and Cultural Consequences of 1492* (Westport, Conn., 1972).

17 Philip D. Curtin, "Epidemiology and the slave trade," *Political Science Quarterly*, 83 (1968), 190–216; Kenneth F. Kiple and Virginia Himmelsteib King, *Another Dimension to the Black Diaspora: Diet, Disease, and Racism* (Cambridge, 1981).

18 A. J. R. Russell-Wood, "Technology and society: the impact of gold mining on the institution of slavery in Portuguese America," *Journal of Economic History* 37, 1 (1977), 59–86.

19 Lobo Cabrera, *La Esclavitud en las Canarias Orientales*, 141–78.

20 Bowser, *The African Slave in Colonial Peru*; Palmer, *Slaves of the White God*; Edmund Morgan, *American Slavery, American Freedom: The Ordeal of Colonial Virginia* (New York, 1975).

21 J. H. Parry, *The Age of Reconnaissance* (London, 1963); C. R. Boxer, *the Dutch in Brazil, 1624–1654* (Oxford, 1957); *The Portuguese Seaborne Empire 1415–1825* (New York, 1969).

22 Richard N. Bean and Robert P. Thomas, "The adoption of slave labor in British America" in Gemery and Hogendorn, *The Uncommon Market*, 377–98; Richard S. Dunn, *Sugar and Slaves: The Rise of the Planter Class in the English West Indies, 1624–1713* (Chapel Hill, 1972); David Galenson, *White Servitude in Colonial America, An Economic Analysis* (Cambridge, 1981); Richard B. Sheridan, *Sugar and Slavery: An Economic History of the British West Indies* (Bridgetown, Barbados, 1974).

For a detailed description of Portuguese trading practices of the seventeenth century in Africa, see Joseph C. Miller, "Capitalism and slaving: the financial and commercial organization of the Angolan slave trade, according to the accounts of Antonio Coelho Guerreiro (1684–1692)," *International Journal of African Historical Studies*, 17, 1 (1984), 1–56.

23 Sidney Mintz, *Sweetness and Power: The Place of Sugar in Modern History* (Harmondsworth, 1985); J.-L. Vellut, "Diversification de l'économie de cueillette: miel et cire dans les sociétés de la forêt claire d'Afrique centrale (*c*. 1750–1950)," *African Economic History*, 7 (1979), 93–112.

24 Some defenders of the slave trade argued that Africa had a population surplus. John D. Fage comes close to the same conclusion in his argument that, for West Africa, "the effect may have been no more than to cream-off surplus population" (Fage, "Effect of the export

slave trade," 20). Henry Gemery and Jan Hogendorn developed a well-known model of slave supply based on the vent-for-surplus model popularized by the development economist Hla Myint. See H. A. Gemery and J. S. Hogendorn, "The Atlantic slave trade: a tentative economic model," *Journal of African History*, 15, 2 (1974), 233–46; and Hla Myint, *The Economics of the Developing Countries* (New York, 1964). The model does not actually require a labor surplus, but only requires that labor be underutilized. Gemery and Hogendorn do, however, use the term "surplus capacity available for export" (for instance on pages 237–9, 246). E. Phillip LeVeen labelled his analogus model an "excess supply" model: LeVeen, *British Slave Trade Suppression Policies, 1821–1865* (New York 1977), 128.

25 For a classic study of shifting cultivation, see Pierre de Schlippe, *Shifting Cultivation in Africa; the Zande System of Agriculture* (London, 1956).

26 Jack Goody, *Technology, Tradition and the State in Africa* (Cambridge, 1971), 25.

27 Jan de Vries has demonstrated this principle nicely for Holland in the early modern period, where the high productivity of agricultural labor (which resulted from capital improvements in the land) raised the general level of wages so high that industrial firms chose to locate in other areas, with the result that Dutch industry never became as brilliant as Dutch commerce: De Vries, *The Dutch Rural Economy in the Golden Age, 1500–1700* (New Haven, 1974), 182–6, 238–40; "Labor in the Dutch golden age" (unpublished paper, Berkeley, 1980), 14–15.

Asian producers of rice, it may be noted, occupied a level of technical efficiency intermediate between those of Europe and Africa. This factor, in addition to the extra distance from Asia to the New World colonies, tended to isolate Asians from being drawn into European-dominated plantation work. There were, nevertheless, important cases of enslavement and plantation work in Asia, notably Dutch slave plantations in Indonesia and Dutch importation of Malaysian slaves into South Africa. Further, as African slave exports came to an end in the nineteenth century, millions of Indian and Chinese workers were recruited as cheap contract laborers for plantations and mines in the Caribbean, the Indian Ocean, Pacific islands, and elsewhere: A. J. H. Latham, *The International Economy and the Undeveloped World 1865–1914* (London, 1978), 105–16.

28 Stefano Fenoaltea has constructed an alternative explanation for slave exports on the assumption that African productivity equalled that in Europe. His model is driven by price differences resulting from African demand for imports. While his assumption on productivity is probably ill-founded, his observations on the relative costs of transporting gold, slaves, and agricultural goods are of importance in explaining the changing nature of African exports in the seventeenth, eighteenth, and nineteenth centuries: Fenoaltea, "Europe in the African mirror: the slave trade and the rise of feudalism" (unpublished paper, Princeton University, 1988).

29 Philip D. Curtin, "The African diaspora" in Michael Craton, ed., *Roots and Branches: Current Directions in Slave Studies* (Toronto, 1979), 15–16.

30 This reasoning has some analogies to Marx's discussion of cost and productivity in wage labor, in which he argued that employers pay workers the cost of their reproduction but keep the difference between that and the value of their output. For the American South, there are numerous studies of the value of slaves: these are based both on the value of goods produced by slaves, and on the cost of raising a slave (in a situation where, in contrast to the case of African captives, slaves were born into the master's household): Robert William Fogel and Stanley L. Engerman, *Time on the Cross*, 2 vols. (Boston, 1974).

31 Philip D. Curtin, Stephen Feierman, Leonard M. Thompson, and Jan Vansina, *African History* (Boston, 1978), 188–9; Davidson, *Black Mother*, 120–52, 224–37.

32 Fenoaltea has implicitly demonstrated the importance of African political and social fragmentation in sustaining slave exports by asking why more slaves were not ransomed by their families or by their own efforts: Fenoaltea, "Europe in the African mirror."

33 Christopher Udry, "The Akan transitional zone" (unpublished paper, Yale University, 1985); Robin Law, *The Oyo Empire, c. 1600–c. 1836* (Oxford, 1977), 158–61; Manning, *Slavery, Colonialism and Economic Growth*, 27–46.

34 Thomas and Bean have used the image of fishing on the high seas to emphasize the competitiveness of the African slave trade; here I offer instead the image of fishing in a river or lake to emphasize the limits on renewing resources. Robert Paul Thomas and Richard Bean, "The fishers of men – the profits of the slave trade," *Journal of Economic History*, 34, 4 (1974), 885–914.

35 Lovejoy, *Transformations in Slavery*, 35–40.

36 The main work on the medieval market for slaves is that of Charles Verlinden. See, for example, "La Traite des esclaves: un grand commerce international au Xe siècle" in *Etudes de civilisation médiévale, IXe – XIIe siècles: mélanges offertes à Edmond René Labande à l'occasion de son départ à la retraite* (Poitiers, 1974), 721–30.

37 David Eltis, "Free and coerced transatlantic migrations: some comparisons," *American Historical Review*, 88, 2 (1983), 251–80.

3 Slavery and the African population: a demographic model

1 Davidson, *Black Mother*; Lovejoy, *Transformations in Slavery*; Reynolds, *Stand the Storm*; Rawley, *Transatlantic Slave Trade*.

2 That is, I have assumed one great slave raid in a given year and then no further enslavement for fifteen years. In more complex versions of the model (presented later in this chapter and in chapter 4), I assume a lower level of enslavement taking place every year, whose effects can be observed continuously. In that extension from a static to an interactive version of the model, some effects will be seen to be reduced and others will be magnified, but the overall picture is remarkably similar to the one presented in the static version of this section.

3 In fact, all across the Savanna from Senegal to Chad there existed regions from which slaves were drawn both into Oriental and Occidental trades. I have assumed that the overlap of the two trades was important only in the Senegambia and, as we shall see below, along the Eastern Coast of Africa.

4 Domestic and Export slaves were thus joint products: both were brought into existence by the same "productive" action of capture. For details and sources on slave prices, see appendix 1.

5 The prevalence of polygyny on the African coast is documented, for instance, in William Bosman, *A New and Accurate Description of the Coast of Guinea* (London, 1967; first published 1705).

6 Two contradictory factors complicate this picture. The large proportion of female slaves who were in their childbearing years tended to increase the crude birth-rate; the low age-specific fertility of slaves in most plantation colonies tended to reduce the crude birth-rate. North American slave populations were unusual in that they had relatively high birth-rates. For a range of New World slave birth-rates, see B. W. Higman, *Slave Populations of the British Caribbean 1807–1834* (Baltimore, 1984), 308–10.

7 For instance, see Roberta Ann Dunbar, "Slavery and the evolution of nineteenth-century Damagaram" in Miers and Kopytoff, *Slavery in Africa*, 161–2.

8 An important and unanswered question is whether males were enslaved in numbers and proportions similar to those for females. I have assumed that the number, age, and sex composition of male and female Captives were similar. For a contrasting viewpoint in the case of Angola, see John Thornton, "The slave trade in eighteenth century Angola: effects of demographic structures," *Canadian Journal of African Studies*, 14 (1981), 423–4.

9 Fisher and Fisher, *Slavery and Muslim Society*; Michael Mason, "Captive and client labour and the economy of the Bida Emirate, 1857–1901," *Journal of African History*, 14 (1973), 467.

189

10 Austen, "Trans-Saharan slave trade," 44–5.
11 Populations of clear African descent survive in some corners of the Orient – in Saudi Arabia, Egypt, and Libya, for instance. But the number of Africans assimilated into the Oriental population was far larger than is suggested by these small groups.
12 Rodney, "Slavery and other forms of social oppression"; John Thornton, "Demography and history in the kingdom of Kongo, 1550–1750," *Journal of African History*, 18, 4 (1977), 507–30; "The demographic effect of the slave trade on Western Africa 1500–1850" in C. Fyfe and D. McMaster, eds., *African Historical Demography* (Edinburgh, 1981), vol. 2, 701–7.
13 David Geggus, "Sex ratio, age, and ethnicity in the Atlantic slave trade: data from French shipping and plantation records," *Journal of African History*, 30 (1989). This study is a major step forward in combining African and New World data on the composition (rather than the aggregate totals) of slaves traded. The development of African demand for slave women needs to be investigated in far more detail, for instance in studies of the sex ratio of slave exports from the fifteenth through seventeenth centuries.
14 See chapter 5 for further discussion of these causes of rising eighteenth-century slave prices.
15 Thornton, "Demographic effect of the slave trade."
16 These results of simulation analysis are discussed in chapter 4 and in Patrick Manning and William S. Griffiths, "Divining the unprovable: simulating the demography of African slavery," *Journal of Interdisciplinary History*, 19, 2 (1988), 177–201.
17 Thornton, "Slave trade in eighteenth century Angola," 426.
18 Klein, "Slavery, the slave trade, and legitimate commerce"; Lovejoy, *Transformation in Slavery*, 159–83.
19 Patrick Manning, "The enslavement of Africans: a demographic model," *Canadian Journal of African Studies*, 15, 3 (1981), 499–526.
20 Allan R. Meyers, "Slave soldiers and state politics in early Alawi Morocco, 1668–1727," *International Journal of African Historical Studies*, 16, 1 (1983), 39–48.
21 Verlinden, *L'Esclavage dans l'Europe médiévale*, vols. 1–2.
22 Based on projections of the simulation model.
23 Nehemia Levtzion, *Ancient Ghana and Mali* (London, 1973); J. O. Hunwick, "Notes on slavery in the Songhay empire," in Willis, *Slaves and Slavery*, vol. 2, 16–32; Olivier de Sardan, "Captifs ruraux et esclaves impériaux au Songhay"; Mordechai Abir, "The Ethiopian slave trade and its relation to the Islamic world" in Willis, *Slaves and Slavery*, vol. 2, 124–5; Getachew Haile, "From the markets of Damot to that of Barara: a note on slavery in medieval Ethiopia," *Paideuma*, 27 (1981), 173–80.
24 Lovejoy, *Transformations in Slavery*, 28–35. R. S. O'Fahey argues that warfare with Wadai initiated the eighteenth-century Dar Fur demand for slaves: O'Fahey, "Slavery and society in Dar Fur" in Willis, *Slaves and Slavery*, vol. 2, 86.
25 R. S. O'Fahey, "Slavery and the slave trade in Dar Fur," *Journal of African History*, 14, 1 (1973), 29–43; Abir, "The Ethiopian slave trade," 128–9. The economic causes of the increased Middle Eastern demand for slaves need to be investigated in more detail.
26 Results of simulation analysis.
27 The magnitude of the male surplus in the Savanna was not as large as the magnitude of the female surplus on the Western Coast. Some Savanna areas, for instance, could sell females to the north and males to the south. Paul E. Lovejoy, "Plantations in the economy of the Sokoto Caliphate," *Journal of African History*, 19, 3 (1978), 341–68; "The characteristics of plantations in the nineteenth-century Sokoto Caliphate (Islamic West Africa)," *American Historical Review*, 84, 4 (1979), 1267–92; O'Fahey, "Slavery and the slave trade in Dar Fur."
28 Martin A. Klein, "Women and slavery in Africa," 67–92; "The demography of slavery in western Soudan: the late nineteenth century" in Dennis D. Cordell and Joel W. Gregory, eds., *African Population and Capitalism: Historical Perspectives* (Boulder, Colo., 1987), 50–61.

29 Edward A. Alpers, *The East African Slave Trade* (Nairobi, 1967), 5–8; Isaacman, *Mozambique: Abdul Sheriff, Slaves, Spices and Ivory in Zanzibar* (London, 1987), 41–5.

30 Mauritius was under French control until 1810, when the British seized it. Gwyn Campbell, "Madagascar and the slave trade, 1810–1895," *Journal of African History* 22, 2 (1981), 203–27; Edward A. Alpers, *Ivory and Slaves in West Central Africa: Changing Patterns of International Trade to the Later Nineteenth Century* (Berkeley, 1975); Cooper, *Plantation Slavery*, 38–46; Sheriff, *Slaves, Spices and Ivory*, 33–76; Beachey, *Slave Trade of Eastern Africa*. On the impact of epidemics and famine, see Gerald W. Hartwig, "Social consequences of epidemic diseases: the nineteenth century in eastern Africa" in Hartwig and K. David Patterson, eds., *Disease in African History* (Durham, 1978), 25–45; and Hartwig, "Demographic considerations in East Africa during the nineteenth century," *International Journal of African Historical Studies*, 12, 4 (1979), 653–72. Hartwig does not, however, include the slave trade as a factor in demographic disruption.

31 Alpers, unfortunately, is able to give no indication of the sex ratio among slave exports. Cooper suggests that sex ratios were fairly equal on Zanzibari plantations and for Eastern Coast exports: Alpers, *Ivory and Slaves*; Cooper, *Plantation Slavery*, 221–3.

32 Based on simulation results.

33 Livingstone and Livingstone, *Narrative of an Expedition to the Zambesi*.

34 Zanzibari planters, however, purchased their slaves, while planters in the Sokoto Caliphate were more closely associated with capturing them: Cooper, *Plantation Slavery*, 4–113.

35 This possibility has been suggested to me orally by a number of scholars, but I have not yet been able to find it in print.

36 Since married couples made no effort to restrict conception, by the same token it was very difficult for them to increase conception. On the concept of natural fertility, see Louis Henry, *On the Measurement of Human Fertility: Selected Writings of Louis Henry*, ed. and trans. Mindel Sheps and Evelyne Lapierre Adamcyk (Amsterdam, 1972), 1–26.

37 Results of the European Fertility Project suggest that the increases in fertility following demographic crises were mostly a result of women ending breast-feeding. Demographic studies of contemporary African populations may be able to validate this conclusion for Africa. Ansley J. Coale and Susan Cotts Watkins, eds., *The Decline in European Fertility* (Princeton, 1986).

38 Michel Garenne and Etienne Van de Walle, "Polygyny and fertility among the Sereer of Senegal" (unpublished paper, University of Pennsylvania n.d.); Manning, "Enslavement" of Africans"; John C. Caldwell, "Comment on Manning," *Canadian Journal of African Studies*, 16. 1 (1982), 128.

39 Philip Curtin has argued – though with qualifications – that "it seems possible and even probable that population growth resulting from new food crops exceeded population loss through the slave trade" *Atlantic Slave Trade*, 270. Simon Ottenberg earlier made a similar assertion for the case of the Igbo.

40 Miller, *Way of Death*, 103; Marvin P. Miracle, *Maize in Tropical Africa* (Madison, 1966); D. G. Coursey, *The Yam* (London, 1967); William O. Jones, *Manioc in Africa* (Stanford, 1959); Bruce F. Johnston, *The Staple Food Economies of Western Tropical Africa* (Stanford, 1958).

41 I. A. Akinjogbin, *Dahomey and its Neighbours, 1708–1818* (Cambridge, 1967), 64–109; Jan Vansina, *Kingdoms of the Savanna* (Madison, 1966), 194–5, 218–20. See the map of the Angolan slaving frontier in Miller, *Way of Death*, 148.

42 Joseph C. Miller, "The significance of drought, disease and famine in the agriculturally marginal zone of west-central Africa," *Journal of African History*, 22, 1 (1982), 17–61.

In *Way of Death*, Miller presents a vivid picture of the interaction of a host of domestic and external variables to bring about a transformation of Angolan life. While the slave trade was evidently crucial in the transformation, and while social welfare would seem to have been compromised, Miller does not portray either the export of slaves or a decline in regional population as essential results. As he puts it (140–1):

> The violence of the revolution – from a political economy in which kings commanded the respect and occasional material tribute of their subjects to one in which warlords drew strength from imported slave mercenaries and guns and in which indebted patrons, elders, and dependent gentry stocked immigrant slaves against future payments on forced loans from powerful merchant princes – probably drove more western central Africans into hiding in the long run than it exposed to seizure and shipment off to the west. Leaving the sufferings of the enslaved aside for the moment, the demographic significance of the transformation for Africa lay less in aggregate population losses than in profound changes in settlement patterns, epidemiological exposure, and the reproductive capabilities of the populations who remained behind.

43 Paul E. Lovejoy and Stephen Baier, "The desert-side economy of the central Sudan," *International Journal of African Historical Studies*, 7, 4 (1975), 551–81; Charles Becker, "Notes sur les conditions écologiques en Sénégambie aux 17e et 18e siècles," *African Economic History* 14 (1985), 167–216.
44 Higman, *Slave Populations*, 322.
45 Ibid., 338.
46 On mortality in the Atlantic slave trade, see Curtin, *Atlantic Slave Trade*, 275–86; Klein, *Middle Passage*, 73–94; and Eltis, *Transatlantic Slave Trade*, 265–8. On captive mortality within Africa, see Thornton, "Demographic effect," 709; Eltis, *Transatlantic Slave Trade*, 65–6.
47 Philip D. Curtin, "Africans at home and abroad" in Daget, *Actes du colleque*; see also *Death by Migration* (Cambridge, 1990).

4   The quantitative impact of the slave trade, 1700–1900

1 See appendix 2. For more details on the methods and results of the simulation, see Manning and Griffiths, "Divining the unprovable"; Patrick Manning, "The impact of slave trade exports on the population of the Western Coast of Africa, 1700–1850" in Daget, *Actes du colloque*; "Local versus regional impact of slave exports" in Cordell and Gregory, *African Population*, 35–49; and "The impact of slave exports: speculation, debate, methods, evidence," *Annales de Démographie Historique* (1988).

  For previous projections of the demographic impact of slavery on Africa, see Fage, "Slavery and the slave trade"; Anstey, *The Atlantic Slave Trade and British Abolition*, 79–82; David Northrup, *Trade Without Rulers: Pre-Colonial Economic Development in South-Eastern Nigeria* (Oxford, 1978); Thornton, "Demographic effect of the slave trade." See also Eltis, *Transatlantic Slave Trade*, 66–71. Further work is in progress by David Richardson.

  Meanwhile David Henige, invoking highly skeptical or "pyrrhonian" standards of proof, has argued that no global estimate of the volume of the slave trade can be proven correct, that the use of inference in studies of slavery yields little more than a restatement of the analyst's presuppositions, and that only micro-studies can add to our meager stock of knowledge about slavery in Africa. Henige's call for caution is well taken. His proposed abandonment of all but micro-studies, however, amounts to renunciation of many established social science techniques. My analysis in this chapter and elsewhere in this book is intended to show that, though one can rarely hope to prove a given figure for African slavery, one may combine global and local analysis to narrow greatly the estimated range of slavery's impact. Henige would almost have us think that the alternatives in history are true and proven certainty as against unsupported speculation. In fact the documented and testable hypothesis remains the heart of historical analysis for African slavery as elsewhere:

192

Henige, "Measuring the immeasurable: the Atlantic slave trade, West African population and the pyrrhonian critic," *Journal of African History*, 27, 2 (1986), 295–313.

2 Sources include Curtin, *Atlantic Slave Trade*; Lovejoy, "Volume of the Atlantic slave trade"; Austen, "Trans-Saharan slave trade"; Eltis, *Transatlantic Slave Trade*; David Richardson, "Slave exports from West and West-Central Africa, 1700–1810: near estimates of volume and distribution," *Journal of African History* 30 (1989). Since I have used new figures from Eltis and Richardson, my estimates here differ in important details from those I published earlier in "Local versus regional slave exports." For the eighteenth century, the present results show a more serious demographic impact for Upper Guinea, the Bight of Biafra, and Loango, and a less serious impact for the Gold Coast and the Bight of Benin.

3 Population figures are drawn from R. R. Kuczynski, *Demographic Survey of the British Colonial Empire*, 3 vols. (Oxford, 1948), and from French, Belgian, and Portuguese colonial records. See note 8 below.

4 E. A. Wrigley *Population and History* (New York, 1969); E. A. Wrigley and R. S. Schofield, *The Population History of England, 1541–1871* (Cambridge, Mass., 1981), 183–4, 214; Ansley J. Coale and Paul Demeny, *Regional Model Life Tables and Stable Populations* (Princeton, 1966); John C. Caldwell, "The social repercussions of colonial rule: demographic aspects" in UNESCO, *The General History of Africa* (Berkeley, 1985), vol. 7; John Thornton, "An eighteenth-century baptismal register and the demographic history of Manguenzo" in Fyfe and McMaster, *African Historical Demography*, vol. 1, 405–15.

5 On the incidence of enslavement, see Philip D. Curtin, *Economic Change in Precolonial Africa: Senegambia in the Era of the Slave Trade*, 2 vols. (Madison, 1975), vol. 1, 158–68; on captive morality, see Dennis D. Cordell, *Dar al-Kuti and the Last Years of the Trans-Saharan Slave Trade* (Madison, 1985), 109–10; on the partition of slaves into domestic and export slaves, see George Metcalf, "Gold assortments and the trade ounce: Fante merchants and the problem of supply and demand in the 1770s," *Journal of African History*, 28, 1 (1987), 27–41; for a comprehensive assessment of enslavement, see Miller, *Way of Death*, 153–67.

6 Depending on the intensity of enslavement, the slave society population ranged from one-third to two-thirds of the total in each region. The adult sex ratio for the entire region, therefore, is in each case somewhat less than that shown in each graph for the slave society population: African regional sex ratios ranged from one-third to two-thirds those of the slave society.

7 I am grateful to Joseph C. Miller for his repeated reminders of the importance and the variability of the march to the coast as a factor determining captive mortality; I hope my simplified index will help to highlight the magnitude of regional differences. For a riveting description of marches to the coast in Angola, see Miller, *Way of Death*, 3–39.

The variable march to the coast is but one example of factors which could be introduced into a more complex and regionally specific simulation model. Other such factors are regional and temporal variations in fertility, in domestic enslavement, or in age and sex composition of slave exports. I have undertaken such work in a separate study.

8 High and low estimates of regional populations were calculated as follows: beginning with estimates of the 1931 population by region (where regions are defined in text and notes below), the high estimate of the 1870 population was calculated by assuming an annual growth rate of 0.49 percent; the low estimate of the 1870 population was calculated by assuming an annual growth rate of 1.1 percent. Growth rates before 1870 are assumed to be 0.5 percent except as modified by the loss of captives. See appendix 2.

9 Boubacar Barry, "The subordination of power and the mercantile economy: the kingdom of Waalo, 1600–1831" in Rita Cruise O'Brien, ed., *The Political Economy of Underdevelopment: Dependence in Senegal* (Beverly Hills, 1979), 39–63.

10 See figures 4.9, 4.10, and accompanying text. On the ethnic and regional origins of Atlantic

slave exports for Senegambia, see Curtin, *Economic Change*, vol. 1, 177–96. On the slave trade generally in Senegambia and the Western Sudan, see also Richard Roberts, *Warriors, Merchants, and Slaves: The State and the Economy in the Middle Niger Valley, 1700–1914* (Stanford, 1987); E. Ann McDougall, "Camel caravans of the Saharan salt trade: traders and transporters in the nineteenth century" in Catherine Coquery-Vidrovitch and Paul E. Lovejoy, eds., *The Workers of African Trade* (Beverly Hills, 1985), 106–10; and Abdoulaye Bathily, "La Traite atlantique des esclaves et ses effets économiques et sociaux en Afrique: le cas du Galam, royaume de l'hinterland sénégambien au dix-huitième siècle," *Journal of African History*, 27, 2 (1986), 269–93.

11 Simulation results; also Walter Rodney, *A History of the Upper Guinea Coast 1545–1800* (Oxford, 1970), 246–50; and Mamadou Saliou Balde, "L'Esclavage et la guerre sainte au Fuuta-Jalon" in Meillassoux, *L'Esclavage en Afrique*, 183–220. Upper Guinea is taken to include the area of modern Guinea, Guiné-Bissau, Sierra Leone, and Liberia.

12 Ray A. Kea, *Settlements, Trade, and Politics on the Seventeenth-Century Gold Coast* (Baltimore, 1982), 139–66.

13 Ibid., 286; Kwame Yeboa Daaku, *Trade and Politics on the Gold Coast 1600–1720* (Oxford, 1970), 36–7. The Gold Coast is taken to include the area of modern Ghana and the Ivory Coast.

14 Manning, *Slavery, Colonialism, and Economic Growth*, 12, 39–43; Daaku, *Trade and Politics*, 150–2. The Bight of Benin is taken to include the area of modern Togo, Benin, and western Nigeria.

15 Through reliance on New World data on the ethnic distribution of slaves, I have concluded that most slaves from both areas came from within 200km of the coast. Lovejoy and Inikori, arguing the contrary, state that the New World data are biased in favor of coastal origins, but they have little alternative documentation: Lovejoy, *Transformations in Slavery*; J. E. Inikori, "The sources of supply for the Atlantic slave exports from the Bight of Benin and the Bight of Bonny (Biafra)" in Daget, *Actes du colloque*; Manning, *Slavery, Colonialism, and Economic Growth*, 30–3, 335–9. For further examples of New World data on slave ethnicity bearing on this issue, see Higman, *Slave Populations of the British Caribbean*, 443–58; Geggus, "Sex ratio"; and Lovejoy, "Impact of the slave trade."

16 Geggus notes that a larger percentage of Bight of Benin slave exports were women than I had suggested in an earlier publication. The sexual disparity projected here for the Bight of Benin accounts for this modification, by assuming 61 per cent of exports were female: Geggus, "Sex ratio."

17 Law, *The Oyo Empire* 255–77; Manning, *Slavery, Colonialism, and Economic Growth*, 30; Lovejoy, *Transformations in Slavery*.

18 Northrup, *Trade Without Rulers*; Latham, *Old Calabar*. Patterson has argued that there were few slave exports from Cameroon and Gabon until the nineteenth century: K. David Patterson, *The Northern Gabon Coast to 1875* (Oxford, 1975), 32–43. The Bight of Biafra is taken to include the area of eastern Nigeria and colonial British Cameroon.

19 On the method of estimating slave exports from Loango, as distinguished from Angolan slave exports, see Manning, "Local versus regional impact," except that Miller's figures for Angola are now subracted from Richardson's West Central Africa totals rather than from Lovejoy's. Loango is taken to include the areas of Gabon, Gongo, Bas-Zaire, colonial Equateur province (a portion), and the Central African Republic (a portion).

20 Phyllis M. Martin, *The External Trade of the Loango Coast* (Oxford, 1972), 86–7, 136–8; Robert Harms, *River of Wealth, River of Sorrow* (New Haven, 1981); Vansina, *Kingdoms of the Savanna*. This projection of the adult sex ratio tends to confirm John Thornton's analysis of the 1778–9 Portuguese census of Angola, which showed an adult sex ratio of roughly fifty; at the same time, the simulation suggests that such drastic sexual disparity was rare at the regional level: Thornton, "Slave trade in eighteenth century Angola."

21 Miller notes that Kasanje was 600 kilometers and four months from the coast by slave

caravan, and that Lunda was another four or five months further inland. Though many slaves came from Lunda in the nineteenth century, I have taken 600 kilometers as the average march since there were still many enslavements of people who lived closer to the coast: Miller, *Way of Death*, 192; Thornton, "Slave trade in eighteenth century Angola."

22 The total Occidental trade (fig. 4.19) exceeds that of the Western Coast by the number of slaves sent to the Occident from the Eastern Coast. For estimates of the free and slave black populations of New World territories at the end of the eighteenth century, see Klein, *African Slavery in Latin America*, 295–6; also Robin Blackburn, *The Overthrow of Colonial Slavery, 1776–1848* (London, 1988).

23 For the high estimate of the 1850 population, the estimated 1931 population is projected back to 1890 at an annual growth rate of 0.1 percent; for the low estimate, the 1931 population is projected back to 1890 at a rate of 1.6 percent. Growth rates before 1890 are assumed to be 0.5 percent except as modified by the loss of captives. For comparison, see note 6 above and appendix 2.

24 For excellent studies of warfare and slavery in this region, see Meillassoux, *Anthropologie de l'esclavage*; Roberts, *Warriors, Merchants, and Slaves*; and David Robinson, *The Holy War of Umar Tal* (Oxford, 1985).

25 Lovejoy, *Transformations in Slavery*, 154–7; LaRue, "Export trade"; François Renault, "La Traite des esclaves noirs en Libye au XVIIIe siècle," *Journal of African History*, 23, 2 (1982), 163–81. The Central Sudan is taken to include the area of colonial northern Nigeria, Niger, Chad, and part of the Central African Republic.

26 The Eastern Sudan is taken to be the area of the modern Sudan republic. For an excellent overview of the slave trade in the region, see Janet Ewald, "The Nile Valley system and the Red Sea slave trade, 1820–1900" (paper presented at the African Studies Association Meeting, Chicago, October 1988). I am grateful to Prof. Ewald for permission to read and cite this paper. See also Toledano, *The Ottoman Slave Trade*, 15–49; LaRue, "Export trade"; Terence Walz, "The trade between Egypt and Bilad As-Sudan, 1700–1850" (Ph.D. dissertation, Boston University, 1975); O'Fahey, "Slavery and slave trade"; Austen, "Trans-Saharan slave trade." Fisher and Fisher, among others, suggest that the Russian occupation of Georgia and the Caucasus, during the late eighteenth and early nineteenth centuries, closed an established source of slaves for the Middle East, and brought higher demand for African slaves: Fisher and Fisher, *Slavery and Muslim Society*, 1.

27 Abir, "Ethiopian slave trade." The Horn is taken to include the area of modern Ethiopia, Somalia, and Djibouti.

28 Eltis, *Transatlantic Slave Trade*, 177–80; Alpers, *Ivory and Slaves*; Isaacman, *Mozambique*; Gill Shepherd, "The Comorians and the East African slave trade" in Watson, *Asian and African Systems of Slavery*, 73–99; Gwyn Campbell, "The East African slave trade, 1861–1895: the 'Southern' complex", *International Journal of African Historical Studies 22*, 1 (1989), 25. Mozambique is taken to include the area of modern Mozambique and Malawi.

29 Sheriff, *Slaves, Spices and Ivory*, 41–73. Tanzania is taken to include the area of modern Kenya and Tanzania (including Zanzibar).

30 Gwyn Campbell estimates Merina exports of 2,000 slaves in 1800, falling to 500 per year until 1820; for the 1870s he notes estimated imports of between 6,000 and 10,000 annually to western Madagascar from Mozambique: Campbell, "The Adoption of Autarky in imperial Madagascar, 1820–1835," *Journal of African History*, 28, 3 (1987), 399–400; "Madagascar and the slave trade," 217; Hubert Gerbeau, "Fabulée, fabuleuse: la traite des noirs à Bourbon au XIXe siècle" in Daget, *De la Traite à l'esclavage*, 2: 467–86.

31 Figure 4.21 thus differs from figures 4.19 and 4.20 in that it is based on estimated population of all of tropical Africa rather than the areas drawn on by the Occidental and Oriental trades.

32 The discussion in the above two paragraphs is based on the following calculations. First, the 1700 populations for each zone (as projected by the simulation) are given in column (a).

Second, in column (b) is given the estimated 1850 population from which the 1700 population was projected. The remaining two columns show the size to which the 1700 population would have grown by 1850 if compounded (c) at an annual growth rate of five per thousand, and (d) at a growth rate of three per thousand. Two comparisons are given, first for the low estimate of the 1700 population (projected back from the low estimate of the 1850 population), and second for the high estimate of the 1700 population (projected back from the high estimate of the 1850 population). Figures given in the text are an average of high and low figures.

Low population estimates

	(a) 1700 pop. (simulation)	(b) 1850 pop. (simulation)	(c) 1850 pop. (0.5 percent growth from 1700)	(d) 1850 pop. (0.3 percent growth from 1700)
Zone				
Western Coast	21.5	16	45.2	33.8
Savanna	15	20	31.5	23.6
Eastern Coast	3.2	4.5	6.7	5.0
Total	39.7	40.5	83.4	62.4

High population estimates

	(a) 1700 pop. (simulation)	(b) 1850 pop. (simulation)	(c) 1850 pop. (0.5 percent growth from 1700)	(d) 1850 pop. (0.3 percent growth from 1700)
Zone				
Western Coast	25	23	52.5	39.3
Savanna	20	32	42	31.4
Eastern Coast	4.5	7.5	9.5	7.1
Total	49.5	62.5	104	77.8

33 Not all African regions grew in the late nineteenth century. North Central Africa, in particular, failed to grow in population until well into the twentieth century.

5 The economics and morality of slave supply

1 Thomas Robert Malthus, *Population: The First Essay* (Ann Arbor, 1959; first published 1798), 19–21, 109–10. Malthus did not discuss Africa or slavery in his first essay. For his later discussion of these topics see Malthus, *An Essay on the Principle of Population*, 2nd edn (London, 1803), 102–16. Elsewhere in his later work, Malthus states his opposition to the slave trade. See B. W. Higman, "Slavery and the development of demographic theory in the age of the industrial revolution" in James Walvin, ed., *Slavery and British Society 1776–1846* (Baton Rouge, 1982), 164–94.

2 Crosby, *Columbian Exchange*; Curtin, "Epidemiology and the slave trade."

3 Emmanuel Karl, *Traditions orales au Dahomey – Bénin* (Niamey, 1974).

4 For instances of resistance to slavery in the nineteenth-century Sokoto Caliphate, including millennial movements, see Paul E. Lovejoy, "Problems of slave control in the Sokoto Caliphate" in Lovejoy, *Africans in Bondage*, 244–64; see also Miller, *Way of Death*, 38, 129.

5 Cooper, *Plantation Slavery*, 215–28; K. Nwachukwu-Ogedengbe, "Slavery in nineteenth-century Aboh (Nigeria)" in Miers and Kopytoff, *Slavery in Africa*, 143–7.

6 Miller, *Way of Death*, 106; Curtin, *Atlantic Slave Trade*, 28–30; Meillassoux, *Anthropologie de l'esclavage*, 79–85; Austen, "Trans-Saharan slave trade." The outstanding exception to naturally declining slave populations was that of the south of the United States, where slave populations became self-sustaining from the early eighteenth century.

7 John Thornton, "The military operations of the slave trade in Angola, 1600–1670: the social, economic and demographic impact" (unpublished paper Montreal, 1985). Of 142 slaves drawn from all over Western Africa and interviewed in Sierra Leone by S. W. Koelle in 1850, 34 percent said they had been enslaved in war, 30 percent said they had been kidnapped, 7 percent said they were sold by relatives or superiors, 7 percent were sold to pay debts, and 11 percent admitted to having been condemned by judicial process. (Hair, in summarizing Koelle's data, did not report the cause of enslavement for the remaining 11 percent.) P. E. H. Hair, "The enslavement of Keolle's informants," *Journal of African History*, 6, 2 (1965), 193–203.

8 Gustav Nachtigal, *Sahara and Sudan*, ed. and trans. Allan G. B. Fisher and Humphrey J. Fisher, 4 vols (London, 1971). This section is from vol. 3, which still awaits publication. See also Jan S. Hogendorn, "Slave acquisition and delivery in precolonial Hausaland" in B. K. Swartz, Jr., and Raymond E. Dumett, eds., *West African Culture Dynamics* (The Hague, 1980), 477–93.

9 Davidson, *Black Mother*.

10 G. I. Jones, "Olaudah Equiano of the Niger Ibo" in Philip D. Curtin, ed., *Africa Remembered* (Madison, 1962), 85–7; Northrup, *Trade Without Rulers*, 69–73, 75–6.

11 Vansina, *Kingdoms of the Savanna*.

12 Austen, "Trans-Saharan slave trade," 31; Law, *The Oyo Empire*, 226.

13 Wyatt MacGaffey, "Economic and social dimensions of Kongo slavery" in Miers and Kopytoff, *Slavery in Africa*, 247; Joseph C. Miller, personal communication.

14 Cooper, *Plantation Slavery*, 126–7; Miller, "Significance of drought"; Becker, "Conditions écologiques'; Lovejoy and Baier, 'Desert-side economy."

15 G. Prunier, personal communication.

16 Meillassoux, *Anthropologie de l'esclavage*, 100. Miller notes that the sheer incapacitation of the captives in transit was one of the means of their subordination to masters: Miller, *Way of Death*, 380–1.

17 The Kongo merchants operating from Cabinda were seen as suffering from affliction because of the anomaly of the commitment to material wealth in slaves and imported goods, in contrast to their agricultural kin. They joined in the *lemba* cult to provide therapy for their affliction. Miller, *Way of Death*, 202. See also Curtin, "The African diaspora," 15–16.

18 Robin Law, "Royal monopoly and private enterprise in the Atlantic trade: the case of Dahomey," *Journal of African History*, 18, 4 (1977), 555–77.

19 Alpers, *Ivory and Slaves*, 229–33.

20 In a quite different approach to explaining the economic logic of supplying slaves, Joseph Miller has drawn out the institutional differences between the mercantilistic economy of the Atlantic and African political economies. The latter, for the case of Angola, were based on use-value economies and "respect" (or symbolic tribute) for one's superiors. The market-places, in Miller's ingenious metaphor, act as semipermeable membranes, allowing slaves and import goods to pass through, but keeping institutions and values distinct: Miller, *Way of Death*, 43–57, 175.

21 Tambo, "Sokoto Caliphate slave trade"; Terray, "Réflexions sur la formation du prix des esclaves."

22 For cases of export slave prices recorded in cash, see Miller, "Slave prices in the Portuguese southern Atlantic," 58; and Sheriff, *Slaves, Spices and Ivory*, 68–9.

23 Marion Johnson, "The ounce in eighteenth-century West African Trade," *Journal of African History*, 7, 2 (1966), 197–214; Miller, *Way of Death*, 299–301.

24 Prices calculated by Bean, LeVeen, Curtin, and Eltis are all based on prime cost.

25 For prices based on prime cost plus transport cost of import goods, see Manning, *Slavery, Colonialism, and Economic Growth*, 332–4; these prices are also reported in Patrick Manning, "Contours of slavery and social change in Africa," *American Historical Review*, 88, 4 (1983), 840; and in Lovejoy, *Transformations in Slavery*, 138. These are c.i.f. (cost, insurance, freight) costs in Africa. They are shown as "Manning, c.i.f." prices in figure 1.2.

Discussion in the text to follow is based on cost plus transport (c.i.f.) for African imports exchanged against slaves, rather than on prime cost (f.o.b.); prices are also standardized to the values of the 1780s. David Eltis has recently emphasized the severe difficulties in estimating a dependable series of c.i.f. prices for African slaves, and he had also noted the difficulty of developing constant-price (rather than current-price) series. Nevertheless, c.i.f. prices – the value of slaves as sold on the African coast, or the cost of the imports (including transport costs) exchanged against slaves – are the relevant figures for evaluating the real costs and benefits of the slave trade to Africans, so I have presented such a series despite the margin of error it entails. Similarly, values of slaves evaluated at constant prices are the relevant measure for comparisons of the slave trade over time, so I have deflated current values by a rough index of British wholesale prices. This procedure doubtless introduces some new errors, but it presents a much more sensible picture of the slave trade in the era of the Napoleonic wars, with its great price fluctuations, than does an approach based on unadjusted figures. David Eltis, "Trade between Western Africa and the Atlantic World before 1870: estimates of trends in value, composition and direction," *Research in Economic History*, 8 (1988); see also appendix 1.

26 One may distinguish, therefore, between "prime cost per average slave' and 'prime cost per prime male" – Bean estimated the latter to have been generally higher by some 19 percent: Bean, *British Trans-Atlantic Slave Trade*, 132–6.

27 English wholesale prices in 1780 were roughly equal to their average for the period from 1680 to 1910. Slave prices in African regions no longer exporting slaves were presumably lower, since Atlantic demand no longer held prices up. For sixteenth-century slave prices, see Lobo Cabrera, *La Esclavitud en las Canarias Orientales*, 386–98.

28 Richard Bean, "A note on the relative importance of slaves and gold in West African exports," *Journal of African History*, 15, 3 (1974), 351–6.

29 Thomas and Bean, "The fishers of men"; Bean, *British Trans-Atlantic Slave Trade*, 58, 86–7.

30 Curtin, *Economic Change*, vol. 1, 156–7; LeVeen, *British Slave Trade Suppression Policies*. Curtin's estimates of slave prices in Senegambia differ significantly from Bean's overall average and even from Bean's estimates for Senegambia. This result tends to undermine the Bean and Thomas view of the uniformity and efficiency of the market.

31 Bean, *British Trans-Atlantic Slave Trade*, 73–5. Other calculations of supply elasticity may be found in Curtin, *Economic Change*; Manning, *Slavery, Colonialism and Economic Growth*, 37–42; Eltis, *Transatlantic Slave Trade*; and in forthcoming work by David Richardson.

32 After 1800, the supply schedule for the Bight of Benin shifted outward, as the Yoruba wars brought increasing numbers of slave exports at any given price. Manning, *Slavery, Colonialism and Economic Growth*, 37–8, 42.

33 I noted this point in earlier work ("Enslavement of Africans," 522; "Contours of slavery," 847). David Geggus, in an important new article, has provided full confirmation of this relationship. He includes in his analysis not only distance, but ethnic identity, descent system, the sexual division of labor, and the mode of capture: Geggus, "Sex ratio, age, and ethnicity."

34 Ibid.; Lovejoy, "Impact of the slave trade"; Manning, "Enslavement of Africans," 517; Curtin, *Economic Change*, 179; Northrup, *Trade Without Rulers*, 239.

35 Manning, "Enslavement of Africans," 522.
36 Eltis, *Economic Growth*, 256–8; Geggus, "Sex ratio, age, and ethnicity"; Lovejoy, "Impact of the slave trade." To phrase the African side of this reasoning in other terms, we may assert that African purchasers of slaves had an inelastic demand schedule for child slaves, but an elastic demand schedule for adult slaves. My thanks to Claudia Goldin for advice on this point.
37 Felix Iroko, "Cauris et esclaves en Afrique occidentale entre les XVIe et XIXe siècles" in Daget, *De la Traite à l'esclavage* 1: 193–204.
38 David Eltis and Lawrence C. Jennings, "Trade between western Africa and the Atlantic world in the pre-colonial era," *American Historical Review*, 93, 4 (1988), 936–59.
39 Paul E. Lovejoy, "Interregional monetary flows in the precolonial trade of Nigeria," *Journal of African History*, 15, 4 (1974), 563–85; Miller, *Way of Death*, 80–1, 180–3; Harms, *River of Wealth*, 85–92; Jan S. Hogendorn and Henry A. Gemery, "Abolition and its impact on monies imported to West Africa" in Eltis and Walvin, *Abolition*, 99–115; Manning, *Slavery, Colonialism and Economic Growth*, 44; Eltis, *Transatlantic Slave Trade*.
40 Jan Hogendorn and Marion Johnson, *The Shell Money of the Slave Trade* (Cambridge, 1986). The estimate of an aggregate £2 million in cowries by 1800 is my own, based on assumed rates of replacement of lost and broken cowries.
41 It should be emphasized that African moneys – whether gold, cowries, or cloth – were general purpose moneys usable in a wide range of transactions. For a contrary view, once influential, see Paul Bohannan, "Some principles of exchange and investment among the Tiv," *American Anthropologist*, 57 (1955), 60–70. For an analysis spanning both mercantile generality and institutional specificity, see Miller, *Way of Death*, 173–88.
42 Hogendorn and Gemery, "Abolition and its impact on monies," 101–3.
43 Harms, *River of Wealth*, 37–9; Dalzel, *History of Dahomy*.
44 Meillassoux, *L'Esclavage en Afrique*.
45 On the Cairo market, Wakalat al-Jallaba, see Terence Walz, "Black slavery in Egypt during the nineteenth century as reflected in the Mahkama archives of Cairo" in Wallis, *Slaves and Slavery*, vol. 2, 137–9. For a detailed description of the Salaga market in Ghana at the end of its days, see Marion Johnson, "The slaves of Salaga," *Journal of African History*, 27, 2 (1986), 341–62. See also Miller, *Way of Death*, 189; Toledano, *Ottoman Slave Trade*, 51–3.
46 Antecedents for this world market for slave labor existed, one could argue, in the medieval and even the ancient Mediterranean; the medieval market extended to the African Savanna, to the Black Sea, and to the Baltic and North Seas. C. Verlinden, "Précédents et parallèles européens de l'esclavage colonial," *O Instituto de Coimbra*, 113 (1949), 1–41; Finley, *Slavery in Classical Antiquity*.
47 Renault, "La Traite des esclaves noirs en Libye."
48 Cooper, *Plantation Slavery*; Sheriff, *Slaves, Spices and Ivory*.
49 For instance, a surplus of captives resulting from warfare might keep prices low in a region for some years; failure of slave ships to arrive in Africa would depress prices; failure of slave ships to arrive in America would raise prices there.
50 Stanley Engerman estimates a total of 2.4 million intercontinental contract labor migrants from 1838 to 1939; of these, 1.6 million were from India and 300,000 from China: Engerman, "Contract labor, sugar, and technology in the nineteenth century," *Journal of Economic History*, 43, 3 (1983), 642–8, and literature cited therein. Larger numbers of Indian and Chinese migrants moved voluntarily within Asia in the same period. See Latham, *The International Economy and the Undeveloped World*, 106–16; Kingsley Davis, *The Population of India and Pakistan* (Princeton, 1951), 98–106; Monica Schuler, *"Alas, Alas, Kongo": A Social History of Indentured African Immigration into Jamaica* (Baltimore, 1980).
51 Engerman, "Contract labor," 642. For the continuation of such labor contracting into the twentieth century, see I. K. Sundiata, *Black Scandal: America and the Liberian Labor Crisis, 1929–1936* (Philadelphia, 1980).

52 Brinley Thomas, *Migration and Economic Growth: A Study of Great Britain and the Atlantic Economy*, 2nd edn (Cambridge, 1973); Davis, *Population of India and Pakistan*.

53 To these effects of slave emigration from Africa must be added the migration of slaves within Africa, and the attendant additional mortality. This internal migration was, in a sense, analogous to the rural-urban migration of industrializing Europe.

54 Eltis, *Transatlantic Slave Trade*.

55 J. Forbes Munro, *Africa and the International Economy 1800–1960* (London, 1976), 38, 62–3, 84.

56 Lovejoy, "The characteristics of plantations"; Sheriff, *Slaves, Spices and Ivory*, 101–10; Vansina, *Kingdoms of the Savanna*; Patrick Harries, "Slavery, social incorporation and surplus extraction: the nature of free and unfree labor in south-east Africa," *Journal of African History*, 22 (1981).

57 It is worth recalling the assumptions of the competitive model of markets: a homogeneous product, fully informed buyers and sellers, no barriers to entry, and no market power for either buyers or sellers. Most of these conditions did not hold in the African slave market. Bean and Thomas, despite their argument that the Atlantic trade was competitive, recognized that monopoly power might be significant on the African mainland: Bean and Thomas, "The fishers of men."

58 Curtin, "The African diaspora," 15–16; Manning, "Contours of slavery," 853–4. On the irregular supplies of slaves recruited through warfare, see Ivor Wilks, *Asante in the Nineteenth Century: The Structure and Evolution of a Political Order* (Cambridge, 1975), 177.

59 Since the slave merchants and the planters were often the same men, they were able to respond to the new economic pressures with relatively conscious choices.

60 Cooper, *Plantation Slavery*.

61 Mortality declined in many tropical areas during the later nineteenth century, for reasons not yet fully understood.

62 Mason, "Captive and client labour"; Cooper, *Plantation Slavery*, 218–25; Latham, *Old Calabar*.

63 On growth in African markets for slave produce, see Lovejoy, *Transformations in Slavery*, 184–219; Roberts, *Warriors, Merchants, and Slaves*.

64 Tambo, "Sokoto Caliphate slave trade," 187–217; Terray, "Réflexions sur la formation du prix"; Eltis, *Transatlantic Slave Trade*, 260–4; Sheriff, *Slaves, Spices and Ivory*, 68–9.

65 Among adult slaves, 60 percent in his sample were female: Klein, "Demography of slavery," 57–8.

6 Patterns of slave life

1 Jones, "Olaudah Equiano."

2 Mettas, *Répertoire*, vol. 1, 165, 167, 260, 277; vol. 2, 257.

3 Pruneau's description is given in Becker, *Mémoire sur le Commerce*, 95; see also Akinjogbin, *Dahomey and its Neighbours*, 87–8.

4 George Brooks, "A Nhara of the Guinea-Bissau region: Mãe Aurelia Correia" in Robertson and Klein, *Women and Slavery in Africa*, 295–319.

5 Pierre Verger, "Le Culte des vodoun d'Abomey aurait-il été apporté à St.-Louis de Maranhon par la mère du roi Ghézo?" *Etudes Dahoméennes*, 8 (1952), 19–24; Judith Gleason, *Agôtîme, Her Legend* (New York, 1970).

6 Nachtigal, *Sahara and Sudan*, vol. 3 (forthcoming).

7 Livingstone, *Last Journals*, vol. 1, 61–2.

8 Edward A. Alpers, "The story of Swema: female vulnerability in nineteenth-century East Africa" in Robertson and Klein, *Women and Slavery in Africa*, 185–219.

9 A. F. C. Ryder has noted that the Edo kingdom of Benin, long treated with respect by

Europeans as a center of African civilization, came from the 1850s to be treated by English writers as a center of barbarity and human sacrifice. Much of this was a simple change in European fashion. On the other hand, the level of human sacrifice seems clearly to have increased in nineteenth-century Benin: Ryder, *Benin and the Europeans 1485–1897* (New York, 1969), 247–51.

10 K. O. Dike, *Trade and Politics in the Niger Delta, 1830–1885* (Oxford, 1954); W. I. Ofonagoro, "Notes on the ancestry of Mbanaso Okwaraozurumba otherwise known as King Jaja of Opobo, 1821–1891," *Journal of the Historical Society of Nigeria*, 9, 3 (1978), 145–56.

11 Claire C. Robertson, "Post-proclamation slavery in Accra: a female affair?" in Robertson and Klein, *Women and Slavery in Africa*, 230–45; Mary F. Smith, *Baba of Karo: A Woman of the Moslem Hausa* (New York, 1955).

12 Patterson, *Slavery and Social Death*.

13 Rattray, *Ashanti Law and Constitution*, 33–46; Robert Harms, "Sustaining the system: trading towns along the Middle Zaire" in Robertson and Klein, *Women and Slavery in Africa*, 105–8.

14 Stanley L. Engerman, "Some economic and demographic comparisons of slavery in the United States and the British West Indies," *Economic History Review*, 29, 2 (1976), 269. In contrast, Perrot reports that in the Akan kingdom of Ndenye, nursing infants were not counted in the prices of their mothers; they were said to be *nvlaswe* or below the market in value: Claude-Hélène Perrot "Les Captifs dans le royaume anyi du Ndenye" in Meillassoux, *L'Esclavage en Afrique*, 365.

15 Meillassoux, *Anthropologie de l'esclavage*.

16 Nachtigal, *Sahara and Sudan*.

17 Lovejoy, "Problems of slave control"; Jan S. Hogendorn, "The economics of slave use on two 'plantations' in the Zaria emirate of the Sokoto Caliphate," *International Journal of African Historical Studies*, 10, 3 (1977), 369–83.

18 On seasoning, see Meillassoux, *Anthropologie de l'esclavage*, 99–116; for an outstanding case of a rebellious slave woman, see Marcia Wright, "Bwanikwa: consciousness and protest among slave women in Central Africa, 1886–1911" in Robertson and Klein, *Women and Slavery in Africa*, 246–67.

19 Meillassoux, *Anthropologie de l'esclavage*, 228. In Muslim Mombasa, however, puberty rites for non-Muslim slave girls served to sustain a slave subculture: Margaret Strobel, "Slavery and reproductive labor in Mombasa" in Robertson and Klein, *Women and Slavery in Africa*, 122–4.

20 Richard Roberts, "Women's work and women's property: household social relations in the Maraka textile industry of the nineteenth century," *Comparative Studies in Society and History*, 26, 2 (1984); Hélène d'Almeida-Topor, *Les Amazones* (Paris, 1984); Edna G. Bay, "Servitude and worldly success in the palace of Dahomey" in Robertson and Klein, *Women and Slavery in Africa*, 340–67.

21 A. G. Hopkins, "Economic imperialism in West Africa: Lagos, 1880–92," *Economic History Review*, 21, 4 (1968), 580–606; Latham, *Old Calabar*, 91–6; George Brooks, "Peanuts and colonialism: consequences of the commercialization of peanuts in West Africa, 1830–70," *Journal of African History*, 16 (1975), 49–50; David Birmingham, "The coffee barons of Cazengo," *Journal of African History*, 19, 4 (1978), 525–31.

22 Nadel, *A Black Byzantium*; Law, *The Oyo Empire*, 68–9.

23 Claude Meillassoux, "Female slavery" in Robertson and Klein, *Women and Slavery in Africa*, 49–66; *Anthropologie de l'esclavage*, 110–14.

24 Hunwick, "Notes on slavery in Songhay," 21–2; Bay, "Servitude and worldly success," 342, 344–7.

25 Patrick Manning, "Slave trade, 'legitimate' trade, and imperialism revisited: the control of wealth in the Bights of Benin and Biafra" in Lovejoy, *Africans in Bondage*, 222–3.

26 Richard S. Dunn, "'Dreadful idlers' in the cane fields: the slave labor pattern on a Jamaican sugar estate, 1762–1831" in Solow and Engerman, *British Capitalism and Caribbean Slavery*, 163–90. Gabriel Debien, *Les Esclaves aux Antilles françaises (XVIIe–XVIIIe siècles)* (Basse-Terre and Fort-de-France, 1974), 363–6; Harms, "Sustaining the system," 106; Latham, *Old Calabar*.

27 Le Herissé, *L'Ancien Royaume du Dahomey*, 182–94; Ryder, *Benin and the Europeans*, 247–51. For a fictional account of the impact of human sacrifice on family life, see Buchi Emecheta, *The Joys of Motherhood* (New York, 1979).

28 Victor Uchendu, "Slaves and slavery in Igboland, Nigeria" in Miers and Kopytoff, *Slavery in Africa*, 129–31; Lovejoy, "Problems of slave control," 256–62.

29 Georges-Edouard Bourgoignie, *Les Hommes de l'eau: ethno-écologie du Dahomey lacustre* (Paris, 1972). The marriage of slaves differed from that of free persons in another respect: where marriage of free Africans usually took the form of alliances among families, slaves by definition had no family. Slave marriages were simply unions of individuals, with no social sanction. The children of such unions belonged to the free partner or to the master.

30 I am indebted to Joseph Miller for clarifications on this issue. For a case of subversion of a matrilineal system, see E. A. Alpers, "Trade, state, and society among the Yao in the nineteenth century," *Journal of African History*, 10, 3 (1969), 405–20. Bilateral families, in which all relatives are counted as kin, lack the corporate structure and chiefs of matrilineages and patrilineages. For the development of bilateral kinship under the influence of slavery, see Wyatt MacGaffey, "Lineage structure, marriage, and the family amongst the central Bantu," *Journal of African History*, 24 (1983), 184. Wilks notes that in Asante, a matrilineal society, slaves mostly remained unmarried – this may refer in particular to male slaves: Wilks, *Asante*, 137.

31 Curtis A. Keim, "Women in slavery among the Mangbetu c. 1800–1910" in Robertson and Klein, *Women and Slavery in Africa*, 146–8; Uchendu, "Slaves and slavery," 126. Historians and anthropologists have paid far less attention to the effect of slavery on patrilineal than on matrilineal descent systems.

32 The dominance of females among slave exports from the Savanna provides presumptive evidence that males dominated the remaining population, and suggests that there may have been concentrations of male slaves. The direct evidence on the sex ratio of the Savanna and desert edge slave populations is, at this point, ambiguous.

33 Lovejoy, "Problems of slave control," 241–3. Polly Hill, in contrast, questions whether it is appropriate to label as slaves those servile workers living in separate villages without daily supervision: Hill, "Comparative West African farm-slavery systems" in Willis, *Slaves and Slavery*, Vol. 2, 33–50.

34 Meillassoux, "Etat et condition des esclaves à Gumbu (Mali) au XIXe siècle" in Meillassoux, *L'Esclavage en Afrique*, 230.

35 Lovejoy, *Transformations in Slavery*, 269; Emmanuel Terray, "Long-distance exchange and the formation of the state: the case of the Abron kingdom of Gyaman," *Economy and Society*, 3 (1974), 315–45; "Class and class consciousness in the Abron kingdom of Gyaman" in Maurice Bloch, ed., *Marxist Analyses and Social Anthropology* (London, 1975), 85–136.

36 Orlando Patterson, while asserting that the society of ancient Greece, for instance, was based on slavery, argues that "slavery never constitutes a distinct mode of production but that it can be used to create and support a new mode." That is, "most attempts to define a slave mode of production really amount to efforts to build a model from the observed process of articulation of a quasi-capitalistic sector into a pre-capitalist formation." Indeed, it is suggestive to consider the nineteenth-century expansion of slavery as the development of a precolonial, "quasi-capitalistic sector" in African economies. Nonetheless, I find that analysis in terms of a slave mode of production is more helpful in specifying Africa's position in the world economy than avoidance of the term: Patterson, "On slavery and slave formations," *New Left Review*, 117 (1979), 48–61.

37 Meillassoux, *Anthropologie de l'esclavage*; Cooper, *Plantation Slavery*; Yves Person, *Samori, une révolution dyula*, 3 vols. (Dakar, 1968–75). In contrast to Meillassoux's conditions is the case of slavery without the slave trade, following the abolition of the slave trade. Such slave systems, as in nineteenth-century United States or in twentieth-century Africa, operated by different rules.

38 Meillassoux, *Anthropologie de l'esclavage*, 163–4.

39 Meillassoux contrasted the number of slaves and of serfs necessary to support 100 free persons, basing his calculations on assumed rates of production and consumption of millet, and assuming that serfs had children to feed while slaves did not; he concluded that forty-three adult slaves could support 100 free persons, and that sixty-one adult serfs (or a total serf population of 122) would be required to support 100 free persons. Ibid., 96–8, 265–9.

40 Brooks, "Peanuts and colonialism." Similarly, the concentration of numerous slaves on the plantations of Zanzibar and the Swahili coast can be seen as the rise of a slave class. Cooper, however, argues that slaves were "unable to coalesce as a class or to confront their masters collectively": *Plantation Slavery*, 266.

41 Ibid., 221–3; Lovejoy, "Characteristics of plantations," 1269, 1290–2.

42 Miller, *Way of Death*, 4–5.

43 Lovejoy, *Ideology of Slavery*; Willis, *Slaves and Slavery*, vol. 1.

44 The case of the Samo of Burkina Faso is instructive: this people held no slaves, yet elders and others sold people in return for cowries: François Héritier, "Des Cauris et des hommes: production des esclaves et accumulation de cauris chez les Samo (Haute Volta)" in Meillassoux, *L'Esclavage en Afrique*, 499–504.

45 Equiano described the slaves carried through his village in the time before he was enslaved: Jones, "Olaudah Equiano," 75.

46 Some of these same areas, on the other hand, converted to Islam as a response to having undergone slave raiding: Cordell, *Dar al-Kuti*; Nehemia Levtzion, "Slavery and Islamization in Africa." Willis, *Slaves and Slavery*, vol. 2.

47 For a case of the strengthening of patriarchy in the context of broader social change associated with slavery, see Susan Herlin Broadhead, "Slave wives, Free sisters: Bakongo women and slavery c. 1700–1850" in Robertson and Klein, *Women and Slavery in Africa*, 160–81. Most of the other articles in that volume demonstrate either explicitly or implicitly the reinforcement of patriarchy through slavery. See also Meillassoux, *Anthropologie de l'esclavage*, 10.

48 Two extraordinary cases from Ouidah were those of Francisco Felix de Souza and Domingo Martins: David A. Ross, "The career of Domingo Martinez in the Bight of Benin, 1833–1864," *Journal of African History*, 6, 1 (1965), 79–90.

49 The historical threads out of which have been woven today's problems of corruption in Africa are perhaps best treated in fictional writing. For instance, the novels of Chinua Achebe, from *Things Fall Apart* (New York, 1959) to *Anthills of the Savanna* (New York, 1988), touch frequently on this theme.

50 Harms *River of Wealth*, 197–215. Harms has developed this theme in greater detail in a further study: *Games against nature: An Eco-Cultural History of the Nunu of Equatorial Africa* (Cambridge, 1987).

7 Transformations of slavery and society, 1650–1900

1 Kopytoff and Miers, "African 'Slavery'".

2 Manning, *Slavery, Colonialism, and Economic Growth*, 4; Eltis, *Transatlantic Slave Trade*, 72–3.

3 This categorization of explanations of social change is inspired by Hugh Kerney's division of scientific theories of causation into the organic, magical, and mechanistic: *Science and Change 1500–1700* (New York, 1971), 17–48.

4 See Chapter 2 above; Alan W. Fisher, "Moscovy and the Black Sea Slave Trade," *Canadian-American Slavic Studies*, 6, 4 (1972), 575–94.
5 Olivier de Sardan, "Captifs ruraux et esclaves impériaux"; Abir, "Ethopian slave trade"; Meillassoux, "Role of slavery."
6 On aristocratic and mercantile slavery, see chapter 6.
7 Raymond Dumett, "Precolonial gold-mining and the state in the Akan region: with a critique of the Terray hypothesis," *Research in Economic Anthropology*, 2 (1979), 37–68; Emmanuel Terray, "Gold production, slave labor, and state intervention in precolonial Akan societies," *Research in Economic Anthropology* 5 (1983), 885–914.
8 Vansina, *Kingdoms of the Savanna*, 124–52.
9 Parry, *The Age of Reconnaissance*.
10 See fig. 1.1 and appendix 1.
11 Kea, *Settlements, Trade and Politics*, 164–6, 286; Akinjogbin, *Dahomey and its Neighbours*, 39.
12 See above, chapter 5.
13 See above, chapter 4.
14 Bean's f.o.b. prices exclude the high cost of transporting, from Europe to Africa, the goods exchanged for slaves, and thus underestimate the real African value of slave exports. Including transportation costs, the equivalent c.i.f. prices rose from roughly £6 in 1690 to £25 in 1740. David Richardson's price estimates (forthcoming) show a slower price increase, thus revising the quantitative but not the qualitative conclusion proposed here. For estimates of British per capita income see Phyllis Deane and W. A. Cole, *British Economic Growth 1688–1959*, 2nd edn. (Cambridge, 1967), 6, 78, 282. See also appendix 1 and Manning, *Slavery, Colonialism, and Economic Growth*, 334.
15 Eltis, "Trade between Western Africa and the Atlantic world"; Hogendorn and Johnson, *Shell Money*; J. E. Inikori, "The import of firearms into West Africa, 1750–1897: a quantitative analysis," *Journal of African History*, 18, 3 (1977), 339–68.
16 Udry, "Akan transitional zone."
17 These growing distinctions – between what may be called court and communitarian traditions – as accentuated by the slave trade, are discussed for West African art in Patrick Manning, "Primitive art and modern times," *Radical History Review*, 33 (1985), 173–7.
18 For a general and thought-provoking investigation into the social effects of low male-to-female sex ratios, see Marcia Guttentag and Paul F. Secord, *Too Many Women? The Sex Ratio Question* (Beverly Hills, 1983). For a general source on sexual division of labor in Africa, see G. P. Murdock, *Africa, its Peoples and its Culture History* (New York, 1959).
  Ester Boserup, in a well-known analysis of women's agricultural work in the twentieth century, reproduces a map of male and female farming in Africa first drawn by Baumann in 1930, and notes that female farming (by far the dominant pattern in Africa) correlated with areas of relatively low population density. Boserup, *Woman's Role in Economic Development* (London, 1970), 18.
19 Joseph C. Miller, *Kings and Kinsmen: Early Mbundu States in Angola* (Oxford, 1976), 195–203; Akinjogbin, *Dahomey and its Neighbours*, 39–67.
20 Daaku, *Trade and Politics*, 96–114.
21 Ibid., 36–7.
22 Kea, *Settlements, Trade and Politics*, 286; Ryder, *Benin and the Europeans*, 65.
23 See above, chapter 4.
24 Northrup, *Trade without Rulers*; Martin, *External Trade*, 136–8; Harms, *River of Wealth*, 24–38; Miller, *Way of Death*, 145–6.
25 Balde, "L'Esclavage et la guerre sainte"; Law, *Oyo Empire*, 227; Manning, *Slavery, Colonialism, and Economic Growth*, 30–3.
26 The cumulative total of cowrie imports increased by over a factor of ten from 1700 to 1800. That represents the maximal estimate of growth in the money supply; in fact it was less

because a portion of cowrie imports went to replacing those lost or destroyed. Cloth was less durable than cowries, and the growth rate of cloth currency supply was consequently a smaller portion of the growth in textile imports than was the case for cowries.

27 Miller, "Significance of drought"; Becker, "Conditions écologiques"; Lovejoy and Baier, "Desert-side economy."
28 Isaacman, *Mozambique*, 86–92; Alpers, *Ivory and Slaves*, 229–33.
29 See fig. 1.2 and appendix 1.
30 "Decreasing effective demand" is a condensed term behind which lurks a very complex situation. The demand for slaves in nineteenth-century Brazil, Cuba, and in the United States was very high and brought ever-rising prices. But the withdrawal of many New World territories from slave purchases (both by legislation and by revolution), and the pressures of the British slave squadron combined to reduce, as time went on, the number of slaves purchased by Atlantic merchants at any given price: Eltis, *Transatlantic Slave Trade*, 154–5, 260–4.
31 For a critique of the indifference of Middle East historians to the role of slavery in the economy, see Cooper, "Islam and cultural hegemony," 271–8.
32 Charles Issawi, "Egypt since 1880: a study in lopsided development," *Journal of Economic History*, 21, 1 (1961), 1–26. For a useful description of Egyptian slavery, see Gabriel Baer, "Slavery in nineteenth-century Egypt," *Journal of African History*, 8, 3 (1967), 417–41.
33 Humphrey J. Fisher, "A Muslim William Wilberforce? The Sokoto *jihad* as anti-slavery crusade: an enquiry into historical causes" in Daget, *De la Traite à l'esclavage* 2: 537–56; O'Fahey, "Slavery and the slave trade."
34 McDougall, "Camel caravans," 109–10.
35 Alpers, *Ivory and Slaves*, 94–8; Gerbeau, "Fabulée, fabuleuse"; Campbell, "Madagascar and the slave trade."
36 Cooper, *Plantation Slavery*; Sheriff, *Slaves, Spices and Ivory*: Alpers, *Ivory and Slaves*, 86–7.
37 Norman R. Bennett, *Mirambo of Tanzania, ca. 1840–1884* (New York, 1971).
38 Christopher Lloyd, *The Navy and the Slave Trade* (London, 1949).
39 See chapter 9 for further discussion of this issue.
40 Manning, *Slavery, Colonialism and Economic Growth*, 30–4; Lovejoy, *Transformations in Slavery*, 199–200; Vansina, *Kingdoms of the Savanna*, 216–27; Cordell, *Dar al-Kuti*, 14–30; Klein, "Demography of slavery."
41 Eltis, *Transatlantic Slave Trade*, 262–4.
42 C. W. Newbury, *The Western Slave Coast and its Rulers* (Oxford, 1961), 38–42.
43 Cooper, "Africa and the world economy," 26–8; Klein, "Demography of slavery"; Sheriff, *Slaves, Spices and Ivory*, 61–72.
44 Henry A. Gemery and Jan S. Hogendorn, "Technological change, slavery and the slave trade" in Clive J. Dewey and A. G. Hopkins, eds., *The Imperial Impact: Studies in the Economic History of Africa and India* (London, 1978), 243–58. Here and in a previous study, I have attempted to locate the particular times and conditions in which innovations were made: Manning "Slave trade, 'legitimate trade'."
45 Meillassoux, *Anthropologie de l'esclavage*, 91–8, 270–95.
46 Abdullahi Mahadi, "Kasr Kano," unpublished paper, Kano, 1987; Richard Roberts, "Long distance trade and production: Sinsani in the nineteenth century." *Journal of African History*, 21 (1980), 169–88; Eugenia W. Herbert, *Red Gold of Africa. Copper in Precolonial History and Culture* (Madison, 1984), 248–9.
47 Martin Klein, "The slave trade in the Western Sudan during the nineteenth century," unpublished paper, Toronto, 1988.
48 M. G. Smith, *Government in Zazzau, 1800–1950* (London, 1960); Hogendorn, "Slave acquisition and delivery."
49 Wilks, *Asante*, 176, 264, 435–6, 451–2; Manning, "Slave trade, 'legitimate' trade," 207–8.

50 C. Daryll Forde, ed., *Efik Traders of Old Calabar* (London, 1956); Peter M. Weil, "Slavery, groundnuts, and European capitalism in the Wuli kingdom of Senegambia, 1820–1930." *Research in Economic Anthropology*, 6 (1984), 77–119; Birmingham, "Coffee barons," 525–31.

51 Manning, "Slave trade, 'legitimate' trade," 222–3; Cooper, *Plantation Slavery*, 202–3. Another early slave revolt took place in Asante in 1818: see Emmanuel Terray, "La Captivité dans le royaume abron de Gyaman" in Meillassoux, *L'esclavage en Afrique*, 422.

52 Cooper, *Plantation Slavery*, 228–40.

53 Ibid., 223–5. Wilks argues that Asante policy was to avoid the organization of a servile class by encouraging the recognition of slave families as lineage fragments. The principle was *obi nkyere obi ase*, "one does not disclose another's origins"; Wilks, *Asante*, 86, 177.

54 J. E. Casely Hayford, *The Truth about the West African Land Question* (New York, 1969; first published London, 1913); Patrick Manning, "L'Affaire Adjovi: la bourgeoisie foncière naissante au Dahomey, face à l'administration" in Catherine Coquery-Vidrovitch, ed., *Entreprises et entrepreneurs en Afrique*, 2 vols. (Paris, 1983), vol. 1, 241–62.

55 Lovejoy, "Characteristics of plantations." See also Hill, "Comparative West African farm-slavery systems."

56 See chapter 4; see also Cordell, *Dar al-Kuti*, 26, 161; and Roberts, *Warriors, Merchants and Slaves*, 134.

57 David Kimble, *A Political History of Ghana. The Rise of Gold Coast Nationalism 1850–1928* (Oxford, 1963), 260, 285; Newbury, *Western Slave Coast*, 54–76.

58 Gabriel Warburg, "Ideological and practical considerations regarding slavery in the Mahdist state and the Anglo-Egyptian Sudan: 1881–1918" in Lovejoy, *Ideology of Slavery*, 250–1; O'Fahey, "Slavery and society"; Cordell, *Dar al-Kuti*, 72–5; Jon R. Edwards, "Slavery, the slave trade, and the economic reorganization of Ethiopia, 1916–1934," *African Economic History*, 11 (1982), 3–14.

59 Cooper, "Africa and the world economy," 26–9. The slave labor system was not, of course, the only linkage of African economies to industrial capitalism: peasant farmers produced much or perhaps most of the peanut and palm oil exported to Europe.

8 The end of slavery

1 This revolt, known as Tacky's Revolt, is described in detail in Michael Craton, *Testing the Chains – Resistance to Slavery in the British West Indies* (Ithaca, 1980), 125–39.

2 Davis, *Problem of Slavery*, 483–93.

3 C. L. R. James, *The Black Jacobins: Toussaint l'Ouverture and the San Domingo Revolution*, 2nd edn (New York, 1963), 85–90.

4 Eugene D. Genovese, *From Rebellion to Revolution: Afro-American Slave Revolts in the Making of the Modern World* (Baton Rouge, 1979).

5 Arthur Zilversmit, *The First Emancipation: The Abolition of Slavery in the North* (Chicago, 1967); Anstey, *Atlantic Slave Trade*; Drescher, *Econocide*; *Capitalism and Antislavery: British Mobilization in Comparative Perspective* (New York, 1987).

6 Svend E. Green-Pedersen, "The economic considerations behind the Danish abolition of the negro slave trade" in Gemery and Hogendorn, *Uncommon Market*, 399–418; Howard Temperley, *British Antislavery 1833–1870* (Columbia, SC, 1972).

7 The anti-slavery committee noted that the *Brookes*, licensed in 1789 to carry 454 slaves, had earlier shipped as many as 600 slaves. Patrick Villiers, however, has demonstrated that the famous engraving shows no room left for gaining access to slaves in order to feed them or remove the dead, nor room to get past the slaves to the hold below them, where the essential supplies of water were kept. He has redrawn portions of the *Brookes* to show how the slaves were more probably stowed: see Villiers, *Traite des noirs et navires négriers au XVIIIe siècle* (Grenoble, 1982), 78–81.

8 Marcel Châtillon, "La diffusion de la gravure du *Brookes* par la Société des Amis des Noirs, et son impact" in Daget, *De la Traite à l'esclavage* 1: 135–48. In fact, French anti-slavery activists and French historians have analyzed several other vessels: *L'Aurore* (1784), *L'Olympe* (1789), and *La Vigilante* (1822). See Jean Boudriot, *Traite et navire négrier. L'Aurore, 1784* (Paris, 1984); and Villiers, *Traite des noirs*, 75–83.

9 Robert Norris, *Memoirs of the Reign of Bossa Ahadee, King of Dahomy* (London, 1968; first published 1789); Dalzel, *The History of Dahomy*; Pruneau de Pommegorge, *Description de la Nigritie*; Robin Law, "Dahomey and the slave trade; reflections on the historiography of the rise of Dahomey," *Journal of African History*, 27, 2 (1986), 247–60.

10 John Lynch, *The Spanish American Revolutions 1808–1826* (New York, 1973); Klein, *African Slavery in Latin America*, 250–4; for case studies see Robert Brent Toplin, ed., *Slavery and Race Relations in Latin America* (Westport, Conn., 1974).

11 Martin Delany, a black American medical doctor, led an 1860 expedition to consider settlement in western Nigeria. Robert G. Weisbord, *Ebony Kinship; Africa, Africans, and the Afro-American* (Westport, Conn., 1973).

12 R. J. M. Blackett, *Building an Antislavery Wall: Black Americans in the Atlantic Abolitionist Movement, 1830–1860* (Baton Rouge, 1983); Temperley, *British Antislavery*. The career of E. W. Blyden in the West Indies, Liberia, and Sierra Leone is an outstanding example of the scope of the black abolitionist movement: Hollis R. Lynch, *Edward Wilmot Blyden, Pan-Negro Patriot 1832–1912* (London, 1967).

13 The details of Henry Williams' story are ironic. He was a well-placed slave, a driver. His punishment came not because he was a Christian, but because he declined to attend services of the official Church of England and instead became a leader in the Methodist church. He was sent to a workhouse by a local magistrate, where he was beaten; the rector of the parish Anglican church was implicated in his punishment. Williams was freed through the efforts of Isaac Whitehouse, an English Methodist missionary who also sent word of the case to England. A similar case arose in 1830 when Sam Swiney, a slave and a Baptist preacher, was arrested. Stiv Jakobsson, *Am I Not a Man and a Brother? British Missions and the Abolition of the Slave Trade and Slavery in West Africa and the West Indies 1786–1838* (Uppsala, 1972), 426–38; Davis, *Slavery and Human Progress*, 197–8.

Earlier major uprisings in the British West Indies were Bussa's rebellion on Barbados in 1816 and the Demerara revolt of 1823. See Craton, *Testing the Chains*, 254–90.

14 Davis, *Slavery and Human Progress*, 198–226. Davis also emphasizes the importance of James Stephen the elder and James Stephen the younger in achieving parliamentary emancipation.

15 For a biographical sketch of Victor Schoelcher (1804–93), see Henry Lemery, *Martinique, terre française* (Paris, 1962).

16 Franklin W. Knight, *Slave Society in Cuba during the Nineteenth Century* (Madison, 1970), 1–24, 47–58; Eltis, *Transatlantic Slave Trade*, 243–5.

17 Knight, *Slave Society*, 154–78; Rebecca Scott, *Slave Emancipation in Cuba: The Transition to Free Labor, 1860–1899* (Princeton, 1985).

18 Robert Conrad, *The Destruction of Brazilian Slavery* (Berkeley, 1972); Robert Brent Toplin, *The Abolition of Slavery in Brazil* (New York, 1972).

19 For the most detailed study of emancipation in Africa – which also reviews the problems of emancipation in the New World – see Frederick Cooper, *From Slaves to Squatters: Plantation Labor and Agriculture in Zanzibar and Coastal Kenya, 1890–1925* (New Haven, 1980).

20 Christopher Fyfe, *A History of Sierra Leone* (London, 1962); Robert Smith, *The Lagos Consulate 1851–1861* (Berkeley, 1979); Sheriff, *Slaves, Spices and Ivory*, 223–38; Cooper, *Plantation Slavery*, 122–30; Melvin E. Page, "The Manyema hordes of Tippu Tip: a case study in social stratification and the slave trade in eastern Africa," *International Journal of African Historical Studies*, 7, 1 (1974), 69–84.

21 The British invasion was not the first step toward abolition in Asante: in about 1808 the Asante monarchy had freed and repatriated all Muslim slaves: Wilks, *Asante*, 263.

22 Livingstone and Livingstone, *Narrative of an Expedition to the Zambezi*. The 1873 illustration, entitled "Slavers avenging their losses" (56) and another, "Slaves abandoned" (62) are in vol. 1 of Livingstone, *Last Journals*.

23 Edward Reynolds, *Trade and Economic Change on the Gold Coast, 1807–1874* (London, 1974), 56–61; Renault, *Lavigerie*, vol. 1, 155–212.

24 Johnson, "The slaves of Salaga," 358–62.

25 Roberts, *Warriors, Merchants, and Slaves*, 180–1.

26 Catherine Coquery-Vidrovitch, *Brazza et la prise de possession du Congo* (Paris, 1969).

27 Ruth Slade, *King Leopold's Congo* (London, 1962); Leda Farrant, *Tippu Tip and the East African Slave Trade* (New York, 1975); Page, "Manyema hordes."

28 Emile Gentil, *La Chute de l'empire de Rabah* (Paris, 1902).

29 Roland Oliver, *The Missionary Factor in East Africa* (London, 1952), 1–50; Warburg, "Slavery in the Mahdist state and the Anglo-Egyptian Sudan," 258–9.

30 Edwards, "Slavery."

31 One exception was Madagascar, where the French abolished slavery in 1897: Maurice Bloch, "Modes of production and slavery in Madagascar: two case studies" in Watson, *Asian and African Systems of Slavery*, 111. For an important set of studies on the end of slavery, published after this book had entered production, see Suzanne Miers and Richard Roberts, eds., *The End of Slavery in Africa* (Madison, 1988).

32 Lovejoy, *Transformations in Slavery*, 261–8; Denise Bouche, *Les Villages de liberté en Afrique noire française, 1887–1910* (Paris, 1968); Klein, "Slave trade in the Western Sudan."

33 The British had not sought to create a more equitable economy through the abolition of slavery, but to fashion a more rational, controllable economy. Instead – largely owing to the efforts of ex-slaves themselves – the domination of an old elite was eroded; but officials, landowners, and ex-slaves alike became bound up in structures that made economic change both difficult and potentially dangerous. Cooper, *From Slaves to Squatters*, 6.

34 Lugard wrote later to justify his position:

> But if every slave can leave his master at will, what, it may be asked, is to prevent a sudden exodus, which would fill the cities with vagrants, criminals, and prostitutes, and pauperise the ruling classes, whom it is our desire to support and strengthen? ... For the sake, therefore, alike of justice to the owners and in the interest of the slaves themselves, the Government ... must do all in its power to make the change as gradual as possible, and to give time for its constructive policy to mature. Lugard, *Dual Mandate*, 372.

For a detailed study of the struggles among British officials in northern Nigeria to work out a policy on slavery, see Jan Hogendorn and Paul Lovejoy, "Sir Frederick Lugard's policies toward slavery in northern Nigeria" (unpublished paper, Waterville, Maine, 1988).

35 Cooper, *From Slaves to Squatters*.

36 Gerald M. McSheffrey, "Slavery, indentured servitude, legitimate trade and the impact of abolition in the Gold Coast, 1874–1901: a reappraisal," *Journal of African History*, 24, 3 (1983), 349–68; Warburg, "Ideological and practical considerations," 258–62.

37 Richard Roberts and Martin Klein, "The Banamba slave exodus of 1905 and the decline of slavery in the western Sudan," *Journal of African History*, 21, 3 (1981), 375–94; Roberts, *Warriors, Merchants, and Slaves*, 184–207.

38 John Grace, "Slavery and emancipation among the Mende in Sierra Leone, 1896–1928" in Miers and Kopytoff, *Slavery in Africa*, 415–34.

39 Patrick Manning, "Un Document sur la fin de l'esclavage au Dahomey," *Notes Africaines*, 147 (1975), 88–92; Claire C. Robertson and Martin A. Klein, "Women's importance in African slave systems" in Robertson and Klein, *Women and Slavery in Africa*, 17–18.

40 E. D. Morel, *King Leopold's Rule in Africa* (London, 1903); *The British Case in French Congo* (London, 1903).

41 The British, following the precedent they set in India, tended to pass legislation which withdrew legal recognition of the status of slavery, but did not go so far as to make slave status illegal. McSheffrey, "Slavery, indentured servitude"; Grace, "Slavery and emancipation."

42 See chapter 1, note 23 on official ethnologists.

43 Lord Frederick Lugard, " 'Slavery in all its forms'," *Africa*, 6, 1 (1933), 1–14.

44 Pierre H. Boulle, "In defense of slavery: eighteenth-century opposition to abolition and the origins of a racist ideology in France" in F. Krautz, ed., *History from Below: Studies in Popular Protest and Ideology* (Oxford, 1988), 219–46.

45 Thomas C. Holt, " 'An empire over the mind': emancipation, race, and ideology in the British West Indies and the American South" in J. Morgan Kousser and James M. McPherson, eds., *Region, Race, and Reconstruction: Essays in Honor of C. Vann Woodward* (New York, 1982), 304–6.

46 Philip D. Curtin, *The Image of Africa: British Ideas and Action, 1780–1840* (Madison, 1963).

47 The leading black intellectual E. W. Blyden, for instance, felt the need to make concessions to the growing white racial feeling during the 1890s: Lynch, *Blyden*, 191–209.

48 Holt, " 'Empire over the mind'," 306.

49 For contributions to this line of thinking, see Curtin, *Image of Africa*; Holt, " 'Empire over the mind' "; Cooper, *From Slaves to Squatters*; and Seymour Drescher, "The ending of the slave trade and the evolution of European 'scientific' racism" (unpublished paper, Pittsburgh, PA, 1988).

50 C. Vann Woodward, *The Strange Career of Jim Crow*, 3rd rev. edn (New York, 1974); E. M'Bokolo, "Peste et société urbaine à Dakar, l'épidémie de 1914," *Cahiers d'Etudes Africaines*, 85–6 (1982), 13–46; Douglas L. Wheeler, " 'Angola is whose House?' Early stirrings of Angolan nationalism and protest, 1822–1910," *African Historical Studies*, 2, 1 (1969), 14–22.

51 Cooper, *From Slaves to Squatters*, 111–24.

52 For a good analysis of this issue, see Marvin P. Miracle and Bruce Fetter, "Backward-sloping labor supply functions and African economic behavior," *Economic Development and Cultural Change*, 18 (1970), 240–51.

53 Gilles Sautter, *De l'Atlantique au fleuve Congo: une géographie du sous peuplement*, 2 vols. (Paris, 1966), vol. 2, 1004–5.

54 Harries, "Slavery, social incorporation, and surplus extraction," 317–20, 328–39. Augé and Terray have interpreted the modern movement of women from Burkina Faso and the interior of the Ivory Coast to marry men of the coastal region as the continuation of a pattern set in the days of the slave trade: Emmanuel Terray, "Commerce pré-colonial et organisation sociale chez les Dida de Côte d'Ivoire" in Claude Meillassoux, ed., *The Development of Indigenous Trade and Markets in West Africa* (London, 1971), 149–50; Marc Augé, "Les Faiseurs d'ombre. Servitude et structure dans la société alladian" in Meillassoux, *L'Esclavage en Afrique*, 456.

9 The world and Africa

1 W. E. B. DuBois, *The World and Africa: An Inquiry into the Part which Africa has Played in World History* (New York, 1946).

2 At the time of his death in Ghana in 1965, at the age of ninety-six, DuBois was working on an encyclopaedia of Africa.

3 The United Nations' world conferences on the status of women, held in Mexico City in 1975 and Nairobi in 1985, are examples of its support for the principle of equality. These efforts are not, of course, necessarily successful in the short term.

4 Oswald Spengler, *The Decline of the West* (New York, 1939); Arnold Toynbee, *A Study of History*, 12 vols. (London, 1961). The recent American concern with the decline of empires – as revealed in the strong response to a survey by a British-born author – gives too much emphasis to the exercise of political power and too little to the social dynamics of participation in a complex world: Paul Kennedy, *The Rise and Fall of the Great Powers: Economic Change and Military Conflict from 1500 to 2000* (New York, 1987).

5 William H. McNeill, *The Rise of the West: A History of the Human Community* (Chicago, 1963). For even stronger reliance on Eurocentric diffusionism in the field of economic history, see Douglass C. North and Robert Paul Thomas, *The Rise of the Western World: A New Economic History* (Cambridge, 1973); and Nathan Rosenberg and L. E. Birdzell, Jr. *How the West Grew Rich: The Economic Transformation of the Industrial World* (New York, 1986). For a comparative approach to the same issues, see E. L. Jones, *The European Miracle: Environments, Economies and Geopolitics in the History of Europe and Asia*, 2nd edn (Cambridge 1987).

6 Wallerstein, *The Modern World-System*. For slavery as seen through a world-system perspective, see Wirz, *Sklaverei und kapitalistische Weltsystem*; see also the monographic and analytic studies in *Review*, the journal of the Fernand Braudel Center in Binghamton, New York.

7 Winthrop Jordan, *White Over Black: American Attitudes toward the Negro 1550–1812* (Baltimore, 1969); Davis, *Slavery and Human Progress*.

8 In this interpretation I seek to emphasize that slavery was a *significant* factor in the evolution of the modern world: it cannot properly be left out of any comprehensive analysis. At the same time, I wish to stop short of arguing that slavery was a *dominant* factor in modern history. There is no need to exaggerate the importance of slavery in modern world history, and it is worthwhile noting some major African and American developments which took place independently of slavery. For instance, many of the interactions which took place between Africa and other continents would have done so even without the slave trade to reinforce them. The spread of diseases in the age of discovery would have taken place regardless. Similarly, the exchange of crops – sorghum, taro, and oranges to the Americas; peanuts, maize, manioc, and tobacco to Africa – would have occurred even without the slave trade, though at a different pace. European and Asian manufactures would have come to Africa in exchange for gold and ivory in the absence of the slave trade, though the quantities would have been smaller.

9 Karl Polanyi, *The Great Transformation* (Boston, 1957). Polanyi's initial vision of the transformation of the world into a system unhappily governed by self-regulating markets did not include Africa. His later work came to focus significantly on Danhomè: he attempted to analyze it as an "archaic" society held at a stage between a non-market society and a market society. This work, while of theoretical interest, does considerable violence to the empirical record on Danhomè. Polanyi, with Abraham Rotstein, *Dahomey and the Slave Trade, an Analysis of an Archaic Economy* (Seattle, 1966); for a useful correction, see Werner Peukert, *Der Atlantische Sklavenhandel von Dahomey, 1740–1797* (Wiesbaden, 1978).

10 This comparison of continental populations is based on A. M. Carr-Saunders, *World Population* (London, 1934). Work emerging from recent international demographic congresses should soon permit the replacement of these dated estimates with more accurate figures.

11 Simulation results. Census figures show that, by 1980, the population of sub-Saharan Africa had risen to over 20 percent of the total for the whole region.

12 Williams, *Capitalism and Slavery*. The large literature on slavery and economic growth in the United States has only recently begun to be linked in depth to the debate on the Williams thesis. See Gavin Wright, "Capitalism and slavery on the islands: a lesson from the mainland" in Solow and Engerman, *British Capitalism and Caribbean Slavery*, 283–302.

13 Drescher, *Econocide*; Anstey, *Atlantic Slave Trade*.
14 Barbara L. Solow and Stanley L. Engerman, "British capitalism and Caribbean slavery: the legacy of Eric Williams: an introduction" in Solow and Engerman, *British Capitalism and Caribbean Slavery*, 1–23.
15 Mintz, *Sweetness and Power*; Marion Johnson, personal communication.
16 Frantz Fanon, *The Wretched of the Earth* (New York, 1968), 95–106. For a remarkably detailed analysis of the issue of reparations within the United States, written by a noted tax lawyer, see Boris I. Bittker, *The Case for Black Reparations* (New York, 1973).
17 Abba Eban, *My Country: The Story of Modern Israel* (New York, 1974), 134. In more recent years the German Democratic Republic has also made reparations payments to Israel.
18 The recent American decision to grant compensation to Japanese–Americans interned during World War II may be seen as a recognition that these people were kin, mistakenly treated as aliens during the war because of their ancestry. The payments are thus best seen not as reparations to aliens, but as grants intended to re-establish ties to injured family members.
19 Elie Wiesel, *Against Silence: The Voice and Vision of Elie Wiesel*, ed. Irving Abrahamson, 3 vols. (New York, 1985), vol. 1, 107.
20 Ibid.

Appendix 1 Slave prices

1 Bean, *British Trans-Atlantic Slave Trade*, 158.
2 LeVeen, *British Slave Trade Suppression Policies*, 8.
3 Miller, "Slave prices," 66.
4 Curtin, *Economic Change*, 159.
5 Eltis, *Transatlantic Slave Trade*, 263.
6 Eltis, personal communication.
7 Manning, *Slavery, Colonialism, and Economic Growth*, 332, based on Bean, *British Trans-Atlantic Slave Trade*, 158, and LeVeen, *British Slave Trade Suppression Policies*, 8, 113.

Appendix 2 The demographic simulation

1 Coale and Demey, *Regional Model Life Tables*.
2 Manning and Griffiths, "Divining the unprovable."

Bibliography

Abir, Mordechai. "The Ethiopian slave trade and its relation to the Islamic world." Willis, *Slaves and Slavery*, vol. 2, 123–36.

Achebe, Chinua. *Things Fall Apart*. New York, 1959.

Anthills of the Savanna. New York, 1988.

Akinjogbin, I. A. *Dahomey and its Neighbours, 1708–1818*. Cambridge, 1967.

Alpers, Edward A. *The East African Slave Trade*. Nairobi, 1967.

"Trade, state, and society among the Yao in the nineteenth century." *Journal of African History*, 10, 3, 1969, 405–20.

Ivory and Slaves in East Central Africa: Changing Patterns of International Trade to the Later Nineteenth Century. Berkeley, 1975.

"The story of Swema: female vulnerability in nineteenth-century East Africa." Robertson and Klein, *Women and Slavery in Africa*, 185–219.

Amin, Samir. *Unequal Development*. New York, 1976.

Anstey, Roger. *The Atlantic Slave Trade and British Abolition, 1760–1810*. Cambridge, 1975.

Augé, Marc. "Les Faiseurs d'ombre. Servitude et structure dans la société alladian." Meillassoux, *L'Esclavage en Afrique*, 455–75.

Austen, Ralph A. "The trans-Saharan slave trade: a tentative census." Gemery and Hogendorn, *The Uncommon Market*, 23–76.

"The Islamic Red Sea slave trade: an effort at quantification." *Proceedings of the Fifth International Conference on Ethiopian Studies*. Chicago, 1979.

"From the Atlantic to the Indian Ocean: European abolition, the African slave trade, and Asian economic structures." Eltis and Walvin, *Abolition*, 117–39.

Austen, Ralph A., and Rita Headrick. "Equatorial Africa under colonial rule." Birmingham and Martin, *History of Central Africa*, vol. 2, 27–95.

Bacon, R. H. S. *Benin, City of Blood*, London, 1897.

Baer, Gabriel. "Slavery in nineteenth-century Egypt." *Journal of African History*, 8, 3, 1967, 417–41.

Balde, Mamadou Saliou. "L'Esclavage et la guerre sainte au Fuuta-Jalon." Meillassoux, *L'Esclavage en Afrique*, 183–220.

Barry, Boubacar. "The subordination of power and the mercantile economy: the kingdom of Waalo, 1600–1831" in Rita Cruise O'Brien, ed., *The Political Economy of Underdevelopment: Dependence in Senegal*, Beverly Hills, 1979, 39–63.

Bathily, Abdoulaye. "La Traite atlantique des esclaves et ses effets économiques et sociaux en Afrique: le cas du Galam, royaume de l'hinterland sénégambien au dix-huitième siècle." *Journal of African History*, 27, 2, 1986, 269–93.

Bay, Edna G. "Servitude and worldly success in the palace of Dahomey." Robertson and Klein, *Women and Slavery in Africa*, 340–67.

Bazin, Jean. "Guerre et servitude à Segou." Meillassoux, *L'Esclavage en Afrique*, 135–81.
Beachey, R. W. *The Slave Trade of Eastern Africa*, London, 1976.
Bean, Richard N. "A note on the relative importance of slaves and gold in West African exports." *Journal of African History*, 15, 3, 1974, 351–6.
The British Trans-Atlantic Slave Trade 1650–1775. New York, 1975.
Bean, Richard N., and Robert P. Thomas. "The adoption of slave labor in British America." Gemery and Hogendorn, *Uncommon Market*, 377–98.
Beck, Lois, and Nikki Keddie, eds. *Women in the Muslim World*, Cambridge, Mass., 1978.
Becker, Charles. "Notes sur les conditions écologiques en Sénégambie aux 17e et 18e siècles." *African Economic History*, 14, 1985, 167–216.
"Notes sur les chiffres de la traite atlantique française au XVIIIe siècle." *Cahiers d'Etudes Africaines*, 26, 4, no. 104, 1986, 633–79.
Becker, Charles, ed. *Mémoire sur le Commerce de la Concession du Sénégal, par Joseph Pruneau 1752*. Mimeographed. Kaolack, Senegal, 1983.
Bennett, Norman R. *Mirambo of Tanzania, ca. 1840–1884*. New York, 1971.
Birmingham, David. "The coffee barons of Cazengo." *Journal of African History*, 19, 4, 1978, 523–38.
Birmingham, David, and Phyllis M. Martin, eds. *History of Central Africa*. 2 vols. London, 1983.
Bittaker, Boris I. *The Case for Black Reparations*. New York, 1973.
Blackburn, Robin. *The Overthrow of Colonial Slavery, 1776–1848*. London, 1988.
Blackett, R. J. M. *Building an Antislavery Wall: Black Americans in the Atlantic Abolitionist Movement, 1830–1860*. Baton Rouge, 1983.
Bloch, Marc. *Slavery and Serfdom in the Middle Ages: Selected Essays*. Trans. William R. Baer. Berkeley, 1975.
Bloch, Maurice. "Modes of production and slavery in Madagascar: two case studies." Watson, *Asian and African Systems of Slavery*.
Bohannan, Paul. "Some principles of exchange and investment among the Tiv." *American Anthropologist*, 57, 1955, 60–70.
Boserup, Ester. *Woman's Role in Economic Development*. London, 1970.
Bosman, William. *A New and Accurate Description of the Coast of Guinea*. London, 1967; first published 1705.
Bouche, Denise. *Les Villages de liberté en Afrique noire française, 1887–1910*. Paris, 1968.
Boudriot, Jean. *Traite et navire négrier. L'Aurore, 1784*. Paris, 1984.
Boulle, Pierre H. "In defense of slavery: eighteenth-century opposition to abolition and the origins of a racist ideology in France" in F. Krautz, ed., *History from Below: Studies in Popular Protest and Ideology*, Oxford, 1988, 219–46.
Bourdillon, M. F. C., and Meyer Fortes, eds. *Sacrifice*, New York, 1980.
Bourgoignie, George-Edouard. *Les Hommes de l'eau: ethno-écologie du Dahomey lacustre*. Paris, 1972.
Bowser, Frederick. *The African Slave in Colonial Peru, 1524–1650*. Stanford, 1973.
Boxer, C. R. *The Dutch in Brazil, 1624–1654*. Oxford, 1957.
The Portuguese Seaborne Empire 1415–1825. New York, 1969.
Broadhead, Susan Herlin. "Slave wives, free sisters: Bakongo women and slavery." Robertson and Klein, *Women and Slavery in Africa*, 160–81.
Brooks, George. "Peanuts and colonialism: consequences of the commercialization of peanuts in West Africa, 1830–70." *Journal of African History*, 16, 1, 1975, 29–54.
"A Nhara of the Guinea-Bissau region: Mãe Aurelia Correia." Robertson and Klein, *Women and Slavery in Africa*, 295–319.
Buxton, Thomas Fowell. *The African Slave Trade and its Remedy*. London, 1968; first published 1839–40.

Bibliography

Caldwell, John C. "Comment on Manning." *Canadian Journal of African Studies*, 16, 1, 1982, 127–30.
"The social repercussions of colonial rule: demographic aspects." UNESCO, *The General History of Africa*, Berkeley, 1985, vol. 7, 458–86.
Campbell, Gwyn. "Madagascar and the slave trade, 1810–1895." *Journal of African History*, 22, 2, 1981, 203–27.
"The adoption of Autarky in imperial Madagascar, 1820–1835." *Journal of African History*, 28, 3, 1987, 395–411.
"The East African slave trade 1861–1895: the "southern" complex." *International Journal of African Historical Studies*, 22, 1, 1989, 1–26.
Carr-Saunders, A. M. *World Population*. New York, 1934.
Casely Hayford, J. E. *The Truth about the West African Land Question*. New York, 1969; first published London, 1913.
Chanana, Dev Raj. *Slavery in Ancient India*. New Delhi, 1960.
Châtillon, Marcel. "La Diffusion de la gravure du *Brooks*, par la Société des Amis des Noirs, et son impact." Daget, *De la traite à l'esclavage*, vol. 2, 135–47.
Chattopadhyay, Amal Kumar. *Slavery in India*. Calcutta, 1959.
Clarkson, Thomas. *The History of the Rise, Progress and Accomplishment of the Abolition of the African Slave Trade by the British Parliament*. 2 vols. London, 1808.
Coale, Ansley J., and Paul Demeny. *Regional Model Life Tables and Stable Populations*. Princeton, 1966.
Coale, Ansley J., and Susan Cotts Watkins, eds. *The Decline in European Fertility*. Princeton, 1986.
Conrad, Robert. *The Destruction of Brazilian Slavery*. Berkeley, 1972.
Cook, Noble David. *Demographic Collapse: Indian Peru, 1520–1620*. Cambridge, 1981.
Cook, Sherburne F., and Woodrow Wilson Borah. *Essays in Population History: Mexico and the Caribbean*. 3 vols. Berkeley, 1971, 1974, 1979.
Cooper, Frederick. *Plantation Slavery on the East African Coast*. New Haven, 1977.
"The problem of slavery in African Studies." *Journal of African History*, 20, 1, 1979, 103–25.
From Slaves to Squatters: Plantation Labor and Agriculture in Zanzibar and Coastal Kenya, 1890–1925. New Haven, 1980.
"Africa and the world economy." *African Studies Review*, 24, 2–3, 1981, 1–86.
"Islam and cultural hegemony: the ideology of slaveowners on the East African Coast." Lovejoy, *Ideology of Slavery*, 271–307.
Coquery-Vidrovitch, Catherine. *Brazza et la prise de possession du Congo*. Paris, 1969.
Cordell, Dennis D. *Dar al-Kuti and the Last Years of the Trans-Saharan Slave Trade*. Madison, 1985.
Cordell, Dennis D., and Joel W. Gregory, eds. *African Population and Capitalism: Historical Perspectives*. Boulder, Colo., 1987.
Coursey, D. G. *The Yam*, London, 1967.
Craton, Michael, ed. *Roots and Branches: Current Directions in Slave Studies*. Toronto, 1979.
Testing the Chains – Resistance to Slavery in the British West Indies. Ithaca, 1980.
Crosby, Alfred W. *The Columbian Exchange: Biological and Cultural Consequences of 1492*. Westport, Conn., 1972.
Curtin, Philip D. *The Image of Africa: British Ideas and Action, 1780–1840*. Madison, 1963.
"Epidemiology and the slave trade," *Political Science Quarterly*, 83, 1968, 190–216.
The Atlantic Slave Trade: A Census. Madison, 1969.
Economic Change in Precolonial Africa: Senegambia in the Era of the Slave Trade. 2 vols. Madison, 1975.
"Measuring the Atlantic slave trade once again." *Journal of African History*, 17, 4, 1976, 595–605.
"The African diaspora." Craton, *Roots and Branches*, 1–17.

214

"Africans at home and abroad." Daget, *De la traite à l'esclavage*, vol. 2, 695–715.

Death by Migration. Cambridge, 1990.

Curtin, Philip D. ed. *Africa Remembered*. Madison, 1962.

Curtin, Philip D., Stephen Feierman, Leonard Thompson, and Jan Vansina. *African History*. Boston, 1978.

Daaku, Kwame Yeboa. *Trade and Politics on the Gold Coast 1600–1700*. Oxford, 1970.

Daget, Serge. *Répertoire des expéditions negrières françaises à la traite illégale (1814–1850)*. Nantes, 1988.

Daget, Serge, ed. *De la traite à l'esclavage: Actes du colloque international sur la traite des Noirs, Nantes 1985*. 2 vols. Nantes and Paris, 1988.

D'Almeida-Topor, Hélène. *Les Amazones*. Paris, 1984.

Dalzel, Archibald. *The History of Dahomy, an Inland Kingdom of Africa*. London, 1967; first published 1793.

Davidson, Basil. *Black Mother: The Years of the African Slave Trade*. Boston, 1961.

Davis, David Brion. *The Problem of Slavery in Western Culture*. Ithaca, 1966.

The Problem of Slavery in the Age of Revolution, 1770–1823. Ithaca, 1975.

Slavery and Human Progress. Oxford, 1984.

Davis, Kingsley. *The Population of India and Pakistan*. Princeton, 1951.

Deane, Phyllis, and W. A. Cole. *British Economic Growth 1688–1959*. 2nd. edn. Cambridge, 1967.

Debien, Gabriel. *Les Esclaves aux Antilles françaises (XVIIe – XVIIIe siècles)*. Basse-Terre and Fort-de-France, 1979.

Deneven, William M. ed. *The Native Population of the Americas in 1492*. Cambridge, 1981.

De Vries, Jan. *The Dutch Rural Economy in the Golden Age, 1500–1700*. New Haven, 1979.

"Labor in the Dutch golden age." Unpublished paper. Berkeley, 1980.

Dike, K. O. *Trade and Politics in the Niger Delta, 1830–1885*. Oxford, 1954.

Diop, Majhemout. *Histoire des classes sociales dans l'Afrique de l'Ouest*. Paris, 1971.

Dobyns, Henry F. "Estimating aboriginal American population: an appraisal of technique with a new hemispheric estimate." *Current Anthropology*, 7, 1966, 395–416.

Domar, Evsey. *"The causes of slavery or serfdom: a hypothesis." Journal of Economic History*, 30, 1, 1970, 18–32.

Drescher, Seymour. *Econocide: British Slavery in the Era of Abolition*. Pittsburgh, 1977.

"The decline thesis of British slavery since *Econocide*." *Slavery and Abolition*, 7, 1, 1986, 3–24.

Capitalism and Antislavery: British Mobilization in Comparative Perspective. New York, 1987.

"The ending of the slave trade and the evolution of European 'scientific' racism." Unpublished paper. Pittsburgh, Pa., 1988.

DuBois, W. E. B. *The Negro*. Oxford, 1970; first published 1915.

The World and Africa: An Inquiry into the Part which Africa has Played in World History. Enlarged edition. New York, 1946.

Dumett, Raymond. "Precolonial gold-mining and the state in the Akan region: with a critique of the Terray hypothesis." *Research in Economic Anthropology*, 2, 1979, 37–68.

Dunbar, Roberta Ann. "Slavery and the evolution of nineteenth-century Damagaram." Miers and Kopytoff, *Slavery in Africa*, 155–77.

Dunn, Richard S. *Sugar and Slaves: The Rise of the Planter Class in the English West Indies, 1624–1713*. Chapel Hill, 1972.

"'Dreadful idlers' in the cane fields: the slave labor pattern on a Jamaican sugar estate, 1762–1831." Solow and Engerman, *British Capitalism and Caribbean Slavery*, 163–90.

Eban, Abba. *My Country. The Story of Modern Israel*. New York, 1974.

Edwards, Jon R. "Slavery, the slave trade, and the economic reorganization of Ethiopia, 1916–1934." *African Economic History*, 11, 1982, 3–14.

Ehrenkreutz, Andrew. "Strategic implications of the slave trade between Genoa and Mamluk Egypt in the second half of the thirteenth century" in A. L. Udovitch, ed., *The Islamic Middle East, 700–1900: Studies in Economic and Social History*, Princeton, 1981, 335–45.

Eltis, David, "Free and coerced transatlantic migrations: some comparisons." *American Historical Review*, 88, 2, 1983, 251–80.

Economic Growth and the Ending of the Transatlantic Slave Trade. New York, 1987.

"Trade between western Africa and the Atlantic world before 1870: estimates of trends in value, composition and direction." *Research in Economic History*, 8, 1988.

Eltis, David, and James Walvin, eds. *The Abolition of the Atlantic Slave Trade*. Madison, 1981.

Eltis, David, and Lawrence C. Jennings. "Trade between western Africa and the Atlantic world in the pre-colonial era." *American Historical Review*, 93, 4, 1989, 936–59.

Elvin, Mark. *The Pattern of the Chinese Past*. Stanford, 1973.

Elwahed, Ali Abd. *Contribution à une théorie de l'esclavage*. Paris, 1931.

Emecheta, Buchi. *The Joys of Motherhood*. New York, 1979.

Engerman, Stanley L., "The slave trade and British capital formation in the eighteenth century: a comment on the Williams thesis." *Business History Review*, 46, 13, 1972, 430–43.

"Some considerations relating to property rights in man." *Journal of Economic History*, 33, 1, 1973, 43–65.

"Some economic and demographic comparisons of slavery in the United States and the British West Indies." *Economic History Review*, 29, 2, 1976, 258–75.

"Contract labor, sugar, and technology in the nineteenth century." *Journal of Economic History*, 43, 3, 1983, 635–59.

Engerman, Stanley L. and Eugene D. Genovese, eds. *Race and Slavery in the Western Hemisphere: Quantitative Studies*. Princeton, 1975.

Ewald, Janet. "The Nile Valley system and the Red Sea slave trade, 1820–1900." Unpublished paper. Durham, NC, 1988.

Fage, John D. "Slavery and the slave trade in the context of West African history." *Journal of African History*, 10, 3, 1969, 393–404.

"The effect of the export slave trade on African populations" in R. P. Ross and R. J. A. Rathbone, eds., *The Population Factor in African Studies*, London, 1975, 15–23.

"Slaves and society in Western Africa, c. 1445 – c. 1700." *Journal of African History*, 21, 3, 1980, 289–310.

Fanon, Frantz. *The Wretched of the Earth*. New York, 1968.

Farrant, Leda. *Tippu Tip and the East African Slave Trade*. New York, 1975.

Fenoaltea, Stefano. "Europe in the African mirror: the slave trade and the rise of feudalism." Unpublished paper. Princeton, 1988.

Finley, M. I., ed. *Slavery in Classical Antiquity*. Cambridge, 1960.

Ancient Slavery and Modern Ideology. London, 1980.

Fisher, Alan W. "Muscovy and the Black Sea slave trade." *Canadian-American Slavic Studies*, 6, 4, 1972, 575–94.

Fisher, Allan G. B., and Humphrey J. Fisher. *Slavery and Muslim Society in Africa*. London, 1970.

Fisher, Humphrey J. "A Muslim William Wilberforce? The Sokoto *jihad* as anti-slavery crusade: an enquiry into historical causes." Daget, *De la traite à l'esclavage*, vol. 2, 537–55.

Fogel, Robert William, and Stanley L. Engerman. *Time on the Cross*. 2 vols. Boston, 1974.

Foote, Peter, and David M. Wilson. *The Viking Achievement*. London, 1970.

Forde, C. Daryll, ed. *Efik Traders of Old Calabar*. London, 1956.

Fyfe, Christopher. *A History of Sierra Leone*. London, 1962.

Fyfe, Christopher and David McMaster, eds. *African Historical Demography*. 2 vols. Edinburgh, 1977, 1981.

216

Galenson, David. *White Servitude in Colonial America: An Economic Analysis*. Cambridge, 1981.

Traders, Planters and Slaves. Cambridge, 1986.

Garenne, Michel, and Etienne Van de Walle. "Polygyny and fertility among the Sereer of Senegal." Unpublished paper. University of Pennsylvania, n.d.

Geggus, David. "Sex ratio, age, and ethnicity in the Atlantic slave trade: data from French shipping and plantation records." *Journal of African History*, 30, 1, 1989, 23–44.

Gemery, Henry A., and Jan S. Hogendorn. "The Atlantic slave trade: a tentative economic model," *Journal of African History*, 15, 2, 1974, 233–46.

"A note on the social costs of imported African monies." Unpublished paper. African Studies Association, Houston, 1977.

"Technological change, slavery and the slave trade" in Clive J. Dewey and A. G. Hopkins, eds., *The Imperial Impact: Studies in the Economic History of Africa and India*, London, 1978, 243–58.

Gemery, Henry A., and Jan S. Hogendorn, eds. *The Uncommon Market: Essays in the Economic History of the Atlantic Slave Trade*. New York, 1979.

Genovese, Eugene D. *Roll, Jordan, Roll: The World the Slaves Made*. New York, 1974.

From Rebellion to Revolution: Afro-American Slave Revolts in the Making of the Modern World. Baton Rouge, 1979.

Gentil, Emile. *La Chute de l'empire de Rabah*. Paris, 1902.

Gerbeau, Hubert. "Fabulée, fabuleuse, la traite des noirs à Bourbon au XIXe siècle." Daget, *Actes du colloque*, vol. 2, 467–86.

Gibb, H. A. R. *Mohammedanism*. 2nd edn. London, 1953.

Gleason, Judith. *Agōtīme, Her Legend*. New York, 1970.

Goody, Jack. *Technology, Tradition and the State in Africa*. Cambridge, 1971.

Grace, John. "Slavery and emancipation among the Mende in Sierra Leone, 1896–1928." Miers and Kopytoff, *Slavery in Africa*, 415–34.

Green-Pedersen, Svend E. "The economic considerations behind the Danish abolition of the negro slave trade." Gemery and Hogendorn, *Uncommon Market*, 399–418.

Guttentag, Marcia, and Paul F. Secord. *Too Many Women? The Sex Ratio Question*. Beverly Hills, 1983.

Haile, Getachew. "From the markets of Damot to that of Barara: A note on slavery in medieval Ethiopia." *Paideuma*, 27, 1981, 173–80.

Hair, P. E. H. "The enslavement of Koelle's informants." *Journal of African History*, 6, 2, 1965, 193–203.

Harms, Robert. *River of Wealth, River of Sorrow*. New Haven, 1981.

"Sustaining the system: trading towns along the Middle Zaire." Robertson and Klein, *Women and Slavery in Africa*, 95–110.

Games against Nature: An Eco-Cultural History of the Nunu of Equatorial Africa. Cambridge, 1987.

Harries, Patrick, "Slavery, social incorporation, and surplus extraction; the nature of free and unfree labour in South-East Africa." *Journal of African History*, 22, 1981, 309–30.

Harris, Joseph H. *The African Presence in Asia: Consequences of the East African Slave Trade*. Evanston, 1971.

Hartwig, Gerald H. "Social consequences of epidemic diseases: the nineteenth century in eastern Africa," in Hartwig and K. David Patterson, eds., *Diseases in African History*, Durham, 1978, 25–45.

"Demographic considerations in East Africa during the nineteenth century." *International Journal of African Historical Studies*, 12, 4, 1979, 653–72.

Hellie, Richard. *Slavery in Russia, 1450–1725*. Chicago, 1982.

Henige, David. "Measuring the immeasurable: the Atlantic slave trade, West African population and the pyrrhonian critic." *Journal of African History*, 27, 2, 1986, 295–313.

Bibliography

Henry, Louis. *On the Measurement of Human Fertility: Selected Writings of Louis Henry*. Eds. and trans. Mindel Sheps and Evelyne Lapierre Adamcyk. Amsterdam, 1972.

Herbert, Eugenia W. *Red Gold of Africa. Copper in Precolonial History and Culture*. Madison, 1984.

Héritier, Françoise. "Des Cauris et des hommes: production des esclaves et accumulation des cauris chez les Samo (Haute Volta)." Meillassoux, *L'Esclavage en Afrique*.

Herskovits, M. J. *Dahomey, an Ancient West African Kingdom*. 2 vols. New York, 1938.

Heusch, Luc de. *Sacrifice in Africa: A Structuralist Approach*. Trans. Linda O'Brien and Alice Morton. Bloomington, Ind., 1985.

Higman, B. W. *Slave Population and Economy in Jamaica 1807–1834*. Cambridge, 1976.

"Slavery and the development of demographic theory in the age of the industrial revolution" in James Walvin, ed., *Slavery and British Society 1776–1846*, Baton Rouge, 1982, 164–94.

Slave Populations of the British Caribbean 1807–1834. Baltimore, 1984.

Hill, Polly. "Comparative West African farm-slavery systems." Willis, *Slaves and Slavery*, vol. 2, 33–50.

Hogendorn, Jan S. "The economics of slave use on two 'plantations' in the Zaria emirate of the Sokoto Caliphate." *International Journal of African Historical Studies*, 10, 3, 1977, 369–83.

"Slave acquisition and delivery in precolonial Hausaland" in B. K. Swartz, Jr., and Raymond E. Dumett, eds., *West African Culture Dynamics*, The Hague, 1980, 477–93.

Hogendorn, Jan S., and Henry A. Gemery. 1981. "Abolition and its impact on monies imported to West Africa." Eltis and Walvin, *Abolition*, 99–115.

Hogendorn, Jan S., and Marion Johnson. *The Shell Money of the Slave Trade*. Cambridge, 1986.

Hogendorn, Jan S., and Paul Lovejoy. "Sir Frederick Lugard's Policies toward Slavery in northern Nigeria." Unpublished paper, Waterville, Me., 1988.

Holt, Thomas C. "'An empire over the mind': emancipation, race, and ideology in the British West Indies and the American South" in J. Morgan Kousser and James M. McPherson, eds., *Region, Race, and Reconstruction: Essays in Honor of C. Vann Woodward*, New York, 1982, 283–313.

Hopkins, A. G. "Economic imperialism in West Africa: Lagos, 1880–92." *Economic History Review*, 21, 4, 1968, 580–606.

Hunwick, J. O. "Black Africans in the Islamic world: an understudied dimension of the black diaspora." *Tarikh*, 5, 1978, 20–40.

"Notes on slavery in the Songhay empire." Willis, *Slaves and Slavery*, 2, 1985, 16–32.

Hutton, James, ed. and trans. *Aristotle's Poetics*. New York, 1982.

Inikori, J. E. "Measuring the Atlantic slave trade: an assessment of Curtin and Anstey." *Journal of African History*, 17, 2, 1976, 197–233.

"Measuring the Atlantic slave trade." *Journal of African History*, 17, 4, 1976, 607–27.

"The import of firearms into West Africa, 1750–1897: a quantitative analysis." *Journal of African History*, 18, 3, 1977, 339–68.

"The sources of supply for the Atlantic slave exports from the Bight of Benin and the Bight of Bonny (Biafra)," Daget, *Actes de colloque*, vol. 2, 25–43.

Inikori, J. E., ed. *Forced Migration*. London, 1982.

Iroko, Felix. "Cauris et esclaves en Afrique occidentale entre les XVIe et XIXe siècles." Daget, *De la traite à l'esclavage*, vol. 1, 193–204.

Isaacman, Allen F. *Mozambique: The Africanization of a European Institution: The Zambezi Prazos, 1750–1902*. Madison, 1972.

Issawi, Charles. "Egypt since 1880: a study in lopsided development." *Journal of Economic History*, 21, 1, 1961, 11–26.

Jakobsson, Stiv. *Am I Not a Man and a Brother? British Missions and the Abolition of the Slave Trade and Slavery in West Africa and the West Indies 1786–1838*. Uppsala, 1972.

James, C. L. R. *The Black Jacobins: Toussaint l'Ouverture and the San Domingo Revolution*, 2nd edn. New York, 1963.

Johnson, Marion. "The ounce in eighteenth-century West African Trade," *Journal of African History*, 7, 2, 1966, 197–214.

"The slaves of Salaga." *Journal of African History*, 27, 2, 1986, 341–62.

Johnston, Bruce, F. *The Staple Food Economies of Western Tropical Africa*. Stanford, 1958.

Jones, E. L. *The European Miracle: Environments, Economies, and Geopolitics in the History of Europe and Asia*. 2nd edn. Cambridge, 1987.

Jones, G. I. "Olaudah Equiano of the Niger Ibo." Curtin, *Africa Remembered*, 85–98.

Jones, William O. *Manioc in Africa*. Stanford, 1959.

Jordan, Winthrop. *White Over Black: American Attitudes toward the Negro, 1550–1812*. Baltimore, 1969.

Karl, Emmanuel. *Traditions orales au Dahomey – Bénin*. Niamey, 1974.

Kaufmann, Walter. *Tragedy and Philosophy*. New York, 1968.

Kea, Ray A. *Settlements, Trade, and Politics on the Seventeenth-Century Gold Coast*. Baltimore, 1982.

Kearney, Hugh. *Science and Change 1500–1700*. New York, 1971.

Keim, Curtis A. "Women in slavery among the Mangbetu c. 1800–1910." Robertson and Klein, *Women and Slavery in Africa*, 144–59.

Kennedy, Paul. *The Rise and Fall of the Great Powers: Economic Change and Military Conflict from 1500 to 2000*. New York, 1987.

Kimble, David. *A Political History of Ghana: The Rise of Gold Coast Nationalism 1850–1928*. Oxford, 1963.

Kiple, Kenneth F., and Virginia Himmelsteib King. *Another Dimension to the Black Diaspora: Diet, Disease, and Racism*. Cambridge, 1981.

Klein, Herbert S. *African Slavery in Latin America and the Caribbean*. New York, 1986.

Klein, Martin A. "Slavery, the slave trade, and legitimate commerce in late nineteenth century Africa." *Etudes d'Histoire Africaine*, 2, 1971, 5–28.

"Women in slavery in the western Sudan." Robertson and Klein, *Women and Slavery in Africa*, 67–92.

"The demography of slavery in western Soudan: the late nineteenth century." Cordell and Gregory, *African Population*. 50–61.

"The slave trade in the Western Sudan in the nineteenth century." Unpublished paper. Toronto, 1988.

Klein, Martin A., and Paul E. Lovejoy. "Slavery in West Africa." Gemery and Hogendorn, *Uncommon Market*, 184–98.

Knight, Franklin W. *Slave Society in Cuba during the Nineteenth Century*. Madison, 1970.

Kopytoff, Igor, and Suzanne Miers. "African 'slavery' as an institution of marginality." Miers and Kopytoff, *Slavery in Africa*, 3–81.

Kuczynski, R. R. *Demographic Survey of the British Colonial Empire*. 3 vols. Oxford, 1948.

Lang, Olga. *Chinese Family and Society*, New Haven, 1946.

LaRue, G. M. "The export trade of Dar Fur, ca. 1785 to 1875" in G. Liesegang, H. Pasch, and A. Jones, eds., *Figuring African Trade*, Berlin, 1986.

Lasker, Bruno. *Human Bondage in Southeast Asia*. Chapel Hill, 1950.

Latham, A. J. H. *Old Calabar, 1600–1891: The Impact of the International Economy upon a Traditional Society*. Oxford, 1973.

The International Economy and the Undeveloped World 1865–1914. London, 1978.

Law, Robin. *The Oyo Empire, c. 1600–c. 1836*. Oxford, 1977.

"Royal monopoly and private enterprise in the Atlantic trade: the case of Dahomey." *Journal of African History*, 18, 4, 1977, 555–77.

"Dahomey and the slave trade; reflections on the historiography of the rise of Dahomey." *Journal of African History*, 27, 2, 1986, 237–67.

Bibliography

Le Herissé, Auguste. *L'Ancien Royaume du Dahomey*. Paris, 1911.

Lemery, Henry. *Martinique, terre française*. Paris, 1962.

LeVeen, E. Phillip. *British Slave Trade Suppression Policies, 1821–1865*. New York, 1977.

Levtzion, Nehemia. *Ancient Ghana and Mali*. London, 1973.

"Slavery and Islamization in Africa." Willis, *Slaves and Slavery*, vol. 2, 182–98.

Lewis, I. M., ed. *Islam in Tropical Africa*. London, 1966.

Livingstone, David. *Missionary Travels and Researches in South Africa*. London, 1857.

The Last Journals of David Livingstone in Central Africa. Ed. Horace Waller. 2 vols. London, 1874.

Livingstone, David, and Charles Livingstone. *Narrative of an Expedition to the Zambesi and its Tributaries*. New York, 1866.

Lloyd, Christopher. *The Navy and the Slave Trade*. London, 1949.

Lobo Cabrera, Manuel. *La Esclavitud en las Canarias Orientales en el Siglo XVI*. Gran Canaria, 1982.

Lovejoy, Paul E. "Interregional monetary flows in the precolonial trade of Nigeria." *Journal of African History* 15, 4, 1974, 563–85.

"Plantations in the economy of the Sokoto Caliphate." *Journal of African History*, 19, 3, 1978, 341–68.

"The characteristics of plantations in the nineteenth-century Sokoto Caliphate (Islamic West Africa)." *American Historical Review*, 84, 4, 1979, 1267–92.

"Indigenous African Slavery." Craton, *Roots and Branches*, 19–61.

"The volume of the Atlantic slave trade: a synthesis." *Journal of African History*, 23, 4, 1982, 473–501.

Transformations in Slavery. A History of Slavery in Africa. Cambridge, 1983. ·

"Problems of slave control in the Sokoto Caliphate." Lovejoy, *Africans in Bondage*, 244–64.

"The impact of the slave trade on Africa in the eighteenth and nineteenth centuries." *Journal of African History*, 30, 1989.

Lovejoy, Paul E., ed. *The Ideology of Slavery in Africa*. Beverly Hills, 1981.

Africans in Bondage: Studies in Slavery and the Slave Trade. Madison, 1986.

Lovejoy, Paul E., and Stephen Baier. "The desert-side economy of the Central Sudan." *International Journal of African Historical Studies*, 7, 4, 1975, 551–81.

Lugard, Lord Frederick. "'Slavery in all its forms'." *Africa*, 6, 1, 1933, 1–14.

The Dual Mandate in British Tropical Africa. 5th edn. London, 1965.

Lynch, Hollis R. *Edward Wilmot Blyden, Pan-Negro Patriot 1832–1912*. London, 1967.

Lynch, John. *The Spanish American Revolutions, 1808–1826*. New York, 1973.

McDougall, E. Ann. "Camel caravans of the Saharan salt trade: traders and transporters in the nineteenth century" in Catherine Coquery-Vidrovitch and Paul E. Lovejoy, eds., *The Workers of African Trade*, Beverly Hills, 1985, 99–121.

MacGaffey, Wyatt. "Economic and social dimensions of Kongo slavery." Miers and Kopytoff, *Slavery in Africa*, 235–57.

"Lineage structure, marriage, and the family amongst the central Bantu." *Journal of African History*, 24, 2, 1983, 173–87.

McMichael, Harold A. *A History of the Arabs in the Sudan*. 2 vols. Cambridge, 1922.

McNeill, William H. *The Rise of the West: A History of the Human Community*. Chicago, 1963.

McSheffrey, Gerald M. "Slavery, indentured servitude, legitimate trade and the impact of abolition in the Gold Coast, 1874–1901: a reappraisal." *Journal of African History*, 24, 3, 1983, 349–68.

Mahadi, Abdullahi. "Kasr Kano." Unpublished paper. Kano, 1987.

Malthus, Thomas Robert. *Population: The First Essay*. Ann Arbor, 1959; first published 1798.

An Essay on the Principle of Population, 2nd edn. London, 1803.

Manning, Patrick. "Un Document sur la fin de l'esclavage au Dahomey." *Notes Africaines*, 147, 1975, 88–92.

220

"The enslavement of Africans: a demographic model." *Canadian Journal of African Studies*, 15, 3, 1981, 499–526.

Slavery, Colonialism, and Economic Growth in Dahomey, 1640–1960. Cambridge, 1982.

"Contours of slavery and social change in Africa." *American Historical Review*, 88, 4, 1983, 835–57.

"L'Affaire Adjovi: la bourgeoisie foncière naissante au Dahomey, face à l'administration" in Catherine Coquery-Vidrovitch, ed., *Entreprises et entrepreneurs en Afrique*, 2 vols., Paris, 1983, vol. 1, 241–62.

"Primitive art and modern times." *Radical History Review*, 33, 1985, 165–81.

"Local versus regional impact of slave exports." Cordell and Gregory, *African Population*, 35–49.

"Slave trade, 'legitimate' trade, and imperialism revisited: the control of wealth in the Bights of Benin and Biafra." Lovejoy, *Africans in Bondage*, 203–33.

"The impact of slave exports: speculation, debate, methods, evidence." *Annales de Démographie Historique*, 1988.

"The impact of slave trade exports on the population of the Western Coast of Africa, 1700–1850." Daget, *De la traite à l'esclavage*, vol. 2, 111–34.

Manning, Patrick, and William S. Griffiths. "Divining the unprovable: simulating the demography of African slavery." *Journal of Interdisciplinary History*, 19, 2, 1988, 177–201.

Mannix, Daniel P., and Malcolm Cowley. *Black Cargoes: A History of the Atlantic Slave Trade, 1518–1865*. New York, 1962.

Martin, Phyllis M. *The External Trade of the Loango Coast*. Oxford, 1972.

Mason, Michael. "Population density and 'slave raiding' – the case of the middle belt of Nigeria." *Journal of African History*, 10, 4, 1969, 551–64.

"Captive and client labour and the economy of the Bida Emirate, 1857–1901." *Journal of African History*, 14, 3, 1973, 453–71.

Mattoso, Katia M. de Queiros. *To Be a Slave in Brazil, 1550–1888*. Trans. Arthur Goldhammer. New Brunswick, NJ, 1986.

M'Bokolo, E. "Peste et société urbaine à Dakar: l'épidémie de 1914." *Cahiers d'Etudes Africaines*, 85–86, 1982, 13–46.

Meek, C. K. *The Northern Tribes of Nigeria*. 2 vols. London, 1926.

Meillassoux, Claude. "Etat et condition des esclaves à Gumbu (Mali) au XIXe siècle." Meillassoux, *L'Esclavage en Afrique*, 221–51.

"The role of slavery in the economic and social history of Sahelo-Sudanic Africa." Inikori, *Forced Migration*, 74–99.

"Female slavery." Robertson and Klein, *Women and Slavery in Africa*, 49–66.

Anthropologie de l'esclavage: le ventre de fer et d'argent. Paris, 1986.

Meillassoux, Claude. ed. *L'Esclavage en Afrique précoloniale*. Paris, 1975.

Metcalf, George. "Gold assortments and the trade ounce: Fante merchants and the problem of supply and demand in the 1770s." *Journal of African History*, 28, 1, 1987, 27–41.

Mettas, Jean. *Répertoire des expéditions négrières françaises au XVIIIe siècle*. Ed. Serge Daget. 2 vols. Paris, 1978-84.

Meyers, Allan R. "Slave soldiers and state politics in early 'Alawi Morocco, 1668–1727." *International Journal of African Historical Studies*, 16, 1, 1983, 39–48.

Miers, Suzanne, and Igor Kopytoff, eds. *Slavery in Africa: Historical and Anthropological Perspectives*. Madison, 1977.

Miers, Suzanne, and Richard Roberts, eds. *The End of Slavery in Africa*. Madison, 1988.

Miller, Joseph C. *Kings and Kinsmen: Early Mbundu States in Angola*. Oxford, 1976.

"The significance of drought, disease and famine in the agriculturally marginal zone of west-central Africa." *Journal of African History*, 22, 1, 1982, 17–61.

"Capitalism and slaving: the financial and commercial organization of the Angolan slave trade, according to the accounts of Antonio Coelho Guerreiro (1684–1692)." *International Journal of African Historical Studies*, 17, 1, 1984, 1–56.

Slavery, A Worldwide Bibliography, 1900–1982. White Plains, NY, 1985.

"Slave prices in the Portuguese southern Atlantic, 1600–1830." Lovejoy, *Africans in Bondage*, 43–78.

Way of Death: Merchant Capitalism and the Angolan Slave Trade, 1730–1830. Madison, 1989.

Mintz, Sidney. "Slavery and the rise of peasantries." Craton, *Roots and Branches*, 213–42.

Sweetness and Power: The Place of Sugar in Modern History. Harmondsworth, 1985.

Miracle, Marvin P. *Maize in Tropical Africa*. Madison, 1966.

Miracle, Marvin P., and Bruce Fetter. "Backward-sloping labor supply functions and African economic behavior." *Economic Development and Cultural Change*, 18, 1970, 240–51.

Mire, Lawrence. "Al-Zubayr Pasha and the Zariba based slave trade in the Bahr al-Ghazal 1855–1879." Willis, *Slaves and Slavery*, vol. 2, 101–22.

Morel, E. D. *The British Case in French Congo*. London, 1903.

King Leopold's Rule in Africa. London, 1903.

Morgan, Edmund. *American Slavery, American Freedom: The Ordeal of Colonial Virginia*. New York, 1975.

Mudimbe, V. Y. *The Invention of Africa*, Bloomington, Ind., 1987.

Munro, J. Forbes. *Africa and the International Economy*. London, 1976.

Murdock, G. P. *Africa, its Peoples and its Culture History*. New York, 1960.

Myint, Hla. *The Economics of the Developing Countries*. New York, 1964.

Nachtigal, Gustav. *Sahara and Sudan*. Ed. and trans. Allan B. G. Fisher and Humphrey J. Fisher. 4 vols. London,1971.

Nadel, S. F. *A Black Byzantium*. Oxford, 1942.

Newbury, C. W. *The Western Slave Coast and its Rulers*. Oxford, 1961.

Nieboer, H. J. *Slavery as an Industrial System*. The Hague, 1910.

Norris, Robert. *Memoirs of the Reign of Bossa Ahadee, King of Dahomy*. London, 1968; first published 1789.

North, Douglass C., and Robert Paul Thomas. *The Rise of the Western World: A New Economic History*. Cambridge, 1973.

Northrup, David. *Trade Without Rulers: Pre-Colonial Economic Development in South-Eastern Nigeria*. Oxford, 1978.

Nwachukwu-Ogedengbe, K. "Slavery in nineteenth-century Aboh (Nigeria)." Miers and Kopytoff, *Slavery in Africa*, 133–54.

O'Fahey, R. S. "Slavery and the slave trade in Dar Fur." *Journal of African History*, 14, 1, 1973, 29–43.

"Slavery and society in Dar Fur." Willis, *Slaves and Slavery*, vol. 2, 83–100.

Ofonagoro, W. I. "Notes on the ancestry of Mbanaso Okwaraozurumba otherwise known as King Jaja of Opobo, 1821–1891." *Journal of the Historical Society of Nigeria*, 9, 3, 1978, 145–56.

Oliver, Roland. *The Missionary Factor in East Africa*. London, 1952.

Oliver, Roland, and J. D. Fage. *A Short History of Africa*, Harmondsworth, 1962.

Olivier de Sardan, Jean-Pierre. "Captifs ruraux et esclaves impériaux du Songhay." Meillassoux, *L'Esclavage en Afrique*, 99–134.

Page, Melvin E. "The Manyema hordes of Tippu Tip: a case study in social stratification and the slave trade in eastern Africa." *International Journal of African Historical Studies*, 7, 1, 1974, 69–84.

Palmer, Colin. *Slaves of the White God: Blacks in Mexico, 1570–1650*. Cambridge, Mass., 1976.

Human Cargoes, the British Slave Trade to Spanish America 1700–1739. Urbana, 1981.

Parry, J. H. 1963. *The Age of Reconnaissance*. London, 1963.

Patterson, K. David. *The Northern Gabon Coast to 1875*. Oxford, 1975.

Patterson, Orlando. "On slavery and slave formations." *New Left Review*, 117, 1979, 31–67.

Slavery and Social Death: A Comparative Study. Cambridge, Mass., 1982.

Perrot, Claude-Hélène. "Les Captifs dans le royaume anyi du Ndenye." Meillassoux, *L'Esclavage en Afrique*.

Person, Yves. *Samori, une révolution dyula*. 3 vols. Dakar, 1968–75.

Peukert, Werner. *Der Atlantische Sklavenhandel von Dahomey, 1740–1797*. Wiesbaden, 1978.

Phillips, William D. *Slavery from Roman Times to the Early Transatlantic Trade*. Minneapolis, 1985.

Polanyi, Karl. *The Great Transformation*. Boston, 1957; first published 1944.

Polanyi, Karl, with Abraham Rotstein. *Dahomey and the Slave Trade, an Analysis of an Archaic Economy*. Seattle, 1966.

Pruneau de Pommegorge, Joseph. *Description de la Nigritie*. Paris, 1789.

Pryor, Frederic L. "A comparative study of slave societies," *Journal of Comparative Economics*, 1, 1977, 25–49.

Pulleyblank, E. G. "The origins and nature of chattel slavery in China." *Journal of the Economic and Social History of the Orient*, 1, 1958, 204–11.

Rattray, Capt. R. S. *Ashanti Law and Constitution*. Oxford, 1929.

Rawley, James. *The Transatlantic Slave Trade: A History*. New York, 1981.

Renault, François. *Lavigerie, l'esclavage africain et l'Europe, 1868–1892*. 2 vols. Paris, 1971.

"La Traite des esclaves noirs en Libye au XVIIIe siècle." *Journal of African History*, 23, 2, 1982, 163–81.

Renault, François, and Serge Daget. *Les Traites négrières en Afrique*. Paris, 1985.

Reynolds, Edward. *Trade and Economic Change on the Gold Coast, 1807–1874*. London, 1974.

Stand the Storm: A History of the Atlantic Slave Trade. London 1985.

Rice, C. Duncan. *The Rise and Fall of Black Slavery*. New York, 1975.

Richardson, David. "Slave exports from West and West-Central Africa, 1700–1810: new estimates of volume and distribution." *Journal of African History*, 30, 1, 1989, 1–22.

Roberts, Richard. "Long distance trade and production: Sinsani in the nineteenth century." *Journal of African History*, 21, 1980, 169–88.

"Women's work and women's property: household social relations in the Maraka textile industry of the nineteenth century." *Comparative Studies in Society and History*, 26, 2, 1984.

Warriors, Merchants, and Slaves: The State and the Economy in the Middle Niger Valley, 1700–1914. Stanford, 1987.

Roberts, Richard, and Martin Klein. "The Banamba slave exodus of 1905 and the decline of slavery in the western Sudan." *Journal of African History*, 21, 3, 1981, 375–94.

Robertson, Claire C. "Post-proclamation slavery in Accra: a female affair?" Robertson and Klein, *Women and Slavery in Africa*, 230–45.

Robertson, Claire C., and Martin Klein, eds. *Women and Slavery in Africa*. Madison, 1983.

Robertson, Claire C., and Martin Klein. "Women's importance in African slave systems." Robertson and Klein, *Women and Slavery in Africa*, 3–25.

Robinson, David. *The Holy War of Umar Tal*. Oxford, 1985.

Rodney, Walter. "African slavery and other forms of social oppression on the upper Guinea Coast in the context of the Atlantic slave trade." *Journal of African History*, 7, 3, 1966, 431–43.

A History of the Upper Guinea Coast 1545–1800. Oxford, 1970.

How Europe Underdeveloped Africa. London, 1972.

Rosenberg, Nathan, and L. E. Birdzell, Jr. *How the West Grew Rich: The Economic Transformation of the Industrial World*. New York, 1986.

Bibliography

Ross, David A. "The career of Domingo Martinez in the Bight of Benin, 1833–1864." *Journal of African History*, 6, 1, 1965, 79–90.

Rotberg, Robert I. *A Political History of Tropical Africa*. New York, 1965.

Russell-Wood, A. J. R. "Technology and society: the impact of gold mining on the institution of slavery in Portuguese America." *Journal of Economic History*, 37, 1, 1977, 59–86.

Ryder, A. G. C. *Benin and the Europeans 1485–1897*. New York, 1969.

Saunders, A. C. de M. *A Social History of Black Slaves and Freedmen in Portugal, 1441–1555*. Cambridge, 1982.

Sautter, Gilles. *De l'Atlantique au fleuve Congo: une géographie du sous peuplement*. 2 vols. Paris, 1966.

Schlippe, Pierre de. *Shifting Cultivation in Africa; the Zande System of Agriculture*. London, 1956.

Schuler, Monica. *"Alas, Alas, Kongo": A Social History of Indentured African Immigration into Jamaica*. Baltimore, 1980.

Scott, Rebecca. *Slave Emancipation in Cuba: The Transition to Free Labor, 1860–1899*. Princeton, 1985.

Shepherd, Gill. "The Comorians and the East African slave trade." Watson, *Asian and African Systems of Slavery*, 73–99.

Sheridan, Richard B. *Sugar and Slavery: An Economic History of the British West Indies*. Bridgetown, Barbados, 1974.

Sheriff, Abdul. "The slave mode of production along the East African coast, 1810–1873." Willis, *Slaves and Slavery*, 161–81.

Slaves, Spices and Ivory in Zanzibar. London, 1987.

Siegel, Bernard J. *Slavery during the Third Dynasty of Ur*, Memoirs of the American Anthropological Association, 66, 1947.

Slade, Ruth. *King Leopold's Congo*. London, 1962.

Smith, Mary F. *Baba of Karo: A Woman of the Moslem Hausa*. New York, 1955.

Smith, Michael G. *Government in Zazzau, 1800–1950*. London, 1960.

Smith, Robert. *The Lagos Consulate, 1851–1861*. Berkeley, 1979.

Société Française d'Histoire d'Outre-Mer. *La Traite des noirs par l'Atlantique, nouvelles approches*. Paris, 1976.

Solow, Barbara L., and Stanley L. Engerman, eds. *British Capitalism and Caribbean Slavery: The Legacy of Eric Williams*. Cambridge, 1987.

Solow, Barbara L., and Stanley L. Engerman. "British capitalism and Caribbean slavery: the legacy of Eric Williams: an introduction." Solow and Engerman, *British Capitalism and Caribbean Slavery*, 1–23.

Spengler, Oswald. *The Decline of the West*. New York, 1939.

Spüler, Berthold. *History of the Mongols*. Berkeley, 1972.

Strobel, Margaret. "Slavery and reproductive labor in Mombasa." Robertson and Klein, *Women and Slavery in Africa*, 111–29.

Sundiata, I. K. *Black Scandal: America and the Liberian Labor Crisis, 1929–1936*. Philadelphia, 1980.

Tambo, David. "The Sokoto Caliphate slave trade in the nineteenth century." *International Journal of African Historical Studies*, 9, 2, 1976, 187–217.

Tauxier, Louis. *Le Noir du Soudan, Pays Mossi et Gourounsi*. Paris, 1912.

Temperley, Howard. *British Antislavery, 1833–1870*. Columbia, SC, 1972.

Terray, Emmanuel. "Commerce pré-colonial et organisation sociale chez les Dida de Côte d'Ivoire" in Claude Meillassoux, ed., *The Development of Indigenous Trade and Markets in West Africa*, London, 1971, 145–52.

"Long-distance exchange and the formation of the state: the case of the Abron kingdom of Gyaman." *Economy and Society*, 3, 1974, 315–45.

"Class and class consciousness in the Abron kingdom of Gyaman" in Maurice Bloch, ed., *Marxist Analyses and Social Anthropology*, London, 1975, 85–136.

"La Captivité dans le royaume abron de Gyaman." Meillassoux, *L'Esclavage en Afrique*, 389–453.

"Réflexions sur la formation du prix des esclaves à l'interieur de l'Afrique de l'Ouest précoloniale." *Journal des Africanistes*, 52, 1–2, 1982, 119–44.

"Gold production, slave labor, and state intervention in precolonial Akan societies." *Research in Economic Anthropology*, 5, 1983, 885–914.

Thomas, Brinley. *Migration and Economic Growth: A Study of Great Britain and the Atlantic Economy*. 2nd edn. Cambridge, 1973.

Thomas, Northcote W. *Anthropological Report on the Ibo-Speaking Peoples of Nigeria; Part IV, Law and Custom of the Ibo of the Asaba District, S. Nigeria*. London, 1914.

Thomas, Robert Paul, and Richard Bean. "The fishers of men – the profits of the slave trade." *Journal of Economic History*, 34, 4, 1974, 885–914.

Thornton, John. "An eighteenth-century baptismal register and the demographic history of Manguenzo." Fyfe and McMaster, *African Historical Demography*, vol. 1, 405–15.

"Demography and history in the kingdom of Kongo, 1550–1750." *Journal of African History*, 18, 4, 1977, 507–30.

"The slave trade in eighteenth century Angola: effects of demographic structures." *Canadian Journal of African Studies*, 14, 3, 1981, 417–27.

"The demographic effect of the slave trade on Western Africa 1500–1850." Fyfe and McMaster, *African Historical Demography*, vol. 2, 691–720.

"The art of war in Angola, 1575–1680." *Comparative Studies in Society and History*, 30, 2, 1988, 360–378.

"On the trail of voodoo: African Christianity in Africa and the Americas." *The Americas*, 44, 3, 1986, 261–78.

Toledano, Ehud R. *The Ottoman Slave Trade and its Suppression*. Princeton, 1982.

Toplin, Robert Brent. *The Abolition of Slavery in Brazil*. New York, 1972.

Toplin, Robert Brent, ed. *Slavery and Race Relations in Latin America*. Westport, Conn., 1974.

Toynbee, Arnold. *A Study of History*, 12 vols. London, 1961.

Uchendu, Victor. 1977. "Slaves and slavery in Igboland, Nigeria." Miers and Kopytoff, *Slavery in Africa*, 121–32.

Udry, Christopher. "The Akan transitional zone." Unpublished paper. Yale University, 1985.

Unruh, Ellen S. "Slavery in medieval Korea." Ph.D. dissertation. Columbia University, 1978.

Vansina, Jan. *Kingdoms of the Savanna*. Madison, 1966.

Vellut, J.-L. "Diversification de l'économie de cueillette: miel et cire dans les sociétés de la forêt claire d'Afrique centrale (c. 1750–1950)." *African Economic History*, 7, 1979, 93–112.

Verger, Pierre. "Le Culte des vodoun d'Abomey aurait-il été apporté à St.-Louis de Maranhon par la mère du roi Ghezo?" *Etudes Dahomeennes*, 8, 1952, 19–24.

Verlinden, Charles. "Précédents et parallèles européens de l'esclavage colonial." *O Instituto de Coimbra*, 113, 1949, 1–41.

L'Esclavage dans l'Europe médiévale, 2 vols. Bruges, Ghent, 1955–77.

Les Origines de la civilisation atlantique. De la Renaissance à l'Age des Lumières. Neuchatel, 1966.

"La Traite des esclaves: un grand commerce international au Xe siècle." *Etudes de civilisation médiévale, IXe – XIIe siècles: mélanges offertes à Edmond René Labande à l'occasion de son départ à la retraite*, 1974, 721–30.

Villiers, Patrick. *Traite des noirs et navires négriers au XVIIIe siècle*. Grenoble, 1982.

Waldman, Loren K. "An unnoticed aspect of Dalzel's *History of Dahomey* [sic]." *Journal of African History*, 6, 2, 1965, 185–92.

Wallerstein, Immanuel. *The Modern World-System*. 3 vols. New York, 1974–89.

Walz, Terence. "The trade between Egypt and Bilad As-Sudan, 1700–1850." Ph.D. dissertation. Boston University, 1975.

Bibliography

"Black slavery in Egypt during the nineteenth century as reflected in the Mahkamat Archives of Cairo." Willis, *Slaves and Slavery*, vol. 2, 137–60.

Warburg, Gabriel R. "Ideological and practical considerations regarding slavery in the Mahdist state and the Anglo-Egyptian Sudan: 1881–1918." Lovejoy, *Ideology of Slavery*, 245–69.

Watson, James L., ed. *Asian and African Systems of Slavery*. Berkeley, 1980.

Weil, Peter M. "Slavery, groundnuts, and European capitalism in the Wuli kingdom of Senegambia, 1820–1930." *Research in Economic Anthropology*, 6, 1984, 77–119.

Weisbord, Robert G. *Ebony Kinship; Africa, Africans, and the Afro-American*. Westport, Conn., 1973.

Wheeler, Douglas L. "'Angola is whose house?' Early stirrings of Angolan nationalism and protest, 1822–1910." *African Historical Studies*, 2, 1, 1969, 1–22.

Wiesel, Elie. *Against Silence: The Voice and Vision of Elie Wiesal*. Selected and ed. Irving Abrahamson. New York, 1985.

Wilbur, Martin C. *Slavery in China During the Former Han Dynasty, 206 BC – AD 25*. Chicago, 1943.

Wilks, Ivor. *Asante in the Nineteenth Century: The Structure and Evolution of a Political Order*. Cambridge, 1975.

Williams, Eric. *Capitalism and Slavery*. Chapel Hill, 1944.

Willis, John Ralph, ed. *Slaves and Slavery in Muslim Africa*. 2 vols. London, 1985.

Wirz, Albert. *Sklaverei und kapitalistische Weltsystem*. Frankfurt-on-Main, 1984.

Woodward, C. Vann. *The Strange Career of Jim Crow*. 3rd rev. edn. New York, 1974.

Woolman, John. *The Journal of John Woolman*. New York, 1954.

The Works of John Woolman. New York, 1969.

Wright, Gavin. "Capitalism and slavery on the islands: a lesson from the mainland." Solow and Engerman, *British Capitalism and Caribbean Slavery*, 283–302.

Wright, Marcia. "Bwanikwa: consciousness and protest among slave women in Central Africa, 1886–1911." Robertson and Klein, *Women and Slavery in Africa*, 246–67.

Wrigley, C. C. "Historicism in Africa: slavery and state formation." *African Affairs*, 80, 279, 1971, 113–24.

Wrigley, E. A. *Population and History*. New York, 1969.

Wrigley, E. A., and R. S. Schofield. *The Population History of England, 1541–1871*. Cambridge, Mass., 1981.

Zilversmit, Arthur. *The First Emancipation: The Abolition of Slavery in the North*. Chicago, 1967.

Index

Index

Index

ideology, 6, 9, 13, 19, 88, 128, 132–3, 157,
    165–6
Igbo, 70, 89, 111, 113, 135
ilari, 116
Il-Khanids, 28
Imbangala, 133
India, 12, 52, 81, 139
Indian Ocean, 21, 24, 52, 79–80, 99, 109,
    136, 138
industrialization, 170–1, 173
inequality, 6, 168–9, 176
initiation, 115, 117
institutional factors (in prices), 34,
    94
institutions, social (see *social institutions*)
International African Association, 159
International African Congress, 159
International African Institute, 163
Iran, 12
Islam (see also Muslims), 10, 28, 50, 117,
    128, 174
Islamic world, 10, 29, 36–7, 51, 161
Israel, 175
Istanbul, 103
Italy, 27
Itsekiri, 144
ivory, 52, 108, 112, 138–9, 159
Ivory Coast (Côte d'Ivoire), 90, 166

Jaga, 3, 113
Jamaica, 149–50, 165
Jews, 176
jihad, 137
Jim Crow, 165
Johnson, Marion, 100, 172
Jolof, 34, 129–30

Kalahari desert, 84
Kamerun, *see* Cameroon
Kano, 115, 143
Kasanje, 133
Kaufmann, Walter, 4
Kea, Ray, 133
Kenya, 53, 161
Khartoum, 76, 137
kidnapping, 88, 91, 131, 160
Kilwa, 103, 112
Kimberley, 167
kinship (see also matrilineal, patrilineal),
    118–20, 142, 178
Kivu, 69
Klein, Martin, 109, 143
Kôli, 89, 112
Kongo, 34, 70, 128
Kopytoff, Igor, 126
Korea, 27–8
Kulibaly, Mamari, 65

labor
    division of, 132
    factor of production, 33
    slave (*see* slaves and slavery)
Lagos, 157, 161, 165
land (factor of production), 33, 49
Lavigerie, Cardinal, 16
law, 118–22
    "customary", 163
    Muslim, 145, 163
League of Nations, 12, 164
Leopold II, 159
LeVeen, E. Phillip, 96, 177
Liberia, 65, 155, 156, 163
liberty villages, 161
Libreville, 155
life-course, 113–18
Lima, 172
Limpopo river, 84
Lincoln, Abraham, 156
littoral, 98
Liverpool, 153, 171
Livingstone, David, 15–16, 112, 158, 161
Loango, 50, 56, 58, 69–70, 90, 94–5, 115,
    134–5, 156
London, 15
London Missionary Society, 160
loss, rates of population, 49, 51, 53
Louis XVI, 15
Lovejoy, Paul, 36, 120, 161
Luanda, 93, 165
Lugard, Lord, 162–3
Luso-Africans, 98

Madagascar, 53, 80, 138, 167
Madeira Islands, 29
Mahdi (Muhammad Hassan), 146, 160
Mahi, 87
maize, 56
malaria, 31
Malawi, 80, 119, 136, 158, 160–1
Malawi, Lake, 112, 139
male supremacy, *see* patriarchy
Malebo Pool, 103
Mali, 29, 50, 63, 74, 128
Malta, 29
Malthus, Thomas, 87
Mamluks, 137
Mangbetu, 143
manioc, 56
manumission, 28, 46, 118, 160
manumitted slaves, 32, 165
Maraka, 91
Maranhão, 111
Maria Theresa thalers (dollars), 100–1, 177
market factors (in prices), 34, 37, 94
markets, 143, 159

Index

Oyo, 35, 56, 67–8, 90, 116, 135

Palestine, 29
palm oil, 50, 108, 116, 140, 142, 146, 148
Pan-Africanism, 3, 25–6, 87
Pascal language, 179
patriarchy, 3, 123, 147
patrilineal descent, 119
Patterson, Orlando, 27, 113
peanuts, 50, 108, 116, 122, 140, 142, 148
Pemba, 53, 139
Persia, 28
Persian Gulf, 52, 81, 103, 139
Peru, 32, 155
Philadelphia, 172
plantations, 53, 57, 129, 143–4, 170
planters, 107, 140, 144
plow, 33
polygyny, 42, 45, 47, 54–5, 98, 120, 132,
    142
population
  by continent, 37, 47, 87, 170–1
  growth and decline, 14, 22, 31, 47, 63–87,
    132, 135, 170–1
  regional, in Africa, 22, 40, 60, 65–6, 136
porters, 116, 166
Portugal, 155, 157
Portuguese, 29–30, 36, 48, 52, 56, 93–4, 101,
    122, 128, 131, 157, 160, 163, 165
prazeros, 136
prices (of slaves), 9, 13, 18–19, 21–2, 31–2,
    42, 48–53, 91–8, 104–9, 128, 130–1,
    133–5, 137–8, 140–2, 177
prime cost, 93, 177
productivity
  in agriculture, 21, 34–5
  of captives and slaves, 21–2, 36
  of labor, 33, 35, 93, 172
profit, 24, 36, 91–2, 94–6, 99, 107, 133, 140,
    143, 162, 171–3
Pruneau de Pommegorge, Joseph, 15, 111,
    152
Puerto Rico, 156

Quakers, 14, 149
Qur'an, 28

Rabih, 159–60
racism, 24, 157, 164–6, 168, 170
Raided (population), 39
Raiders (population), 39
raids, 65, 76–7, 88–9, 106, 133
rebellions, 117–18, 130, 138, 144, 149–50,
    155, 165
reconquista, 29
Red Sea, 21, 50, 77
Reform Bill of 1832, 155

Regional population (Sources, Captors, and
    Domestics), 40, 66, 68–70, 80–1
religion, 10, 28, 126, 150, 173
remembrance, doctrine of, 174
rent, economic, 95–6
reparations, doctrine of, 174
reproduction
  biological, 22, 73, 121
  social, 106, 121, 173
Reunion (see also Mascarene Islands), 21,
    52, 81, 136
Rhode Island, 156
rinji, 114–15
Rio de Janeiro, 103
Robertson, Claire, 113
Rodney, Walter, 13–14, 20
Rome, 27, 29
rubber, 108
Russia, 29
Rwanda, 84

sacrifice, 4–6, 16, 174
  human, 16, 108, 112, 117, 118
Sahara desert, 21, 29, 36, 50, 58, 62, 64–5,
    74–5, 84, 138, 160
Sa'id, Sayyid, 138–9
St.-Domingue (see also Haiti)
Salaga, 159
Salvador, 172
Samori, see Toure, Samori
São Thomé, 29
Savanna and Horn, 18, 23, 41, 45–53, 56–7,
    59, 61–2, 72–3, 75, 77–8, 82, 84, 90,
    106, 115, 120, 127, 130, 136–7, 145,
    147, 156, 167, 181
Schoelcher, Victor, 155
seasoning, 88, 113–14, 173
Segu, 65
self-enslavement, 88, 160
Senegal, 15, 22, 63, 159, 167
Senegambia, 41, 49, 57, 63–5, 73–5, 89–90,
    94, 96, 98, 103, 116, 122, 134, 144
seniority, 118, 120
Sennar, 50–1
serfdom, 145
sex ratio, 22–3, 31, 45–6, 48–9, 51, 55, 59,
    61–2, 64–82, 85, 97–8, 109, 119, 128,
    132, 134–6, 142, 167, 170, 173, 180
sexuality, 22, 43, 116, 130
Shaba, 69
Shaka, 138
Shangaans, 138
Sheriff, Abdul, 109
Shona, 52
Sidama, 77
Sierra Leone, 65, 139, 154, 157, 163, 165
simulation, demographic, 60–2, 179–81

232

Index

OTHER BOOKS IN THE SERIES